P9-BYY-118

FREUD
AND
JUNG

LINDA DONN

FREUD AND JUNG

Years of Friendship, Years of Loss

CHARLES SCRIBNER'S SONS
NEW YORK

Permissions acknowledgments appear on page 237

Charles Scribner's Sons
Macmillan Publishing Company
866 Third Avenue, New York NY 10022
Collier Macmillan Canada, Inc.

Library of Congress Cataloging-in-Publication Data
Donn, Linda.
Freud and Jung: years of friendship, years of loss / by Linda Donn.
p. cm.
Includes index.
ISBN 0-684-18962-3
1. Freud, Sigmund, 1856–1939—Friends and associates. 2. Jung, C. G. (Carl Gustav), 1875–1961—Friends and associates. 3. Psychoanalysts—Austria—Biography. 4. Psychoanalysts—Switzerland—Biography. 5. Psychoanalysis—History. I. Title.
BF173.F85D6 1988
150.19'52—dc19
[B] 88-19739 CIP

Macmillan books are available at special discounts for bulk purchases for sales promotions, premiums, fund-raising, or educational use. For details, contact:

Special Sales Director
Macmillan Publishing Company
866 Third Avenue
New York, NY 10022

10 9 8 7 6 5 4 3 2 1

Printed in the United States of America

For my husband, Tony, and our children, Cassie, Alex and Michael.
With all my love.

CONTENTS

PREFACE

THE FRIENDSHIP between Sigmund Freud and Carl Jung was an intersect of genius. It fixed an emotional space that had at times great height and intoxicating airs, and at others narrow passages, mazelike turns and the sudden monolith of stone. It became my pleasure to try to find my way, to look through a window of an evening and see Freud and Jung laughing over coffee in the warmth of a Vienna café. They scrape their wooden chairs back from the table and toss down their coins, impatient to be off. I began with scenes like these, imagined. But slowly they were replaced by others, grounded in a reality however distant.

One afternoon in the stacks of the New York Society Library, I took down a small, worn volume and found the American poet Hilda Doolittle in Freud's Vienna in the tense days before Austria fell to Hitler. Walking home that afternoon I carried Hilda's book, moved by the image of her alone in the streets of Vienna, going to see Sigmund Freud on the eve of terror.

There were times when difficulties overlaid the visual display. Research could be frustrating, even treacherous. It is easy to make mistakes and hard to catch them. The images I was pursuing came from an altogether different place than my doctoral courses in academic psychology. I began to envy those whose projects evolved from their scholarship and not the other way around. But there were moments of satisfaction. Some of the restrictions on the Sigmund Freud Collection at the Library of Congress were beginning to lift when I started my research, and I was able to study letters previously difficult to obtain, among them the correspondence between Freud and his daughter Anna, and Freud's letters to his colleagues and friends Eugen Bleuler, Ludwig Binswanger and Ernest Jones. I also read the correspondence between Freud and his confidant Sándor Ferenczi. Conceptual riches are to be found in these many letters and they have informed this story. But I also read passages of great color and warmth, of sudden, heart-stopping rage, the quick burst of gossip and the calm of truth.

At the Francis A. Countway Library of Medicine in Boston I was introduced to the work of Dr. Eugene Nameche, interviews with more than a hundred colleagues, relatives and friends of Carl Jung. The talks had been conducted for the most part in the late 1960s and early 1970s and had been restricted for varying numbers of years, but many of the curbs had run their course by the time I began my research. The probing conversations with people such as Sir Arnold Toynbee were an absorbing and invaluable journey into Jung's mind. During the course of four research trips to Europe, I gained the friendship of Freud's maid, Paula Fichtl, who lives in a nursing home just outside Salzburg. Aged eighty-three, still remarkably articulate and vivacious, she had been with the Freuds since the age of twenty-eight. Paula drew a human portrait of Freud, and together we watched night fall on Austria and the Freud family. Elsewhere, in Switzerland, Franz Jung told me stories about his father over a dozen afternoons. Franz's feeling for the small facts of everyday life placed me in a little village in Switzerland with Carl Jung at the turn of the century.

In time, over a period of four years, I came to the end of the book. It is strange that I can trace its development yet not know where the idea for it first came nor why. I remember, as a college student, staying in a London townhouse owned by the relative of a friend. It was quite grand, and one evening our host gave a dinner party. I was startled when the party picked itself up from the table and moved as one to a television set: Carl Jung was being interviewed. There was excitement in the air, and conversation about the friendship; even, I like to think, a breath of mystery.

Accounts of why things are written can be boring. There is the attempt at logic to get reasons down and make the work presentable. The lovely truth is so much otherwise, often elusive even to its possessor. At a party in London, people had found in the friendship between Freud and Jung an occasion of mystery and drama: that brief memory of an evening when I was young, like a piece of bark floating downstream, collected other bits and drew me in. I was attracted to the idea of friendship between men of genius, a joining of intellect and passion, but I stayed because I grew to cherish the company of Freud and of Jung.

What follows is a selective account of their friendship. However scrupulous my attention to the facts, my choice of images was personal. One day someone will walk the terrain of Freud and Jung at its farthest boundary and include it all. Until then, perhaps something can be said for standing in one place and describing the scene. There were times when the street was dark, but I tried to see as well as I could.

ACKNOWLEDGMENTS

WHEN IT is tied to chronology, thanking people tells its own story. William Schneider, a member of the faculty of the New School for Social Research, was kind enough to tell me that he saw the possibility of a book in a paper I wrote for him on the friendship betwen Freud and Jung. Steven Frimmer, the former editor of Reader's Digest Press, looked the paper over and made suggestions at different junctures. He then put me in touch with Julian Bach, who became my literary agent and who, with patience and humor, taught me how to write a book proposal, and more. Julian remained very much with the project throughout, as enthusiastic and helpful at the end as he had been at the beginning. Dr. Bernard Weitzman of the New School Graduate Faculty also gave me good advice early on. I am grateful to all of these people for their help.

William McGuire was generous on several occasions in sharing his considerable knowledge about the subject of this book. Winifred Clark put me in touch with members of the Jungian community. Eliat van de Velde was kind enough to share information about Jung and Freud with me, as was Dr. John Rosen. I kept their suggestions in mind as I began my research.

I traveled in Europe several times during the course of the project. In London, I visited Mrs. Eveline Bennet, who had just published her husband's meticulous notes, *Meetings with Jung*. I spent a day in Aldeburgh, England with Sir Laurens van der Post and his wife, both of whom had known Jung well. In Salzburg, I met Paula Fichtl, who had been Freud's maid, fluent in English and charming. I am obliged to them for sharing their memories and for making those memories come alive.

In Switzerland, I visited Franz Jung, and he talked about his father over many hours and days. Franz gave me a stable and continuous image of his family life, and his thoughtful, careful memories were bedrock. I am grateful for his thorough attention and for his friendship. He will know where to find himself in these pages. Through Aryeh Maidenbaum, Executive Director of the C. G. Jung Foundation for Analytical Psychology of New York, I met Dr. Robert Hinshaw, an American analyst practicing in Zürich. With a quickness that makes everything possible, Bob introduced me to people in Zürich it might otherwise have been difficult to meet, among them Aniela Jaffé, the gifted editor of Jung's *Memories, Dreams, Reflections* and a repository of factual detail about Carl Jung. Loyal to Jung's memory yet gracious to those who might disturb it, Frau Jaffé was particularly kind. In Zürich as well, the writer and analyst Dr. Liliane Frey-Rohn and Dr. Siegmund Hurwitz described Jung as they had known and understood him. Dr. C. A. Meier, an eminent analyst and a close colleague of Jung for many years, also had his own portrait of Carl Jung. All of these people were generous in sharing their memories with me, but if there are lines misdrawn, they are my own.

Within the libraries and archives, daunting places for the uninformed, Dr. Ronald S. Wilkinson, a manuscript historian who specializes in cultural history and science, made my work at the Manuscript Division of the Library of Congress a pleasure. Dr. Harold Blum, Executive Director of the Sigmund Freud Archives, Inc., was unfailingly helpful, and I am mindful that in his busy day there was always time for a word with me. The Jung Biographical Archive in the Francis A. Countway Library of Medicine in Boston is in the firm care of Mr. Richard Wolfe. His knowledgeable, energetic presence encouraged questions and assured answers. Mary E. Van Winkle, assistant curator of archives and manuscripts at the time I was working on this book, was a friendly presence during a long day's research and coped reliably with the details of my work. At the Countway, I also met Eugene Taylor, a scholar on the development of scientific psychotherapy in America and generous with his knowledge and sources of information. Dr. Frank Mecklenburg of the Leo Baeck Institute in New York City was helpful early on in my research. The staff of the New York Society Library in New York City dealt efficiently with the details of shipping microfilm from one library to another and solved the procedural problems that inevitably occur. My thanks to all of these people for their competence and good cheer.

I would like to thank the translators who worked on this project. I am particularly obliged to Magda Jones. Keeping track of hundreds of letters, accomplishing transcriptions from gothic German to everyday German, translating from there into English with a sensitivity to clarity and style, and all the while maintaining an orderly pursuit was time-consuming and tedious, moments of translating excitement aside. At Wesleyan University, Dr. Krishna Winston handled other translations, while her secretary, Hilda Damiata, worked dependably and accurately on transcriptions. Ilse Schutz and Almut Fitzgerald translated other materials. At the end, Krishna, Magda and Almut reviewed the work as a whole. I appreciate their expertise and their combined goodwill.

Annie Rohrmeier, Montie Mills and Steve Kellogg read the manuscript with a view to the story itself. Dr. Robert Hinshaw and William Schneider read the manuscript and contributed their particular concerns. I am grateful to them for their comments. But there are debts of even greater magnitude which cannot be repaid. Tom Crider, a partner in writing ventures in other years, stepped in several times to help. No detail was too slight for Tom's attention, and, as in earlier times, humor prevailed. Tom is a wonderful friend and a man to whom words matter much, but even he cannot work miracles: the snags in the pages to come belong to me.

To Janet Foster fell the task of coordinating the end notes. It is work filled with loose ends and a constantly changing text. I thank her for her sharp eyes, her tenacity and her friendship. Mieke Maas researched the photographs for this book, and her sense of design determined the final selection. The project became, during the last months, more than ever a team effort. Janet Foster, Suzy Kane, Almut Fitzgerald, Annie Rohrmeir and Avra Matsoukas devoted themselves to the time-consuming details of photograph and text permissions and fact-checking. I am indebted to them all.

Gladys Alvarez, Debbie Kusa, Alice Seeley and Maria Royek kept our household lives in order at various times during the course of this project. My work could not have been accomplished without their help, but who would know that better than they?

I thank my father for his encouragement and support. And through it all, no one was kinder or more patient than my husband, Tony. A physician, busy enough, no one listened better or more critically. Tony understood and sympathized, but most important he gave, always, an unvarnished view, honest and uncomplicated. It is quite a boring matter to have a wife writing a book, but it is worse to have your mother writing one. Cassie and Alex, now thirteen, did their best to keep life interesting. They suggested titles and cover designs. They told me to get on, and stay on, a word processor, and they sat with me during the first perplexing days. Most particularly, they are interested in all aspects of the writing process—from setting a scene to annotation techniques—an unexpected delight.

I appreciate the fact that Scribners, in particular my editor Robert Stewart, provided me with the opportunity to write this book. There are many who gave a hand along the way, and I thank them all. It is peculiarly moving to have reached the end and realize it was accomplished with so much genuine help.

PART ONE

SETTINGS

CHAPTER ONE

HILDA DOOLITTLE often wore bright-colored stockings, loosely belted dresses she found in thrift shops, silk ribbons strung with lockets and the careless extravagance of furs. But one day late in October 1934 when she dressed in Vienna, she chose old tweeds instead. She walked out of the Hotel Regina onto Freiheitsplatz carrying a sturdy leather case because the students and professors at the university across the square used them, and she liked to feel part of their world.

It was nearly five o'clock in the afternoon, and Hilda Doolittle was on the way to her hour with Professor Sigmund Freud. When she turned the corner onto his street, she saw swastikas before her on the narrow old sidewalk. Her days in Vienna had been punctuated by such signs. One morning confetti-like bits of paper had showered from the skies. They reminded her of the little slips of paper English children receive in Christmas favors promising wealth and good fortune. But these messages predicted a different future: "Hitler gives work." "Hitler gives bread." Gilded paper swastikas had floated down on her once as well. But the swastikas Hilda saw on this October day were different. "They were the chalk ones now; I followed them down Berggasse as if they had been chalked on the pavement especially for my benefit." Hilda walked on, her tall figure solitary in the deserted streets. The swastikas sketched in bold strokes on the sidewalk led her to Freud's door.

Long ago the poet William Carlos Williams had remarked upon Hilda's "bizarre beauty." Nearly six feet tall but somehow fragile, her eyes intensely glittering yet her gaze awkwardly childlike, the contradictions only heightened her beauty. Now forty-eight years old, Hilda had sailed from America to England in 1911, a young and untried poet eager to visit her friend and former fiancé, Ezra Pound. One day after visiting the Greek friezes in the British Museum, Hilda and Pound sat together over tea and she showed him her newest poems. With a spare and quiet hand, Hilda had omitted everything inessential and gained the simple line of the Greek statues she loved. Elated, Pound struck out her signature on one of her poems and wrote "H.D. Imagiste." With his gesture, a new movement in poetry had begun. H.D.'s unique style as a woman and a poet inspired several writers to use her as a character in their fiction. One of her biographers would write that *Lady Chatterley's Lover* was the story of H.D.'s life during her first years in England.

But the sensitivity that imbued H.D.'s poems with grave charm had an effect on her emotional well-being. Hilda would struggle her life long to measure her own myth against the legends of ancient Greek heroes, and at times the chasm was too wide. "She is like a person walking a tight-rope," her friend D. H. Lawrence said. "You wonder if she'll get across." Troubled, often sad, Hilda Doolittle arrived in Vienna late in 1934 to resume an analysis begun the year before with Dr. Freud.

Hilda often thought of the first time she had visited Berggasse 19. "Paula has opened the door (though I did not then know that the pretty little Viennese maid was called Paula). . . . She has shown me into the waiting room with the lace curtains at the window. . . . There is the modest, treasured, framed diploma from the small New England university, which I examined later." It was, Doolittle learned, the honorary degree bestowed upon Freud by Clark University when he journeyed to America in 1909 with his closest friend, Carl Jung. H.D. had been nervous as she sat in the waiting room. "I know that Prof. Dr. Sigmund Freud will open the door which faces me. Although

I know this and have been preparing for months for this ordeal, I am, nonetheless, taken aback, surprised, shocked even, when the door opens."

The man standing before her now, consummately polite, impeccable in a dark suit and vest, with his old-fashioned gold watch chain and tiny locket, had once been handsome. Yet Hilda had been disturbed from the first by something enigmatic in Freud's nature. His mouth seemed to be slightly smiling, but his eyes—dark and deep-set—revealed little. "But why did you come?" Freud asked her. "No one has come here today, no one. What is it like outside?" Ever since Hitler had taken control of Germany in January 1933, people in Vienna watched for signs that would tell whether or when or how he might enter Austria.

Freud had reason to worry about conditions in the city. As a Jew, Freud had lived among the realities of anti-Semitism all his life. His friend Oskar Pfister had written him recently, "I paid a brief visit to Germany last week, and it will be a long time before I am able to get rid of the feeling of disgust I got there. . . . Cowardly towards the outside world, it wreaks its infantile rage on defenceless Jews." Freud knew that his grandson in Berlin was called on in school as *Jud Freud*—Jew Freud. It was used as a form of address, as one might say Herr Freud.

Seventy-eight years old in 1934, Freud had come to Vienna as a small boy. When he had grown and married, he had, after a few years, brought his young wife, Martha, to live with him here in this large, comfortable apartment. Now, more than forty years later, swastikas led to his door. Quite possibly Freud would have to leave Vienna; offers of refuge had already been made. "The only thing I can say," he had written his half-nephew Samuel Freud in England the year before, "is that we are determined to stick it out here til the last. Perhaps it may not come out too badly." And yet, he was not sure. Some seventy thousand Jews had been forced to flee Germany, among them many psychoanalysts. Freud feared that the movement he had worked his life to build was beginning to come apart and that his death would mark its end. Once he had hoped that his friend Carl Jung would carry on after him, but they had quarreled years ago; now there was no one to take Freud's place.

Freud and Doolittle weighed the meaning of the swastikas that day. England and France were pledged to stand together, and it seemed unlikely that Hitler would dare to challenge them. "Well we had better go on with your analysis," Freud told H.D. finally, shrugging his shoulders. "It is the only thing now." Hilda Doolittle interested Freud.

With her love of mysticism, she was irresistibly drawn to the edge of rational possibility, happy to surrender herself to the magical world of alchemy and spiritualism. Freud, too, had been interested in such things, had participated in séances and experiments in thought transference and come away convinced. But he had always fought the irrational side of his nature. Something in it frightened him. Years ago he had lost Carl Jung to this strange and mystical world. And so with Hilda Doolittle, while they would "go backward or go forward into alchemy," as she later wrote, Freud would always return her to what he believed was the rational side of psychoanalysis, the structure of which he had created himself. Freud had accomplished this at great cost, and for the most part, he had done it alone.

HILDA DOOLITTLE's hour with Freud was over, and the long afternoon had drawn to a close. Sometimes Freud walked with her into his study, continuing their discussion for a moment or two. At first glance it seemed a conventional room, with old-fashioned horsehair chairs soft with wear. But it was more than that. Freud's study fascinated Hilda, for all around, in cabinets and on shelves, hundreds of strange and lovely little carved faces gazed upon her. Mythological figures, ancient Assyrian deities, wooden toys from Egyptian tombs, saints and gargoyles, the eloquent symbolism of serpents and Gothic dragons—Freud told her these "little statues and images helped stabilize the evanescent idea, or keep it from escaping altogether." Once, he picked up an elegant little bronze statue standing among several others in a grave semicircle on his desk. "*This* is my favorite," he said, and placed it in her hands. It was Pallas Athena, Doolittle knew, "to be venerated as a projection of abstract thought . . . born without human or even without divine mother, sprung full-armed from the head of her father . . . Zeus." Perhaps, in these troubling days, the little statue symbolized for Freud his belief in reason against all odds, against the irrationality of the world that lay beyond his door.

Here in his study Freud had tunneled beneath the surface of conscious life and discovered the world of the unconscious, governed by instinctual needs and fueled with sexual energy. To account for human behavior as Freud observed it had been a massive undertaking. "Mine," he said, "was the devil's lot. I had to get the stones out of the quarry as best I could and was glad when I succeeded in arranging them willy-nilly so that they formed something like a building." Now he wondered who would finish it.

Freud had met with an intellect capable of the task, a mind akin to his, a man whose ideas had complemented, extended and largely confirmed his own. Years ago, on a Sunday in March 1907, the Swiss psychiatrist Carl Jung had come with his wife to pay Sigmund Freud a visit. Already drawn to the principles of the infant science of psychoanalysis, captivated by the mysteries of spiritualism, possessed of originality and the defiant, stubborn assertiveness of youth, Carl Jung—then thirty-two years old—possessed qualities of mind that Sigmund Freud admired. The men had closeted themselves in Freud's study and talked on that first visit for thirteen uninterrupted hours. Freud, self-assured at the age of fifty-one, sat smoking cigars, picking up from time to time one little figure or another from the small collection on his desk and gazing with growing wonder upon the voluble and enthusiastic man whose ideas seemed so nearly to match his own. The loneliness of the years fell away as the men talked on past midnight, as the tall young Swiss, unself-conscious and unknowing, laid claim to Freud in a way that no one ever would again.

Together Freud and Jung would try to unravel the mysteries of the psyche, and they would defy the established order of psychiatry. They were revolutionaries whose course was bold and imaginative, and their personalities were suited to the task. "I am by temperament nothing but a conquistador—an adventurer," Freud once confessed. Jung met this essential lawlessness with his own. Their conversation that evening was the beginning of an intimate friendship and a powerful alliance. But the love that gripped the men erupted in anger in 1913; the complex and vital friendship lay in a tangled ruin. The passage of time obscured the pain but did not fully ease it. In 1932 a visitor came to Freud and asked about the friendships that had foundered during the early days of psychoanalysis. What about Alfred Adler, Wilhelm Stekel and Carl Jung, the visitor, Dr. E. A. Bennet, asked? Freud answered easily that Adler did not matter, and as for Stekel, his personality had made him impossible to work with, and then Freud stopped. And Jung? After a pause, Freud said, "Jung was a great loss."

In 1933 there was a different kind of pain. Carl Jung had accepted the position as president of the international General Medical Society for Psychotherapy, located in Germany and dominated by Germans, whose contingent would soon formally reorganize to exclude Jewish membership. Jung wielded considerable power, for along with undertaking the presidency, he became the editor of the Society's influential journal, the *Zentralblatt für Psychotherapie*, a position he would share after 1936 with Dr. Matthias Heinrich Göring, cousin of field marshal Hermann Göring. Jung was strongly condemned for his relationship with M. H. Göring, who assumed the presidency of the

German Society just months after Jung became president of the international umbrella association. In 1933, Dr. Göring published a manifesto in the German supplement to the *Zentralblatt* urging the members of the German Society to adopt Hitler's ideological principles. By mistake or by design, a slightly altered version also appeared in the international edition of the *Zentralblatt*. What the world saw was a journal under Jung's editorship carrying the Nazi manifesto; Jung maintained the addition had been made without his knowledge.

Not only were people saying that Jung was anti-Semitic and collaborating with the Nazis in Berlin, many also felt he was casting aspersions upon Freudian psychology. "I have fallen foul of contemporary history," Jung said. "People now think I am a blood-boltered anti-Semite because I have helped the German doctors to consolidate their Psychotherapeutic Society and because I have said there are certain differences between Jewish and so-called Aryan psychology which are mainly due to the fact that the Jews have a cultural history that is 2,000 years older than the so-called Aryan." Jung wrote in the *Zentralblatt* in 1933, "The factual and well-known differences between Germanic and Jewish psychology should no longer be blurred, which can only benefit science." In the next volume of the *Zentralblatt*, published in 1934, Jung wrote, "The Jew, who is something of a nomad, has never yet created a cultural form of his own and as far as we can see never will, since all his instincts and talents require a more or less civilized nation to act as host for their development." Jung's words were considered by many to be anti-Semitic. Some people would wonder whether these statements, and others Jung made, were not in part the result of anger at Freud.

Roy R. Grinker, who would one day practice psychoanalysis in Chicago, was coming to Freud for analysis in 1933, and they discussed Jung's connection with the *Zentralblatt*. Jung's controversial actions may not have come as a surprise to Freud. He told Grinker of a dream he had had in the months before his rupture with Jung: a gladiator had appeared, dressed in a Swiss costume and brandishing a sword. "That [Freud] hadn't immediately recognized the meaning of the dream," Grinker remembered, "he regarded as a 'very serious breach of insight.' " The man Freud met in his study years ago and loved like a son had been a stranger for many years. Now it seemed Jung had become an enemy as well.

NIGHT WAS falling as Hilda Doolittle walked back through the empty streets of Vienna to the Hotel Regina, but she could still see the swastikas on the sidewalk. "It is not so easy," she thought, "to scrub death-head chalk marks from a pavement." Vienna was a powder keg in 1934. The year before, Austrian chancellor Engelbert Dollfuss had officially rejected the idea of *Anschluss*, of uniting with Germany. He declared the National Socialist movement illegal, and Nazis in Vienna resorted to acts of terror; Dollfuss was killed. The new chancellor, Kurt von Schuschnigg, though well-intentioned, was unable to cope with the growing threat of Hitler within and outside the Austrian border.

Part of Hilda's ritual after her hour with Freud was to relax in the familiar comfort of her hotel room and write in her diary, an etching of Freud propped on the dressing table. In a few weeks she would leave Vienna, but Freud never lost his affection for her. When she sent him orchids on his eightieth birthday, he would thank her gently. "Life at my age is not easy, but spring is beautiful and so is love." One day H.D. would look over the old diaries of her stay in Vienna and write a moving memoir of Freud in these solemn days before Austria was taken by Hitler, and a world and more was lost.

CHAPTER TWO

WHEN PAULA Fichtl woke up in the Freud apartment on the morning of March 12, 1938, she took off the sheets and comforter as usual and put them away in a drawer. She had been a maid in the Freud household for ten years and she spent each night on a couch in the waiting room where Freud received his patients. "I slept very well on that couch," she said, and her brown eyes danced. "After all, it was the Professor's, wasn't it?" Paula had been in her twenties, charming in a Tyrolese dirndl, her hair in a thick dark braid, when she had first come from Salzburg to work in Vienna. Now she knew the family in ways no stranger ever would. "The Professor teased me all the time, always making jokes. I went about swishing my skirts, and he would pull my ear or pull my braid, and I always screamed. Of course, I never teased him back. I had too much respect for him because you see, I loved him. He was like a father to me."

"Quick, Paula—get me the *Abend*," Freud called later that day. As Paula ran down the steps, she saw Austrian storm troopers in the street. A month before, Hitler had summoned Austrian chancellor Schuschnigg to the Berghof, his Bavarian mountain retreat near Berchtesgaden. His message to Schuschnigg was plain: either Austria would accept a National Socialist "coalition" government or Hitler would invade. Schuschnigg did not want Austria to unite with Germany and he declared a plebiscite on the issue of an independent Austria. Sidewalks and walls were covered with pro-Schuschnigg slogans, but on March 11, Hitler had ordered Schuschnigg to call off the vote. Schuschnigg was forced to resign. "God save Austria," he said that evening: his country had fallen to Hitler and to Germany. By dawn the next morning, German tanks were rumbling across the Austrian border.

Now, taking the *Abend* from Paula gently, Freud read through the headlines, then crushed the paper and threw it in a corner. Freud's son Martin picked up the crumpled sheets while the rest of the family sat in silence. Martin quickly saw that the *Abend*, a pro-Schuschnigg newspaper, was jubilant over the news of Hitler's victory. Moreover, throughout the paper, accusations of terrible crimes were leveled against Jews.

"Hitler in Vienna," Freud wrote in his journal on March 14. Thousands of Viennese ran through the streets singing and cheering. Foreign newsmen wrote of an atmosphere of celebration in the city, and worse. People gathered to watch and hurl abuses as Jews were forced to take toothbrushes or use their bare hands to scrub pro-Schuschnigg slogans from the pavements and buildings of Vienna.

The following weeks marked the end of a life Sigmund Freud and his family treasured. As efforts were made to leave the city, the quiet routine born of forty years' repetition was played out for the last time. The apartment had been home to Sigmund and Martha since the early years of their marriage, and its seventeen rooms covered the entire second floor of Berggasse 19. The six Freud children were proud that eleven desks could be found in their home. Now only Freud's youngest daughter, Anna, still lived with her parents. She too was a psychoanalyst, working long hours in a room near her father's. Anna, Paula remembered, sewed many of her own clothes during the hours she spent with her patients. The blouses and dresses, slips and nightgowns, were handmade in exactly the same way, each with a seam down the right and left sides of the bodice, a square neck, and buttons down the back, the buttonholes neatly stitched, the dresses sashed in back.

One evening as Anna sat sewing after the last patient had left, Paula said to her, " You were so pretty when you were young. You come from a fine family. Why did you never marry?" Anna answered, "When I was young, I wanted to marry, but the men I loved were all older than I, and already married." Like Anna, Martha's sister, Minna Bernays, was unmarried and living at Berggasse 19. Over the years Minna had helped raise the children and look after the large household. Now, with the children grown, her days were quiet. She passed the time with needlepoint in her comfortable sitting room. Paula always wondered why Auntie Minna had not chosen this room to sleep in instead of the little room behind that of the Professor and his wife.

"I always thought it very strange, Auntie Minna's bedroom right next to theirs. She had to pass right through to get to her room. And at night, in her nightclothes, she would have to enter their room to get to the bathroom." Although Paula loved the other members of the family, she had a difficult time with Minna. Auntie Minna was hard, Paula remembered, but the Professor's wife "was quiet and gentle. She was shy. She did everything for the Professor, but she was always very serious. She never joked, and she never talked much at all. Herr Professor always wanted to give a little gift, to be jolly and tell jokes. She was not like that." Martha took pleasure in housewifely details, tying her beautifully laundered linens carefully with colored ribbons and going to the market herself. "Frau Professor liked to save everything —string, paper. We had big boxes of it in the kitchen. She didn't like to waste anything. Every morning Herr Professor would give his boiled egg to Lün [the family chow]. Frau Freud would get annoyed. 'I cooked it for *you*!' But every day, slice by slice, he gave it to Lün. And then he would always laugh, because he had saved only a little bit for himself."

Paula felt sorry for Frau Freud. "Nobody ever made a fuss over her. It was as if she were pushed aside. Not even the children made a fuss over her. *They* loved the father, Miss Freud loved the father, Auntie Minna—they all, all of them, loved the father." And Paula did too. "Of them all," she said, "I always liked him the best. He was so kind."

FRAIL AND gravely ill with the cancer of the mouth that had afflicted him since 1923, Freud remained the calm presence his family had always known. On March 15 four Nazis came to the door. Paula took their rifles and put them in the umbrella stand. Frau Freud invited the Nazis to sit down, but by the end of the hour's visit, the apartment had been ransacked by the Nazis, the Freuds' money and passports confiscated. The storm troopers had taken six thousand schillings from Freud's safe. When Frau Freud told her husband of this, he said merely, "That is more than I ever got for a single visit."

As both a psychoanalyst and a Jew, Freud was particularly vulnerable to Nazi persecution, and people moved quickly to help him. John Cooper Wiley, the American consul general in Vienna, cabled Secretary of State Cordell Hull in Washington, FEAR FREUD, DESPITE AGE AND ILLNESS, IN DANGER. President Roosevelt intervened immediately and had Hull wire the American ambassador in Berlin, THE PRESIDENT HAS INSTRUCTED ME TO ASK YOU TO TAKE THE MATTER UP PERSONALLY AND INFORMALLY WITH THE APPROPRIATE OFFICIALS IN THE GERMAN GOVERNMENT.

Roosevelt also turned to William C. Bullitt, the American ambassador to France. Bullitt was called the Champagne Ambassador because of the lavish private parties he held at the embassy in Paris, international society balls where six hundred people drank nearly five hundred bottles of Pommery in an evening. Bullitt's pink cheeks and blue eyes called up a lighthearted image, but he had telephone access to Roosevelt at any hour. His thorough reports on the growing threat of Germany made a decisive impression on the President, and he became an important go-between in the plan to get Freud out of Vienna. Bullitt was happy to be of use. He had consulted with Freud in the 1920s because of psychological problems; the men had also collaborated on a book about Woodrow Wilson, an undertaking that many would feel bore more the impress of Bullitt than of Freud.

Despite the efforts of Bullitt and others, harassment of the family continued. On the afternoon of March 22, the Gestapo were at the door again; "I tried to push them away," Paula remembered. "I would always do anything to protect the family. But then the Professor came out and said, 'Paula, what are you doing? Let them in.' *He* was not afraid. And then one of the Nazis said to me, 'Yes, you are a cheeky one, aren't you? Watch out, I might kill you.' " Within minutes, Nazis were all over the apartment. Martha, finding a storm trooper going through her tidy linen closet searching for money, told him what she thought of such behavior. The storm trooper, embarrassed, turned away.

The Nazis arrested Anna, then forty-two years old, and took her to Nazi headquarters. Seeing her go off in the open car flanked by Nazis tore at Paula's heart: "She was such a little thing." Freud paced for hours in his rooms smoking cigars endlessly. Perhaps his daughter was being tortured, perhaps she was on her way to a concentration camp. Quite possibly she would die. Freud did not know that Anna and her brother Martin, anticipating arrest, had gone to their father's physician. At their request, Max Schur had given them Veronal, a strong barbiturate, to take if their lives were threatened.

Freud had been a struggling young physician of thirty-five when he bought the apartment at Berggasse 19 in 1891. Forty-seven years later, as he waited there for news of his daughter, he was one of the most renowned men in the world. The irony that his fame as the founder of psychoanalysis now served only to endanger Anna's life would not have escaped him. After some time, he said quietly, "They've kept her too long." Paula set off for Gestapo headquarters. "I peeped in the windows," Paula said, "and the Nazis asked me what I was doing there. 'Well,' I said, 'I'm looking for Fräulein Freud. She has been away so long, and the Professor is so worried.' They told me to go away, but I wouldn't. I told them that the Professor was an old man and needed his daughter to help him." Finally Paula returned to Berggasse 19, where the family waited in the dark, old-fashioned rooms, a profusion of orchids blooming pale and delicate in the early spring twilight. Anna was delivered back home that evening at seven o'clock after five hours of interrogation.

In the days that followed, the family began to make arrangements to leave the country. A story, perhaps apocryphal, is sometimes told about one offer to help Freud. At Jung's direction, it is said, the son of his colleague Franz Riklin was dispatched to Vienna. Young and Nordic-looking, Franz junior carried the equivalent of ten thousand dollars in a money belt into Austria. When he arrived at Freud's house, Anna greeted him at the door. Riklin told her he had come on behalf of Jung and his father, who wanted to give money to Freud so that he could go to England. Anna returned to Riklin after speaking to Freud and told him that her father refused the offer. Riklin pleaded with Anna, and then Freud stepped to the door. "I refuse to be beholden to my enemies," he said. Jung was saddened: "He would not take help from me under any circumstances."

A devoted friend, the Princess Marie Bonaparte, arrived to help the Freud family. Descended from Napoleon Bonaparte's brother and married to Prince George of Greece, the princess had undergone an analysis with Freud and supported the psychoanalytic cause financially and emotionally. Now, against her husband's wishes, she spent her days with Freud, facing the dangers of being involved with a Jewish family, although she was not herself a Jew. The princess, Anna and Freud began the painstaking work of going through Freud's papers, labeling, packing and shipping them out of the country. Marie Bonaparte noticed that Freud threw many papers away. Disturbed by the possibility that historic documents might be lost forever, she recovered from the wastebasket the letters and manuscripts Freud threw out each day.

There was among the papers half of an exchange of more than three hundred and fifty letters between Sigmund Freud and Carl Jung. The letters in Freud's possession, Jung's letters, chronicled an intellectual odyssey undertaken by men of genius; but they also told the story of a most intimate, complex and mysterious friendship. It was strange that Freud had kept the letters so long. They reflected a vulnerability and intensity he would prefer to forget. It is not difficult to imagine Freud's summary allocation of the relationship to the wastebasket. Nor is it difficult to imagine the princess, watchful and loyal, restoring to history a haunting and provocative tale.

MUSIC DRIFTS across the pastures and down the Swiss hills that slope toward the Zürichsee at its eastern shore. Sometimes there is a single note, and sometimes all the cowbells ring when a wandering dog disturbs the peace of the cows. In days gone by, a farmer often gave his cows particular notes on the musical scale, and his stature could be measured by the rich harmony of the tones that echoed down his valley. Carl Jung loved the sound of the bells. One day in April 1938, he left Küsnacht and set out for Bollingen, a tower he had built at the edge of the lake among fields of grazing cows. Normally he would sail to Bollingen in the eighteen-foot yawl of his own design, complicated to handle and very fast. Jung would let the red sails fill and sail before the wind the twenty miles to the end of the lake. But an illness Jung had contracted on a visit to India that year persisted, and this time he went to Bollingen by car. There he would follow a regimen of fresh air and exercise recommended by his doctor, Edwin Schmid.

Jung had within months to present a paper in England, and the solitude of Bollingen would give him uninterrupted hours to write. The issues confronting him in the speech he would deliver in the summer of 1938 were serious. Hitler's rise to power threatened to destroy the psychoanalytic movement in Germany. The Nazis had barred Jewish psychiatrists from membership in medical societies; Freud's writings had been included in the Burning of the Books in Berlin. Controversy surrounded some of the actions Jung had taken, and some of his statements had been interpreted as supporting the Nazi formulation of racial differentiation. Jung would attempt to make his position clear in the speech he would write at Bollingen.

In a house half a mile from Jung's tower, a young Swiss, Hans Kuhn, would be waiting patiently. As soon as he saw Jung's car, he would take a basket packed with bread, milk and meat and cross the pastures to the tower at Bollingen. Flanked on either side by tall trees, the gray stone building with its courtyard facing the Zürichsee had been the work of Jung himself. He had bought the land in 1922 and sailed across the lake to a quarry to learn how to work with stone. Patiently cutting the heavy rocks, raising and fitting them carefully into place, he had built the first part of the tower with the help of relatives. "Old Jung, down there by the lake," the son of a stonemason would say years later, "he knew the right way to take a stone in your hand."

Dressed as he often was in worn drill trousers stuffed into laced boots, his socks with holes in them, an old blue apron tucked to one side and a leather jacket on, Jung at sixty-three was a massive and arresting figure. Rumpled, often dirty, he was the meat and marrow of Bollingen. The shopkeepers of Schmerikon, where Jung sailed for provisions, called him Professor, but there any concession to his stature ended. Jung would often go with the hotel owner and wine merchant, Franz Kuster, down into his cellar, each man carrying a candle and a glass. They would sit for an hour or so on the stairs tasting and discussing the wines. Jung would sometimes say excitedly, "But this one is really *chaib* [goddamned] good!" Herr Kuster would remonstrate gently. "Herr Professor, but you don't say of a wine that it is *chaib*!" Jung was contrite. "You are right . . . because it's a gift of nature that we got."

Jung would sail back to Bollingen with his prizes. If friends were staying with him or family members, Jung sat himself on a small child's chair before the primitive fireplace, and from there he would direct, imprecate and sometimes despair over the dinner operations in his command. No one escaped his watchful eye, not even Toni Wolff, a woman he had once treated as a patient and whom he dearly loved. One evening he instructed her to go to the garden to gather a few chives to sprinkle on the soup. Toni returned instead with a quantity, enough to fill a large bowl. Jung was dumbfounded by such a blatant example of the ineptitude he suspected in his kitchen help. He teased Toni with such earthy finality that she began to cry. Jung's son, Franz, took her outside the next morning and together they sprinkled the offending chives in the garden, restoring her good humor in the mistaken belief new chives would grow. A day or so later, unobserved, Franz bought new chive plants and put them in the garden.

Despite the amateur help, meals at Bollingen were very good. Jung's hand was everywhere, mixing garlic with oil and vinegar into a big wooden spoon, and stirring wine into a pan with the meat, which he preferred full of gristle, bone and fat. Lean veal or chicken disturbed his sensibilities: "This is not meat!" Once at a dinner during which much wine was drunk, and people had exclaimed at the wonderful taste of the meat, Jung told them delightedly it was cows' udders and offered them more.

But on this visit to Bollingen in 1938, Jung was alone. He turned over the earth in his garden at the edge of the lake, spread manure and set out potatoes. Following his doctor's instructions, Jung scrubbed himself daily with a hard brush, sunbathed in the warmth of his courtyard when the sun was high and walked for hours in the hills. Life at Bollingen was grounded in the satisfactions of hard physical work, but there were quiet, nearly idle times as well. Everywhere Jung had carved—into the outside walls of the tower, on little pillars half hidden by trees and on boundary markers—the mysteries of alchemy: brief quotations and symbolic figures "to make these troublesome things steady and durable."

It was Jung's habit to sit near the tower beside threads of water that ran down a slope, clearing and widening the small channels with a shepherd's spade. His creative life had become connected with the flow of the little streams, and he sat there for hours at a time. Here Jung had developed some of the ideas that distinguished his psychology from that of Sigmund Freud. Several of his concepts had come about as a result of the parting with Freud and his struggle to understand it. Jung's formulations of introversion and extroversion defined two perceptions of reality: the extrovert, he thought, was Freud; the introvert, himself. In one, the reliance was upon an inner, the other upon an outer reality. Jung had concluded sadly that between the two, as between himself and Freud, lay a tragic lack of understanding.

During the troubled years after his separation from Freud, Jung became convinced that not everything he encountered in his dreams and fantasies could be explained by Freud's theories. Jung did not agree with Freud's belief that the sole contents of one's dream life were early childhood experiences. Jung was sure he saw more. He saw his major dreams arranged by instinctual patterns of behavior not amenable to Freudian explanation. Jung expanded upon Freud's concept of the unconscious to include what he called the collective unconscious: "I call it 'collective' because, unlike the personal unconscious, it is not made up of individual and more or less unique contents but of those which are universal and of regular occurrence."

Over the years Jung continued to explore what he thought were the inadequacies of Freudian theory. When he tried to understand the psychological reasons for the rise of the Nazi movement in Germany, Jung concluded that Freud's psychology, with its emphasis on sexuality and early childhood experiences, was not sufficient to explain the behavior of the German people. "Where was that unparalleled tension and energy while as yet no National Socialism existed?" Jung asked himself; he concluded that it had lain deep in the collective unconscious of the German people, "in a pit that is anything but a garbage-bin of unrealizable infantile wishes and unresolved family resentments." Despite their theoretical differences, Jung did not lose his high regard for Freud. Jung's friend Sir Laurens van der Post recalled years later, "The respect and love of Freud flared up wherever the long years of controversy gave him the calm to allow it . . . to re-emerge in his life."

In fine weather Jung wrote outside at a plain wooden table in his courtyard beside the lake, a yellow flag raised on his roof to warn friends he was not to be disturbed. Because the medical society would meet that year in Oxford, Jung was writing his paper in English, a language he felt was more precise than his native German. He wrote slowly and with total concentration, rarely changing a word. But Jung was prepared to be misunderstood. "The written word," he told a friend, "is a damnable tricky thing because one never knows exactly how to read it. Primitive language needs as you know a lot of gesticulation. People therefore can't talk to each other in the night, so they light a fire, because mere sound won't do. So when you want to understand one of my papers you better light a fire first, so that you can see where I am serious and where I smile."

Images conflicted of Jung in 1938, and enigma still surrounded the ruptured friendship of the two giant figures of psychoanalysis, one a gentile, the other a Jew; enigma of a magnitude that a quarter century of silence between them had done nothing to dispel. One can only guess what Jung's actions during the past few years, wrong at times and misinterpreted at others, meant to Freud in Vienna that spring of 1938 as the relentless force of Hitler threatened to engulf him, his family and his people.

CHAPTER THREE

IT WAS not a simple matter for the Freud family to leave Vienna. At times the attempt seemed doomed. "Wouldn't it be better," Anna asked her father one day, "if we all killed ourselves?" "Why?" Freud asked her in turn. "Because they would like us to?" Ernest Jones, Freud's colleague and friend in London, began to draw on a complex network of powerful friends and associates involving the lord privy seal and the home secretary. When Jones flew to Vienna four days after the *Anschluss*, he was preceded by a telegram sent from London to the British ambassador: DR. JONES IS ANXIOUS ABOUT THE FATE OF DR. FREUD AND IF HE APPLIES TO YOU FOR ADVICE LORD PRIVY SEAL WOULD BE GRATEFUL FOR ANYTHING YOU CAN DO.

After weeks of negotiation, permission was granted for the Freud family to leave the country. It was just in time. Freud's son Martin, publisher of the *Verlag*, which printed papers and books on Freudian psychology, had been exiled from Vienna. He was free to visit the city daily, however, and he maintained that his years of mountain climbing were particularly helpful now; Jews were no longer allowed to ride in elevators and were forced to climb the stairs. Freud had not left his house in weeks. News of torture circulated, and each knock on the door signaled danger and possible death. Anna went to Gestapo headquarters for the official release papers and returned with the news that all Jews obtaining such permission were required to go to the police daily. Freud was intractable. "You, Anna, have of course refused to obey so humiliating an order," he said.

But finally the necessary plans were complete. Minna Freud would precede the family to London on May 5, and Martin Freud would leave on May 14 to join her. Mathilde, Freud's eldest child, was to follow with her husband on May 24. Ernst, Freud's youngest son, had been in London making arrangements for the family and was about to go to Paris; Oliver, the second oldest son, was already in France. (Sophie, the next to youngest child, had died in 1920 in Hamburg, Germany.) With his family guaranteed safety, Freud permitted himself a last defiant gesture. The Gestapo brought a document to Freud's door and demanded his signature. The paper stated that he had been properly treated, and he signed it, but he added a phrase of his own. "I can recommend the Gestapo very much to everyone," Freud wrote, adopting the style of a commercial advertisement. The irony, Martin Freud thought, was lost on the Nazi soldiers, "although they were not altogether sure as they passed the certificate from man to man." Freud's most difficult moments were taking leave of four of his old sisters, who would stay behind in Vienna. Sadly, he had provided enough money to assure them a comfort they would never enjoy. The brother they adored was not to know they would die, all four, in concentration camps.

On June 4, 1938, the Freud family was ready to leave the city. An American envoy arrived to accompany them to Paris and safety. Years later an observer wrote, "When I saw [this U.S. official] just after World War Two, he told me about the trip and also vehemently described his personal feelings of repugnance for Freud, his friends and relatives, Jews and psychoanalysis." At the train station the Freud party, including Paula Fichtl, boarded the Orient Express for Paris. At 3:00 A.M. on June 5 they crossed the frontier into France at Strasbourg. "Over the Rhine bridge and we were free," Freud wrote. He said nothing to Paula sitting quietly beside him that morning at breakfast.

The family was met in Paris by William Bullitt, Freud's son Ernst, his nephew Harry Freud and Marie Bonaparte. Wearing a green felt hat and an overcoat, Freud took the princess's fur-draped arm and waved away the stretcher she had brought. He carried his cane but did not use it. Bullitt, dapper and smiling, a white flower in his buttonhole and carrying gloves, walked with Freud along the platform. After a twelve-hour visit in Marie Bonaparte's home, Freud left "proud and rich, under the protection of Athena": the princess had smuggled the statue Freud and Hilda Doolittle loved out of Vienna. That night the Freud party crossed the English Channel by ferry and went directly to London. Security was such that Martin Freud could not welcome his father when he first got off the train. Only Ernest Jones was standing on the platform to greet him, while reporters and well-wishers waited at the other end of Victoria Station. "It's good to be in this lovely England," Freud said.

The little chow Lün had made the trip to England as well. She was placed in quarantine for six months at Mr. Kevin Quinn's Kennels in the west of London. "If you want to know where things are happening abroad," a reporter wrote, "you can get a good idea by visiting the kennels. Two years ago there was an invasion of dogs from Spain. Then came a rush of German dogs. Now Austrian dogs are arriving at the kennels almost daily." Freud visited Lün there several times over the next months, among the few excursions his health permitted him.

The setting of Freud's temporary new home at 39 Elsworthy Road charmed him. In back of the house was a tree-lined garden, which ended at Primrose Hill. The green slopes of Regent's Park lay just beyond. But there was a note of sadness. Minna was confined to her bedroom upstairs with pneumonia, and Freud was not yet able, for reasons of his own fragile health, to see her. "The pain in the heart," he admitted, "turns into an unmistakable depression." The Freud family was greeted warmly. Freud wrote, touched, "We are buried in flowers." Among them one day was a cluster of gardenias from Hilda Doolittle. Living in England herself, H.D. visited Freud soon after he arrived. "The Professor was sitting at a table just exactly like in Wien with a row of gods." When she told him how happy she was that he had gotten the little statues out of Austria, he replied, "I did not bring them. . . . The Princess had them waiting for me in Paris, so that I should feel at home there."

Worry over those left behind them, Freud said, cast "a deep shadow over our happiness." As the summer of 1938 wore on, he heard rumors that his sisters were not allowed access to the money he had left for them in Vienna. Anxious, knowing little of conditions there, he arranged for the diamonds belonging to his dead daughter Sophie to be sent from Vienna to a bank in Zürich and safety. When he learned that his sisters had been to the police to register, Freud was alarmed. "Register what?" he asked his daughter Anna. "What new malice is afoot here?"

CARL JUNG arrived in Oxford in July 1938 to present the speech he had prepared that spring at Bollingen. On the first evening, he attended a reception at Christ Church hosted by His Majesty's government, "dinner jacket and medals required." The recent history of the General Medical Society for Psychotherapy was a microcosm of the drama being enacted in Germany and soon throughout all of Europe: events in the association chronicled the ascendance of Nazi power, the pervasiveness of anti-Semitism and the moral dilemma of collaboration with the enemy. Jung maintained that he had accepted the presidency of the Society because he believed his neutrality as a Swiss would allow him to help his Jewish colleagues in ways no German could. By 1934 the former, predominantly German organization had shifted officially under Jung's leadership to an international umbrella association composed of different national societies. The Nazified German Society became one among several other national groups. Another of Jung's official acts in 1934 was to permit German-Jewish doctors, excluded from the German association, to become individual members of the new International Society.

Jung's colleague C. A. Meier remembered that at one of the meetings of the International Society, Jung had been asked to have a psychiatric consultation with Hitler. Meier recalled that M. H. Göring had arranged for Jung and Hitler to meet in Berlin on the occasion of a big military parade. Jung and Meier had come to Berlin as planned. The night before the parade, Meier recalled, the hotel room he shared with Jung was carefully searched by secret police. The next day Jung was fascinated by his glimpse of Hitler standing at the parade only yards away. "Hitler made upon me the impression of a sort of scaffolding of wood covered with cloth, an automaton with a mask, like a robot." And then Jung said, "With Hitler, you are scared. You know you would never be able to talk to that man; because there is nobody there." Meier was never sure whether it was Jung or Hitler who at the last moment refused to participate, but the consultation did not take place.

Jung would comment in October 1938 on the way to treat a man like Hitler therapeutically: "It is extremely difficult to deal with this type of phenomenon. It is excessively dangerous. . . . Now, when I have a patient acting under the command of a higher power, a power within him, such as Hitler's Voice, I dare not tell him to disobey his Voice. He won't do it if I do tell him. He will even act more determinedly than if I did not tell him. All I can do is attempt, by *interpreting* the Voice, to induce the patient to behave in a way which will be less harmful to himself and to society than if he obeyed the Voice immediately without interpretation."

Although Jung never treated Hitler, he proposed a cure for him. "I say let him go East," he would tell an American correspondent in October 1938. "Turn his attention away from the West, or rather, encourage him to keep it turned away. . . . That is the logical *cure* for Hitler. . . . Nobody has ever bitten into Russia without regretting it. . . . Meanwhile we should be safe, and by we, I mean all of Western civilization. . . . How to save your democratic U.S.A.? It must, of course, be saved, else we all go under."

AS JUNG stood before the Society at Balliol College on July 30, 1938, the controversial actions he had taken were a matter of record. He had been joined by M. H. Göring on the *Zentralblatt*. He had said that there were differences between the Germanic psyche and the Jewish, and his distinctions had played into the Nazis' hands. He had criticized Freudian psychology in its most vulnerable hour. But on this occasion, Jung addressed the Society in a spirit of compromise. He called upon the members to find those truths that were common to all schools of psychology, Jungian and Freudian alike. It was a mistake, Jung told the audience, to let differing theories obscure the fact that each psychotherapist follows a line that is common to his colleagues. Differences fell away to reveal Jung's central concern. "Today," he said, "we ought to think hard and make a serious effort to bring together all men of good will in our profession, in order to meet the needs and demands of the time."

It is doubtful that Jung had said enough on that July morning in England in 1938. When he finished addressing his audience of Americans, Nazi-Germans, British, Swiss and Scandinavians, some among them—and history—would remember what Jung did not say, and had not said during the years before. In a few months Jung would describe Hitler as a dangerous phenomenon and declare that Western civilization should at all cost be saved. But on that warm summer day in Oxford, as in the past, Jung's voice of human outrage was still, and his silence would not be forgotten on other, cold days.

Neverthless, Jung had made a gesture, and before the morning session ended, he made another. He wanted to honor Sigmund Freud, the man he loved and still admired. Days before, he had dispatched Dr. E. A. Bennet to Freud to ask him if he would accept a cable from Jung and the medical association. Now Jung arranged for it to be sent. THE TENTH INTERNATIONAL MEDICAL CONGRESS FOR PSYCHOTHERAPY IN SESSION AT OXFORD EXTENDS YOU VERY HEARTY GREETINGS, the cable went. WE RECOGNIZE OUR INDEBTEDNESS TO YOU FOR YOUR BRILLIANT CONTRIBUTION TO PSYCHOLOGICAL MEDICINE AND WISH YOU HEALTH, HAPPINESS, AND TRANQUILITY IN YOUR NEW SURROUNDINGS IN ENGLAND. Hours later when the meeting reconvened, Jung inquired after the telegram. The secretary of the Congress confessed he had forgotten to send it. Jung became instantly enraged. Friends present said he was angrier than they had ever seen him. Jung ordered the cable sent at once. The telegram itself had hardly been spontaneously phrased nor was Freud's reply. "The Oxford P.therapeutic Congress which Jung presides over," Freud told his daughter Anna, "sent me the obligatory welcome telegram to which I replied with a cool answer, prepared by Dr. Bennet."

A year later, Freud was dead. His age and long struggle with cancer did little to lessen the shock. His daughter Anna wrote sadly, "It is really not so that we had known for a long time that he would die. He was very ill but then he had been very ill many times before." Missing the daily interchange with her father, she said, "It is much more difficult to see things in their right light without his help."

ANNA FREUD collected bits of shrapnel during World War II. A bowl in the front hall was "piled nearly a foot high," a reporter noticed, "with sharp, irregular fragments of shell and bomb casings" that had been picked off the roof or raked from the lawn. A pail of sand to put out incendiary bombs stood beside the door. Like Anna Freud, Hilda Doolittle lived in England during the war. As the months and years wore on, she returned from forays into séances and spiritualism with a bounty she hoped would help end the war: she received word of where the bombs were to fall; she heard messages from airmen and from a Viking ship. Her fragile grasp on reality began to fail. She had a nervous breakdown in 1946 and was flown to a sanitorium in Switzerland on the shore of the Zürichsee a few steps from Carl Jung's door.

Most of the last fifteen years of H.D.'s life were spent at the Nervenklinik in Küsnacht, Switzerland. She regained her creative energy and turned to write an affectionate portrait of Sigmund Freud, but she was never again strong enough to live for long without the humane constraints of the Nervenklinik. Hilda was happy there. The houses were sober, elegantly appointed with antique furniture and porcelain stoves with painted tiles. The grounds were a sweep of green where narrow paths wound around tall trees. Patients played tennis and croquet on the lawn or sat on a terrace beside the lake. Each evening they joined Dr. Theodor Brunner at his long table, immaculate in a white cloth. Zürich bankers, European noblemen, visiting physicians and family members had dined there in benign accord with Dr. Brunner and his patients for more than thirty years.

Sometimes among the guests was Carl Jung. He had built a house in Küsnacht overlooking the lake. Terraces led down to a boathouse, and swans idled in the waters below. From time to time, Jung put patients up at Brunner's Klinik, and they walked down the road with a nurse for their hour with him in his upstairs study. Brunner consulted with Jung about his own patients from time to time, and Jung stepped in to help. Brilliant and original, with the sure magnetism of the born healer, Jung's presence was everywhere felt in Küsnacht. When Hilda came to Küsnacht in 1946, Jung was an analyst still; but more than that, he had become a renowned thinker whose view of the human psyche was steeped in the language of alchemy and open to the world of mysticism. Tales of Jung had taken on a legendary quality. At the heart of the legend lay his friendship with Freud and its strange, dramatic end. People heard that Jung had come close to madness after their quarrel, though few knew what had driven the men apart. Jung rarely spoke of those days with Freud, but people close to him sensed his suffering even many years later. "Yes," Jung's colleague C. A. Meier said. "The pain was enormous." Freud would still be a vivid memory "even for the very old Jung. If you spoke about Freud," the Swiss educator Karl Schmid saw, "then you touched something very living; it always remained that for him. . . . [It] was still living."

HILDA DOOLITTLE remained a Freudian, committing herself daily to the rigors of self-analysis; and yet there was a strong thread of religion and the occult in her writings. She barely knew her neighbor, Carl Jung, but H.D.'s psychiatrist Dr. Erich Heydt attributed her interest in mysticism partly to Jung's influence. Hilda's restless quest had drawn her into the worlds of both Freud and Jung. She had walked the gray streets of Vienna to visit Sigmund Freud, and she had sought solace strolling on a green lawn in Küsnacht a stone's throw from Carl

Jung's door. She knew their weathers, the damp Viennese chill and the winds that blew across the Zürichsee. More than that, she knew the inner terrain of Freud and Jung. She had absorbed with them the intellectual and cultural life of Europe, was drawn to their particular concerns and embodied even their conflicts. Hilda understood the value of Freud's insistence upon rational thought, and she shared Jung's interest in the occult. She knew the dry, restraining hand of reason, and she knew the joy in casting it off as well. "Here is the alchemist's key," she had written. "It unlocks secret doors . . . the elixir of life, the philosopher's stone is yours if you surrender sterile logic, trivial reason."

Hilda's room at the Nervenklinik looked out over the water; a photograph of Freud hung on her wall. She worked at a table by the window finishing the book that Freud's biographer Ernest Jones would call "the most delightful and precious appreciation of Freud's personality that is ever likely to be written." Sometimes, if she wished, she could see Jung in his small two-masted boat, unmistakable with its red sails, setting out on the long trip to Bollingen. Perhaps Freud would say it was a matter of chance that Hilda Doolittle had come to live out her life next door to Carl Jung. Jung might have called it fate that had brought her to Küsnacht, to the shore of the lake he loved.

ON A cold snowy day many years after Carl Jung's death, his son, Franz, stood silently in the library in Küsnacht. The long, narrow room looked much as it had when his father worked there, with the same gray walls and shelves of old leather books, tall windows and little balconies overlooking the Zürichsee. The afternoon and the days before had been full of talk about Jung and Freud. Franz had pointed out the "secret cache" in the wall of the study where Jung many years before had kept Freud's letters. He had told with warmth the story of how the correspondence between his father and Freud was finally joined. Jung's letters to Freud had made the move to London in 1938 under the supervision of Marie Bonaparte. In late 1969 Freud's son Ernst and Franz Jung decided to publish the letters between their fathers. Franz then flew to London, where Ernst Freud, gravely ill, received him. The two sons liked each other. "He was an architect like myself," Franz said, "and so there was a kind of common ground. Years ago Father had placed Freud's letters in a portfolio that was covered in a linen cloth, and he had written on it in large capitals 'FREUD'S LETTERS.' When I came with them, Ernst Freud was touched. Those letters were the most important thing in the world to him, and I think he stayed alive long enough to receive them."

Twilight was near and lights had begun to flick on in the houses across the Zürichsee, but the library was dim and full of memories. A low table was filled with snapshots of family camping trips: of Franz's mother and sisters in long white dresses looking on as he and his father built little villages with stones. There were road maps on the table and a tray filled with tea things. Franz had reached back into his childhood, to the years before the mystery that surrounded Jung and Freud had hardened into legend, and he had remembered what he could. Franz put a log in the old tile stove and stood gazing silently out over the lake he had sailed all his life, first with his father and later with his four sons. He turned from the window and said to me finally, "My father would not confess it, but he probably never got over Freud in all those years."

PART TWO

MEMORIES

CHAPTER FOUR

IN SUMMER the mountains of Bavaria beyond Salzburg are smooth and green as a crayon drawing, and broad valleys lie open to the sun. In 1899 Sigmund Freud was spending a few months in the country with his wife and children, writing a book he would one day call *The Interpretation of Dreams*. For the first time, Freud was demonstrating in a systematic way that dreams have meaning, and the dreamer he was relying on most was himself. An accounting of the facts of his early life, and even of his secret fears and wishes, was called for in order to document his dream theory. Confessing that "there is some natural hesitation about revealing so many intimate facts about one's mental life," Freud saw no way out of the dilemma. He was forty-three years old in 1899, and in the pages he was writing were many of the events and dreams of his life up to that summer. The extent of his unwilling self-disclosure was such that the book would later be described—with good reason—as Freud's disguised autobiography.

Work on the book had not gone well in Vienna. "I have great difficulties with it," Freud wrote in July 1899. "I cannot manage more than two hours a day without calling on Friend Marsala for help. 'He' deludes me into thinking that things are not really so bleak as they appear to me when sober." Freud was not a drinking man, but before Martha went on to Bavaria ahead of him, she counted the wine bottles carefully. Freud felt much better when he finally joined his family at Riemerlehen, a large old farmhouse set back on a hill at the edge of the village of Berchtesgaden. There he contented himself with walks with his children morning and evening and indulged his passion for mushroom hunting, which his eldest son recalled taking on the grandeur and excitement of a big-game hunt, his father invariably capturing the best one in his old felt hat and summoning his young troops with a silver whistle to admire his prize.

But at the center of Freud's life that summer of 1899 lay the dream book, as he called it, the chapters spread out on a table in the large ground-floor room of the cottage, windows framing the mountains he loved. "My old and grubby gods, of whom you think so little," Freud wrote a friend describing the antique statues he had begun to collect, "take part in the work as paperweights for my manuscripts." Here at Riemerlehen, amid the noise and activity of his children ("The rascals are making an unholy row in the meadow," he complained fondly), Freud wrote of each man's debt to his childhood. "The deepest and eternal nature of man . . . lies in those impulses of the mind which have their roots in a childhood that has since become prehistoric." His dreams and memories revealed aspects of his character that would draw him into a friendship with Carl Jung and aspects, too, that would contribute to its tragic undoing. "And now," he wrote, "I must ask the reader to make my interests his own for quite a while, and to plunge, along with me, into the minutest details of my life."

FREUD'S BIRTHPLACE was Freiberg, a little town in Moravia in what would one day become Czechoslovakia. He was born on May 6, 1856, to Jacob Freud, a wool merchant then forty-one years old, and Amalia, Jacob's third wife, who was twenty-one. Although Jacob already had two grown sons, one of whom was living nearby, Sigmund was Amalia's firstborn. Freud would retain his early belief that "a man who has been the indisputable favorite of his mother keeps for life the feeling of a conqueror, that confidence of success that often induces real success." Because of Jacob's marriages, family relationships were complicated. Freud's first playmate was his nephew John, a year older than himself. Theirs was a demanding relationship, with each boy vying for the upper hand; eldest sons both, neither wished to defer to the other. Their play was rough. Freud, though smaller and younger, was combative and unyielding. "Why," his father asked Sigmund, during a particularly damaging battle, "are you hitting John?" Freud, with the belief in vigilante justice common to aggressive little boys, retorted simply, "I hit him 'cos he hit me!"

Although Sigi, as he was known in his family, fought with John, he loved him too. This swing between love and hate would mark his relations with other friends in the years to come. Freud referred to his experiences with John several times in his dream book. "My emotional life has always insisted that I should have an intimate friend and a hated enemy. I have always been able to provide myself afresh with both, and it has not infrequently happened that the ideal situation of childhood has been so completely reproduced that friend and enemy have come together in a single individual—though not, of course, both at once or with constant oscillations, as may have been the case in my early childhood."

When Freud was nearly two years old, his younger brother Julius died; one day Freud would come to realize that he had been jealous of the baby and that a deep sense of guilt had been with him since Julius's death. When Sigmund was three, Jacob Freud and his family left Freiberg and went to live in Leipzig, then moved on to Vienna in 1860. Life in the city was not to Freud's liking. He missed the rural freedom and his heroic play with John. But his home had begun to fill with sisters, and he moved into his role of older brother with authority. He was a well-behaved boy and recalled few acts of defiance. One occurred when he was seven or eight. Immodest, he relieved himself in a glass urinal in his parents' bedroom while they were present. Freud never forgot Jacob's angry words, "The boy will come to nothing!" He regarded them as an important spur to his later achievement: "You see, I *have* come to something."

Freud's intellectual life began at the age of seven under the careful guidance of his father. Two years later, when at the age of nine Freud entered school, it was clear that Jacob Freud had prepared his son well: for eight years at the Sperlgymnasium, Freud sat on the front bench, at the top of his class. The envy and resentment he sensed from those who sat behind him was a vivid memory many years later. Freud's unrivaled position at school confirmed his mother's choice of him as her favored child. *Mein goldener Sigi* she would call him to the end of her long life and very nearly to his own.

During these early years, Freud began in schoolboy fashion to master the complexities of the world around him. His youthful notion of the hero—in part a legacy of his brave combat with John—was played out in endless battles with wooden toy soldiers. With them, Freud traced Napoleon's campaigns by the hour, favoring Napoleon's marshal André Masséna because he believed him a Jew born on his own birthdate a century before. The young boy's relationship with his father was largely untroubled. Yet, on one occasion when Freud was twelve, his father disappointed him. Jacob Freud recounted an incident when a gentile had come up, brushed his new fur cap into the mud and shouted, "Jew! get off the pavement!" Young Sigmund asked Jacob, "And what did you do?" His father replied quietly, "I went into the roadway and picked up my cap." It was not the answer Freud wanted to hear. He lived among heroes in his books and games and would seek them in the faces of the friends he knew. But more than that, he wanted to find a hero in his father.

The story did not end in simple disappointment, for as great as Freud's need to find a hero was his need to displace him. When he was fourteen, he play-acted a powerful drama with his nephew John, then fifteen, who had come to visit the family in Vienna. Before an audience of children, they presented a scene from a play by Schiller in which Sigmund played the role of Brutus, and John, Caesar. Years later Freud struggled to understand the nature of his intense involvement with John—the presence of so much hostility along with the love. "Where was an antithesis of this sort to be found," Freud asked himself as he turned to his books, "a juxtaposition like this of two opposite reactions towards a single person . . . ?" He found it, finally, "only in one passage in literature," in Brutus's famous lines in Shakespeare's *Julius Caesar*: "As Caesar loved me, I weep for him; as he was fortunate, I rejoice at it; as he was valiant, I honour him; but as he was ambitious, I slew him."

Freud drank black coffee and ate grapes as he studied for his final exams at the Sperlgymnasium, and he confessed in the dream book that his brilliant performance on the oral history examination had been aided by the kindness of his master. He "did not fail to notice that on the paper of questions which I handed him back I had run my fingernail through the middle one of the three questions included, to warn him not to insist upon that particular one." (In Freud's recurrent dreams of school examinations, the subject would always be history.) He graduated first in his class.

In the autumn of 1873, Freud enrolled in the University of Vienna as a medical student, and during the following eight years he pursued the usual courses of anatomy, physics, chemistry, biology and zoology.

Freud's choice of career confused his father. "When the Professor was a boy he used to say he wanted to be a doctor," Freud's sister Anna remembered. "But my father asked him how he could be when he was of such a sensitive nature he could not stand by and watch a splinter taken out of the hand of one of us children if the blood came." Freud continued to live at home during these years at the University, and when his family moved to a larger apartment, he was the only one given his own room. Long and narrow, the "cabinet" was large enough for a bed, a desk, a few chairs and shelf upon shelf of growing numbers of books.

His position in the household as the eldest of seven children prefigured his life years later as a family man at Berggasse 19. Always he would be the favorite, and now, in his late teens, he had his own room and the only lamp as well; the rest of the family used candles. He ate his supper in his room so that he could continue to study. Although he tunelessly hummed Viennese folk songs while he worked, the sound of his sisters playing the piano disturbed his concentration. The lessons ceased and the piano was removed. Despite his seeming arrogance, Sigmund was a devoted brother. Family finances were often precarious and he worried that his sisters were too thin. He found it difficult once, dining out at the invitation of a friend, to eat roast meat knowing how hungry his sisters were at home.

Sigmund Freud was the consummate older brother—self-assured, brilliant and lordly. Slender and well-proportioned, his adult height was five feet seven inches. His hair was dark brown, nearly black, and though he brushed it back from his brow, a thick shock of straight hair often fell across his forehead. His features were strong, but it was his eyes that people noticed; dark, intense at times and at others remote, they reflected as much as he would care to reveal and rarely more. Freud was a singularly passionate man and would always be, but already his self-control was nearly complete, and the emotions that played on his face were subtle and fleeting.

Franz Joseph presided over a worn-out empire during Freud's youth, but Vienna was experiencing a kind of cultural renaissance: within its reverence for the past, a modern sensibility was beginning to emerge. Gustav Klimt and Oskar Kokoschka were painting distinctive visions. Ludwig Wittgenstein, a wealthy young Viennese who would cast aside his fortune in order to live purely, would be called the most demanding philosopher of the twentieth century. Richard Strauss and Gustav Mahler composed and conducted in Vienna. Opera was so popular that people who wanted the cheapest places had to spend half a day in line for tickets. Herbert Graf, who would one day be Freud's famous case, "Little Hans," remembered his father, Max Graf, in a cultural juxtaposition common in Vienna: "on the crowded footboard of a trolley headed for the Sunday soccer match at the Hohe Warte, one hand on the railing, the other clutching his most cherished book, a well-worn, annotated copy of Kant's *Critique of Pure Reason*."

Living in Vienna with adoring parents, with respectful younger sisters and now a little brother; a medical student with early, clear success; a gifted, acknowledged intellect: for Freud on the edge of manhood, the future was alive to his touch. He turned nineteen in May 1875; in July of that year Carl Gustav Jung was born in a little village in Switzerland.

CARL JUNG'S first memory was of the bright leaves and blue sky of Laufen, Switzerland. Many years later he remembered lying in his pram on a summer day. "I see the sun glittering through the leaves and blossoms of the bushes. Everything is wholly wonderful, colourful, and splendid." Jung wrote these words with the greatest reluctance when he was a very old man. He had been silent about his early life, rarely speaking of it even to his family, and when he finally began his autobiography at the age of eighty-three, he hesitated even then. The instinct to hoard his memories was strong, for Jung, like Freud, realized how much of the character of the man derived from the early experience of the child. "I have guarded this material all my life, and have never wanted it exposed to the world; for if it is assailed, I shall be affected even more than in the case of my other books."

Yet in the end Jung spared himself little. He wrote much of his autobiography, *Memories, Dreams, Reflections*, at his tower at Bollingen. He would sit outside on his terrace thinking back eighty years to the boy he once had been, growing up in a little village in Switzerland. Jung was often motionless as he sat there in the sun, so quiet, a friend remembered, that once or twice birds swooped down and tugged at his white head for a few hairs to line their nests. The old man was like a piece of nature, and so they had no fear. What Jung remembered gave him pain at times, for his childhood had been plagued with fear and loneliness. Jung had not been well practiced in friendship when he met Freud. His lonely childhood had left scars.

CARL JUNG'S father was a minister of the Reformed Church of Zwingli. Paul Jung's vicarage at Laufen looked out over the Rhine River and the ceaseless drama of cascading falls dropping hundreds of feet below. It was a heady sight for a young child and the backdrop of Jung's early memories. Once, he recalled, a lovely young woman with blonde hair and blue eyes had taken him walking down by the Rheinfall, through chestnut trees gold in the autumn sun. The woman, whose youthful image he retained all of his life, was Berta Rauschenbach; she would one day be his mother-in-law. These early memories were forever vivid, suspended in warmth and sunlight, but other, darker images intruded. "The muted roar of the Rhine Falls," Jung remembered, "was always audible, and all around lay a danger zone. People drowned, bodies were swept over the rocks." One day when he was very young, as he was walking across the bridge that stretched above the falls, Carl put his leg under the railing. Only the quickness of his maid prevented the little boy from dropping down into the river far below. The incident, Jung later believed, pointed to "an unconscious suicidal urge or, it may be, to a fatal resistance to life in this world."

Carl was sometimes distressed at home and didn't know why, although "dim intimations of trouble in my parents' marriage hovered around me." In 1878 his mother went to a hospital in Basel for several months, and Jung would later conclude that her illness was connected with difficulties with her husband. Young Carl, then three years old, missed his mother terribly. "From then on," he wrote, "I always felt mistrustful when the word 'love' was spoken. The feeling I associated with 'woman' was for a long time that of innate unreliability." The boy became ill during this separation. He was troubled by eczema and was often feverish, unable to sleep at night. His father would carry him in his arms, pacing up and down and singing his old student songs, "*Alles schweige, jeder neige* . . ." Jung wrote many years later, "To this day, I can remember my father's voice, singing over me in the stillness of the night."

At about this time Jung had the first dream he would remember, and it would affect him for the rest of his life. He dreamed he was in a familiar meadow, where he saw a hole in the ground with a stone stairway leading down to a doorway covered in a material like green brocade. Beyond was a rectangular stone room with a red carpet stretching to a golden throne, where at first Carl thought a tree trunk reached nearly to the ceiling. He was terrified to discover it was made of naked flesh. "On the very top of the head was a single eye, gazing motionlessly upwards." The boy stood paralyzed, sure that it might at any moment crawl toward him like a giant worm, when his mother cried out in his dream, " Yes, just look at him. That is the man-eater." The little boy awoke in terror and covered with sweat. The dream haunted Jung. He was sure that the strange creature was a subterranean god.

In 1879, when Jung was four, his father became the Protestant chaplain of the Friedmatt Mental Hospital, and the family moved to Klein-Hüningen, a small village on the Rhine near Basel. The atmosphere at home continued to trouble Carl. "All sorts of things were happening at night, things incomprehensible and alarming. My parents were sleeping apart." And, evidence that distrust of his mother had not disappeared, "I slept in my father's room." Carl became sick with what he would later describe as "pseudo-croup" and had bouts of choking. "I see in this," he later wrote, "a psychogenic factor: the atmosphere of the house was beginning to be unbreathable." Driven to rely more and more upon himself, uncomfortable with his parents and the sense of oppression at home, the boy spent much time outside and was troubled if anyone watched him at his solitary play. Hour after hour he constructed houses and towers with bricks and then delighted in destroying them with mock earthquakes.

Jung began to go to school in 1881, his companions the children of the peasants and fishermen in the village. But there, as at home, his feelings of estrangement continued. He felt the children's play was different from his own. Their concerns were not his, and he tried in childish bewilderment to preserve that part of himself he knew was crucial to his identity. Within the rituals of his childhood play lay the need to keep others, who might tamper with his fragile sense of self, at bay. On a slope near Jung's house was embedded a stone to which he returned time and again, sitting on it for hours on end and playing an imaginary—and compelling—game. Bereft of adequate definitions of himself from his school and family, he would say, "I am sitting on top of this stone and it is underneath." But he empowered the stone to respond as well: "I am lying here on this slope and he is sitting on top of me." After a while the distinction between outer and inner reality began to blur. "Am I the one who is sitting on the stone," the boy asked himself, "or am I the stone on which *he* is sitting?" Finally he would stand up, wondering which was which, a dark and fascinating question he was unable to resolve.

Young Carl wanted to make tangible the self that seemed so vulnerable to the world outside. He needed to secure proof that his inner self was inviolate and safe. One day he took up the yellow wooden pencil box that schoolchildren always carried, slid the ruler off, and carved a manikin at one end of it, inking in a black frock coat, top hat and shiny black boots. Then he sawed off the little figure and nested him in the pencil case, together with a small stone he had painted. He slid the ruler back in place and hid the box up in the attic on one of the roof beams. Carl felt immediately better. "The tormenting sense of being at odds with myself was gone." From this gesture was born Jung's idea of the "Other," an "other" self, a manikin with his black stone, sequestered in the far reaches of an eighteenth-century attic. While Jung struggled to understand his inner self, Freud was trying during the same years to find his place in the outer world of love and work.

IN 1882, Freud was a young doctor living at home with his parents, teaching and continuing his medical research. In that year Freud met Martha Bernays, the woman who would become his wife. In 1882 as well, a physician Freud knew, Josef Breuer, told him how he had treated a patient's symptoms in a novel way. The consequences of these events would shape the rest of Freud's life.

Sigmund Freud's first experience with love took him by surprise. Ordinarily, when he came home each day, he went directly to his room with only a brief greeting for his family. But one day in the spring of 1882, Freud caught sight of an attractive girl laughing with his sisters and peeling an apple at the family table, and this time he joined them. Martha Bernays, five years younger than Freud, came from a distinguished Jewish family who had moved to Vienna from Hamburg, Germany. Freud's love for Martha, who was then twenty-one years old, was a series of psychic shocks for which he was completely unprepared. He told her ruefully that he had never paid much attention to girls before, and now he was paying heavily for this neglect. He sent her a red rose every day, and when he visited her on the day of their engagement and the next, he told her he had given her more kisses on those two occasions than to his sisters in the twenty-six years of his life. Freud once wrote about the kind of woman who appealed to him, and his description fit Martha very well: "A robust woman who in case of need can single-handed throw her husband and servants out of doors was never my ideal, however much there is to be said for the value of a woman being in perfect health. What I have always found attractive is someone delicate whom I could take care of."

Martha was slender and pale, and her health would worry Freud always. "I really get quite beside myself when I am disturbed about you," he wrote one day, fearing she was ill. "I lose at once all sense of values, and at moments a frightful dread comes over me lest you fall ill. I am so wild that I can't write much more." A day later, learning she was in good health after all, he told her sheepishly, "So I was quite wrong in imagining you to be ill. I was very crazy. . . . One is very crazy when one is in love." Separated from Martha for three years of their four-year engagement because her family moved back to Hamburg, Freud wrote her at least once a day, often twice, sometimes even three times, and he wrote at length. A dozen closely written sheets was common, and one letter was twenty-two pages long. During their courtship Freud would send Martha more than nine hundred letters. The long months and years of their engagement took their toll. "I am like a clock that hasn't been repaired for a long time, dusty in every joint," he wrote Martha gravely.

Often in his letters to Martha, Freud mentioned the name of Josef Breuer, a man fourteen years older than himself whom he had met during the course of his studies. Breuer was a distinguished physician with deep cultural interests in music, art and literature. Well known in Vienna, and wealthy, he was nevertheless described by those who knew him as "the most unassuming man one can imagine." Breuer had embarked upon a promising scientific career only to abandon it, giving up his position as private docent because, it was thought, he did not wish to spend too much time away from his patients. One woman in particular had interested him, and as the friendship between Freud and Breuer deepened, the older man told her story often. Freud was fascinated.

Bertha Pappenheim was born in 1859 to wealthy Jewish parents. She had developed a variety of nervous symptoms as she cared for her ailing father during the summer of 1880, and her symptoms worsened when he died. The eminent professor of psychiatry Richard von Krafft-Ebing was brought in as a consultant, but it was Josef Breuer who listened to her complaints. In these years before the turn of the century, the strange complaints and bizarre behavior of the mentally ill were believed to be born of physiological causes: mishandlings at birth, hereditary defects, tragic accidents—damages for which there was no hope of repair. Physicians' offices everywhere were filled with patients like Bertha, whose physical complaints often shifted daily and sometimes even hourly. Nothing really helped the anxious woman newly married or the young girl who could not sleep, the man with a persistent nervous tic or the young boy who fainted. There was no known cure for their myriad problems, only the placatory effect of hot baths, rest and, more rarely, electrical stimulation.

Breuer decided upon a different treatment for Bertha Pappenheim. One day when she was in a hypnotic state, he listened to her complaints, a recital of stunning, seemingly arbitrary chaos. At times a profound darkness settled in her head; at others she could not move three of her limbs. Her vision fluctuated strangely and she believed she was turning blind and deaf. Worse, she had a pervasive fear that two selves—one of them evil—inhabited her body. She told these things daily to Breuer under hypnosis and in English, because somewhere in her labyrinthine difficulties she had abandoned all memory of her native German.

One day Bertha complained of thirst but could drink nothing. The list of her symptoms, already long, included a final eccentricity: she now ate only fruit. Under hypnosis, "Anna O.," as Breuer referred to her, "grumbled about her English lady-companion, whom she did not care for, and went on to describe with every sign of disgust, how she had once gone into that lady's room and how her little dog—horrid creature!—had drunk out of a glass there. . . . After giving further energetic expression to the anger she had held back, [Anna O.] asked for something to drink, drank a large quantity of water without any difficulty and woke from her hypnosis with a glass at her lips; and thereupon the disturbance vanished, never to return."

By taking each of Bertha's complaints and slowly tracing it, incident by incident and in order, back to its first occurrence, "the symptom," according to Breuer, "was permanently removed." The process apparently worked for the problem of Bertha's two selves as well. Alleviation of this symptom was achieved—like the others—by moving back through recent memory, past the tremors of adolescence to the sanctuary of childhood, to a moment long forgotten and now, with Breuer, suddenly remembered. Freud, struck by Breuer's tale, could not know that Jung, like Bertha, was struggling to make sense of his two selves. In the story of Bertha Pappenheim—Anna O.—Freud would find his future. Now he simply wanted to know more, to hear it all again, to puzzle with Breuer over why it had helped Bertha so to purge her mind by talking her way through nearly forgotten memories. "Chimney sweeping," she called it; her "talking cure." Breuer called it her catharsis.

In January 1884, Freud joined the Vienna General Hospital's department of nervous diseases, and after his first week he wrote, "Today I put my case histories in order at last and started on the study of a nervous case; thus begins a new era." The study of nervous diseases was not a prominent field in Vienna; on October 11, 1885, Freud went to Paris on a travel grant to study under Jean Martin Charcot, a neurologist who worked among the insane in an asylum called the Salpêtrière. Charcot had begun to transform the lunatic asylum into a humane effort. He attempted to see clearly, beyond the filth and degradation and random violence, the patient who stood before him. Freud would say of Charcot, "He used to look again and again at the things he did not understand, to deepen his impression of them day by day, till suddenly an understanding of them dawned on him."

Freud noticed that the German practice of ascribing physiological causes to all conditions of the body was not followed in France. Freud had seen Charcot treat patients who had for years endured physical pain or tics or limps, and by the power of his suggestion under hypnosis, the ailment was cured, the muscle ceased its ticking, the patient walked normally. The effect of mental life upon the body's well-being was demonstrable. What Charcot had done was to put before Freud the possibility that many physical complaints might well have a psychological basis, and this reminded him of Bertha Pappenheim's "talking cure."

When Freud returned to Vienna four and a half months later in 1886, he resumed his work at the hospital; according to the custom of the day he wore a silk top hat and white gloves to grand rounds. In the same year he opened his office and began to see private patients. That he was not immune to the charms of women besides Martha became apparent when, during the course of treating an American doctor for a nervous ailment, Freud asked to see the man's wife. She turned out to be both beautiful and interesting. "It seemed weird to me," Freud told Martha, describing the wife's two visits to him, "that on both the occasions . . . your photograph, which has otherwise never budged, fell off the writing table. I don't like such hints, and if a warning were needed—but none is needed."

Within the year Freud would marry Martha. "I don't want to be much longer without you," he wrote her. "I can put up with any amount of worry and hard work, but no longer alone." Their life together would seem quite ordinary, even prosaic. But beneath his outward conformity to white gloves and top hat, to the bourgeois trappings of career, marriage and soon, family, Sigmund Freud felt anything but ordinary.

CHAPTER FIVE

ANTON CHEKHOV visited Vienna for the first time in 1891 when he was thirty-one, not yet the famous writer he would one day be. Four years younger than Freud, the young doctor had grown up in Russia beside the Sea of Azov. Russians called Taganrog a "deaf town." Few ships put into port there anymore, the roads were muddy spring and fall, and the tumble-down houses reflected the inertia of the provinces. Chekhov marveled at the size of the apartment houses in Vienna, "all six or seven storeys high, and the shops—they are not shops but utter dizziness, dreams! They have millions of neckties alone in the windows!" Vienna convinced the young Russian that architecture was an art. The churches, he thought, "seem to be spun out of lace." Two of them he called "not buildings, but petits fours." Chekhov liked the charming little carriages and found the women stylish and beautiful. He wondered what they thought of him, in his "grizzly-furred cap." He missed only his vodka.

Freud never spoke of Vienna with the enthusiasm of Anton Chekhov, but his world brightened in 1886. He married Martha Bernays, and their family life was warm and fruitful. Babies were born in swift succession to a household that welcomed them with pride. Mathilde, the first, was born in 1887; Martin, named for Charcot, two years later. Oliver would arrive in 1891; Ernst in 1892; Sophie and Anna would follow in 1893 and 1895.

During the 1880s a new friendship emerged in Freud's life. Wilhelm Fliess was a young doctor in Berlin acquainted with Josef Breuer, who, on one of Fliess's visits to Vienna, recommended the lectures of the brilliant neurologist Sigmund Freud. Fliess was just starting out in practice as an ear, nose and throat specialist, and he was immersed in scientific theory as well. Fliess thought the biology of sexuality played a key role in human behavior. He contended that man was essentially bisexual, and Freud would come to agree with him. Fliess also maintained that the nose as an organ affected the condition of the rest of the body, and Freud seemed to subscribe to Fliess's view for a time. To believe, in the 1880s, in the bisexuality of man and the dominance of the nose as influencing human health was to test the limits of acceptability in science. But to defend Fliess's periodicity theory—his conviction that events occurred at given numerical intervals—went beyond the scope of the science of the day. Freud tried to be loyal to Fliess's strange version of predestination, juggling numbers and dates faithfully in attempts to have events fall where he felt they should. For a time, Freud's natural yet uneasy disposition to superstition held him to Fliess's theory, though never wholeheartedly. But Fliess was a learned man and a dedicated scientist; despite reservations about some of Fliess's ideas, Freud admired the man from the first. In the friendship that ensued, Freud gave voice to deep personal concerns and to the psychological issues that dominated his intellectual life.

Freud was secure in friendship and peacefully married with children on the way, but he was not able to shake off the sense that he was different from other men. "I regard it as a serious misfortune that Nature did not give me that indefinite something which attracts people," he had confessed to Martha. "If I think back on my life it is what I have most lacked to make my existence rosy. It has always taken me a long time to win a friend, and every time I meet someone I notice that to begin with some impulse . . . leads him to underestimate me. It is a matter of a glance or a feeling or some other secret of nature, but it affects one very unfortunately." Such feelings plagued him. Freud saw in himself a degree of passion greater than that of other men, though unexpressed. "I have often felt," he explained to Martha, "as if I had inherited all the passion of our ancestors when they defended their Temple, as if I could joyfully cast away my life in a great cause. And with all that I was always so powerless and could not express the flowing passions even by a word or a poem. So I have always suppressed myself, and I believe people must notice that in me." Freud would contain his passion for several more years until he found his cause, psychoanalysis, and he would find it within himself, within the shadows of his childhood loves.

IF FREUD was disturbed by his feeling that other people found him strange, Jung, eleven years old in 1886, was similarly troubled. "My 'unusualness,'" Jung remembered, "was gradually beginning to give me the disagreeable, rather uncanny feeling that I must possess repulsive traits, of which I was not aware, that caused my teachers and schoolmates to shun me." Jung's loneliness was sealed with secrets he could not as a child confess and later as a man would find difficult to share. "More than ever I wanted someone to talk with," Jung remembered. "But nowhere did I find a point of contact; on the contrary, I sensed in others an estrangement, a distrust, an apprehension which robbed me of speech."

At the age of eleven, Carl began to walk several miles to school along the green Rhine River, the hills of the Black Forest on one side, and ahead of him the slender towers and brilliantly colored new roof of Basel's red sandstone cathedral. The city had an illustrious past. During the Renaissance, under the cultural example of Erasmus and Paracelsus and the painter Hans Holbein, Basel was the center of European humanism. The city fell into decay after a time, but in the eighteenth century Jung's grandfather, Carl Gustav Jung the Elder, played a role in Basel's revival when he restored the medical school to its previous luster and became rector of the University. In 1886 Basel was still small enough for everyone to know each other and Jung's family was greatly respected, but the boy was uncomfortable at school. For the first time he encountered the expansive lives of the rich, boys whose homes were large and whose clothes, unlike his own, were elegant and well-fitting. Carl's shirt-sleeves were often above his wrists as he grew beyond six feet, and he realized with sudden shame that as a poor pastor's son he was not like the other boys. The feeling persisted when he and his parents, and now a little sister nine years younger, visited family friends in the village of Schaffhausen. Berta Rauschenbach, the blonde woman who had walked with Carl along the Rhine years before, now had two children. At her home in Schaffhausen, the carriages drawn by spirited horses and tended by footmen in green livery represented a life utterly unlike Carl's own. The elder daughter, Emma, Carl thought, was like a fairy princess, and he felt the gulf widen further between himself and others.

During Carl's twelfth year the situation worsened. One sunny day after school he crossed the cathedral square in Basel thinking, "The world is beautiful and the church is beautiful, and God made all this and sits above it far away in the blue sky on a golden throne and . . ." Then he paused, for a feeling of terror overcame him, and he did not want to finish his thought. All the way home from school he pushed his thoughts away; he did not want to know what might come next. In torment and alone he tried to consider what God wanted of him. Suddenly he remembered Adam and Eve, whom He had created. They were perfect creatures, and yet they had sinned. "How was that possible," Jung wondered. "They could not have done it if God had not placed in them the possibility of doing it. . . . *Therefore it was God's intention that they should sin.*" Was it God's intention that he too should sin, should, after all, think the unthinkable? The image of God on His golden throne high above the world returned to Jung, and he resolutely finished his thought: God had befouled the cathedral of Basel with an enormous turd, which shattered the roof and broke the walls. Strangely, Jung felt God's grace immediately and knew in the same moment that his pastor father had never experienced this miracle of divine intervention "which heals all and makes all comprehensible."

With this secret image of God alive in his mind, Jung's disappointment was acute as he listened to his father discuss religious matters with relatives. Their platitudes contained none of the moral drama Carl knew was bound up in true religious experience. "Yes, yes, that is all very well," he thought to himself. "But what about the secret? . . . None of you know anything about that. You don't know that God wants to force me to . . . think abominations in order to experience His grace." The boy began to believe that he knew God in a way that his father did not, and the realization saddened him. The terrible and demanding God Jung had discovered was not the God of his father and his pastor uncles. Jung's God was found in the Old Testament, but that was considered "old-fashioned" and "Jewish" by his relatives. Jung's God—the God of Freud's tradition—had been, the boy realized, "long since superseded by the Christian message of God's love and goodness."

Jung continued to feel alienated at school. He began to do well in his studies; unlike Freud, he tried never to be at the top of his class, preferring to go unnoticed and sympathizing with the boys who struggled along behind him. But his efforts to remain in the background failed, and he was regarded with growing suspicion by his fellow students. He found himself singled out for punishment by his teacher and accused of cheating on his papers. Jung could find no plausible solution to his problems until one day in the cathedral square he was knocked down in fun by a classmate; he hit his head on the curbstone and fainted. Jung's first thought was, "Now you won't have to go to school anymore."

Carl began to have fainting spells with such frequency that he was unable to study or go to school. One day when he had been out of school for six months, a man stopped by to visit his father. "And how is your son?" Jung heard the friend ask. "Ah, that's a sad business," his father answered. "The doctors no longer know what is wrong with him. . . . It would be dreadful if he were incurable. I have lost what little I had, and what will become of the boy if he cannot earn his own living?" Carl's reaction was immediate: he would cure his fainting spells himself. He went quietly to his father's study and began to read his Latin. A fainting spell ensued, and when he picked up his book again, another. He worked for an hour and experienced a third attack, but he continued to study. "Suddenly I felt better than I had in all the months before. And in fact the attacks did not recur. . . . That was when I learned what a neurosis is."

DURING THESE same years, Freud was struggling with a puzzle that would not come together, and the pieces he had in hand were provocative. He had returned from the Salpêtrière with the impression that mental states could produce physical effects. Moreover, in a curious remark freighted with assumption, Freud had overheard Charcot say of a patient, "But in this sort of case it's always a question of the genitals—always, always, always." It reminded Freud of a comment Breuer had made several years before when speaking of the neuroses: "These things are always *secrets d'alcôve*"—secrets of the marriage-bed.

Freud worked with his private patients, using the old methods of massage and electrical stimulation. In 1889 when he resumed his work on one of his patients, Frau Emmy von N., he experimented for the first time with Breuer's cathartic method. He asked his patient under hypnosis to recall the first time her symptoms had occurred. When she was finally able to do so, her symptoms abated. After several such cases, Freud became convinced that the cause of much hysteria was psychological. Alleviation was therefore to be accomplished through the psyche. If one could engage the mind in the search backward in time, there was here to be found a powerful ally. If intellect, emotion, will and the associative links of memory could be drawn into the enterprise, something might be accomplished. "Be calm," Charcot had written him in 1888, "hysteria is making its way and one day it will occupy, gloriously in full sun, the important place which is due it." It seemed that Charcot had been right.

Encouraged by his confirmation of Breuer's cathartic method, Freud tried to enlist the older man's support in publishing their findings. But Freud sensed a reluctance in Breuer and felt it stemmed from the fact that Bertha Pappenheim, needing and depending on Breuer, had been drawn to him, had loved him; Breuer, confused, possibly attracted to the beautiful, troubled girl, was hesitant to disclose this, did not wish even to recall it. Perhaps Breuer was reassured by Freud's own account of a patient who had thrown her arms around him in a mute declaration of love; or perhaps he was relieved by Freud's promise not to examine publicly the sexual implications of these cases. Finally, in 1893, Breuer and Freud together published a paper in which they stated that "hysterical patients suffer mainly from reminiscences." These patients were not possessed. Their complaints did not issue from malfunctions of the uterus or from genetic defects or even from forgotten trauma. Their buried memories had made them suffer and now, according to Breuer and Freud, it was their memories unearthed that would make them well. It was not the whole story, Freud knew, but it was a beginning. Two years later, in 1895, the two men published their accounts of the cathartic method in *Studies in Hysteria*. There, richly disguised, pseudonymous, were five patients whose tangled, misshapen lives had been ordered and eased by the technique of psychical analysis. "Much will be gained," Freud wrote in the last chapter, "if we succeed in transforming . . . hysterical misery into common unhappiness."

After slow hard years of discovery, Freud in the next decade would have insight upon insight in rapid succession, binding his theories with the substance of exchanges with his patients. His sureness was the fruition of genius coupled with passionate and stubborn work. It must have been daunting at times to be his friend. "Now listen to this," Freud reported to Fliess in October 1895. "During an industrious night last week . . . the barriers suddenly lifted, the veils dropped, and everything became transparent—from the details of the neuroses to the determinants of consciousness. Everything seemed to fall into place, the cogs meshed, I had the impression that the thing now really was a machine that shortly would function on its own." Breuer, conceptually brilliant himself and honored among his peers, wrote a friend in quiet awe: "Freud's intellect is soaring at its highest. I gaze after him as a hen at a hawk."

AS JUNG moved into his later teenage years in the 1890s, outside influences began to ease the pain and isolation of his childhood. His mother, who at times displayed an acute awareness of her son's inmost needs, suddenly said, "You must read Goethe's *Faust* one of these days." There in *Faust* the fifteen-year-old Jung found for the first time confirmation of his own experience with the dark side of God that other people seemed unwilling to discuss. For the rest of his life Jung would collect such signs. The philosopher Schopenhauer, like Goethe, gave Jung sanction for a world he knew, a world in which suffering and pain were real and ever-present, part of the human condition now and always.

Perhaps because of this affirmation of his secret world, Jung began to change. He read constantly and indiscriminately. His father worried. "The boy is interested in everything imaginable, but he does not know what he wants." There was little that Jung and his father genuinely shared, and toward the end of his high school years Jung's closest confidant was a man of about fifty, a friend of his family. It meant a great deal to the boy to know someone older whom he admired and trusted; but one day the friend made a homosexual advance and Jung, in fright and disgust, broke off the friendship. Only Jung knew the effect on a shy teenager just beginning to reach out to others of a sexual gesture beyond his experience, and unwelcome. One day he would talk about it and he would talk about it with Freud; but not now, and not for years to come.

During the latter part of his son's childhood, Paul Jung had suffered from a variety of physical complaints, and Jung suspected finally that they were psychosomatic. His father's condition worsened during the summer of 1895 as Jung began his medical studies at the University of Basel. One day several months later, in January 1896, Jung came home from his lectures at the University to find his father delerious. Jung remembered, "There was a rattling in his throat, and I could see that he was in the death agony. I stood by his bed, fascinated. I had never seen anyone die before. Suddenly he stopped breathing. I waited and waited for the next breath. It did not come." Several days later his mother, in a remark that chilled him, said, "He died in time for you."

Jung stepped into a more expansive role in the years following his father's death. Tall and sandy-haired, with piercing brown eyes that people often, remembering later, would mistake for blue, Jung was handsome and impetuous. He would always trust his instincts, and this sureness gave his personality definition and purpose. During his first year at the University Jung joined the Zofingia, the Swiss student club, and became its president. Nicknamed "the barrel," he took strong positions on all manner of topics, some of which would occupy him for the rest of his life. He debated Schopenhauer and Kant; he was concerned with the problem of evil and convinced that the soul, though immaterial and transcendent, could be approached scientifically.

His first talk before the student club in November 1896 was entitled "On the Limits of the Exact Sciences" and called for the investigation of hypnotic and spiritualistic phenomena, places he felt the soul might be captured and examined. The undertaking he proposed knitted together his two seemingly contradictory interests: his demand for scientific discipline and his need, soul deep, to examine the ineffable. For the moment he was alone in his quest; few people understood, and even fewer thought it could be done. The soul, after all, was not the domain of science but of religion and literature.

Jung took an interest in any and all evidence that spoke to him of the spirit world. He shared this predisposition with his mother. One day in 1898, as she sat knitting in the dining room and Carl studied in an adjoining room, the round dining table suddenly split across the grain with a loud cracking noise. Mother and son were stunned. Two weeks later he was told of a second deafening report, seemingly from the sideboard in the same room. When he opened the cupboard, he was shocked to find that the blade of the bread knife had broken in several places, although it had been used only hours before. Moreover, while the knife lay as usual in the rectangular bread basket, "the handle lay in one corner . . . and in each of the other corners lay a piece of the blade." Physical conditions could not explain what had happened; the broken knife for Jung was testimony, however mute, that not all occurrences could be traced to material causes.

While Jung seemed open to all manner of influences, one he shunned. He had heard discussions of Nietzsche, who had been a professor of Greek philology at the University of Basel when Jung was a little boy. But when Jung read Nietzsche's *Thus Spake Zarathustra*, it was as if he had collided with a part of himself, and the knowledge haunted him. Zarathustra, he thought, was morbid. Jung worried that in a deep and intractable way he was morbid as well. "This possibility," Jung realized, "filled me with a terror which for a long time I refused to admit but the idea cropped up again and again at inopportune moments, throwing me into a cold sweat, so that in the end I was forced to reflect on myself. . . . Among my friends and acquaintances I knew of only two who openly declared themselves adherents of Nietzsche. Both were homosexual; one of them ended by committing suicide, the other ran to seed as a misunderstood genius." Jung had spent his boyhood feeling different and being different. He wanted, at the age of twenty-three, to be like others. He turned away from Nietzsche and away from a part of himself he had seen reflected in Zarathustra. Nearly twenty years later, in the excess of confusion and pain connected with his break with Freud, he would confront this aspect of himself that he suppressed and, over time, reclaim it. But now he only moved on.

Nor would Freud read Nietzsche. "I denied myself the study of Nietzsche," Freud would say late in his life, "even though or actually because it became obvious that I would find there insights very similar to those of psychoanalysis." The Greek myth of Oedipus runs through Nietzsche's work. Laius, king of Thebes, is told by an oracle that he will be killed by his son. When a baby is born to his wife, Jocasta, Laius orders Oedipus killed, but a shepherd rescues him. When Oedipus becomes a young man, he learns from an oracle that he will kill his father and marry his mother. Troubled by this news, Oedipus flees, and on his journey he quarrels with a man and kills him, not knowing he is Laius, his true father. Oedipus is then posed a riddle, which he solves; he is made king of Thebes and marries the widowed Queen Jocasta, unaware that she is his mother. The story would dominate Freud's work; more than that, he would discover its significance within his memories and his dreams. Freud's hesitations about reading Nietzsche reminded one later observer of the creative habits of two other men: Lenin gave up chess because it was too fascinating and might take his mind off the goal of revolution; Gustav Mahler chased the birds away from his house when he wanted to compose. Nietzsche was fascinating to both Freud and Jung, like chess; and he was threatening as well, like the incomparable beauty of birdsong.

Jung put Nietzsche behind him and struggled to be like others, but he was haunted by fears. He would sit in the Brio, the local student pub on the south bank of the Rhine, drinking beer and still talking hours after midnight. Unwilling to begin the long walk home alone through the woods, he would charm someone into accompanying him. When they had arrived safely at his door, he would offer his companion the use of his revolver for protection on the way back. Jung's friend Albert Oeri was never quite sure whether the safety catch was on or off, and so he rarely accepted Jung's pistol. Years later, a friend looking back upon Jung's fears would wonder whether as a young man Jung had been plagued by visions and anxieties.

In 1900 Carl Jung was studying for his state examinations, after which he planned to move to Munich and specialize in internal medicine. He had saved his psychiatry textbook to study last because the subject was distasteful to him. Care of the insane, people disturbed for life by physiological defect, anomalous and incurable, was graceless at best. Why a man would lock himself up with the mad and enter their reasonless existence was beyond him. But one evening he finally picked up Krafft-Ebing's *Lehrbuch der Psychiatrie*, and his future was transformed by the first paragraphs. "My heart," Jung wrote, "suddenly began to pound. I had to stand up and draw a deep breath." What he saw there was confirmation of a kind. Krafft-Ebing had, by way of apology, written that textbooks in psychiatry were inevitably stamped with the subjective character of their author. "So," Jung thought, "the textbook is in part the subjective confession of the author. With his specific prejudice, with the totality of his being, he stands behind the objectivity of his experiences and responds to the 'disease of the personality' with the whole of his own personality." Since childhood, Jung had taken seriously the value of his own view. The possibility of bringing this to bear on the complexity of human personality was irresistible. He applied immediately for a post at the Burghölzli Mental Hospital in Zürich.

DURING THE 1890s, as Jung turned from that part of himself that was troubling, Freud in the same years was compelled to confront his conflicts. The simplicity of his family life, his open and natural exchange with Wilhelm Fliess and the lucid elegance of his intellectual work belied his turmoil. Freud had frequently to deal with bouts of depression and he was plagued with migraine headaches. Moreover, ostensibly because of Breuer's hesitation over the possible sexual etiology of hysteria, Freud began to withdraw from the man who had meant and given so much. Perhaps Breuer was hesitant, but he was also brave. "I confess that plunging into sexuality in theory and practice is not to my taste," he was to say. "But what have my taste and feeling about what is seemly and what is unseemly to do with the question of what is true?"

Nothing Breuer had done or failed to do could explain Freud's growing hostility toward his old friend. Years later Breuer, out walking, would chance to see Freud and, ever fond, reach out his arms to embrace his old friend. Freud, aloof, affecting not to see, would drop his eyes and pass without speaking. Not by nature inclined to self-doubt, Freud mentioned his difficulties with Breuer to Fliess, but he saw in them no fault of his own. He did not know that one day soon the serenity of his relationship with Fliess would quicken into accusation and injured pride.

Freud's problems increased when his father died in 1896. Jacob Freud's death did not occasion in his son the feelings of liberation that Paul Jung's death had released in Jung the year before. Freud did not know why the old man's death continued to trouble him so; as the months went by, there were days when he could do no work and spent them playing chess or pouring over his collection of antique maps. He was withdrawn, lethargic and indifferent. Control over his thoughts slipped away for hours at a time and he was often anxious. "Curious states incomprehensible to [consciousness], twilight thoughts, veiled doubts, with barely a ray of light here or there," he wrote to Fliess. Freud managed his routine with his patients and family at times with the greatest effort, and within he despaired.

His relationship with Fliess was implicated in his distress. At one point, disoriented, Freud admitted to his friend, "I still do not know what has been happening in me. Something from the deepest depths of my own neurosis set itself against any advance in the understanding of the neuroses, and you have somehow been involved in it." Freud had been close to Fliess for nearly ten years and was disturbed by his realization that the friendship was bound up in neurosis. His inner fragmentation, precipitated by Jacob Freud's death and exacerbated by his relationship with Fliess, echoed that of his patients. Finally, like them, Freud was forced to confront his early memories. As Freud reached into his unconscious by examining his dreams, he drew out the concepts that would later establish his preeminence. Now they served to order his confusion and save his life.

Freud found, beneath the respectful love of his father, hostility toward the man who had possessed his mother. He was forced to acknowledge in himself the sexual wish of the child for his mother. Unthinkable, raw, humiliating—the images continued to emerge in his dreams, a panoply of childish desires, forbidden and incestuous wishes, urges of a sexuality disguised. "Many a sad secret of life," he wrote, "is here followed back to its first roots; many a pride and privilege are made aware of their humble origins. All of what I experienced with my patients, as a third [person] I find again here—days when I drag myself about dejected because I have understood nothing of the dream, of the fantasy, of the mood of the day."

As the long months of self-analysis went on, Freud began to wonder if he was threading not just his own themes but those of mankind as well. His, he finally concluded, was a universal story, played out with the clarity of Greek drama. "I cannot convey to you," he confessed to Fliess, "any idea of the intellectual beauty of this work." Freud began writing his dream book, heartened by the progress he had made. Years later he would say of the death of his father, "It revolutioned my soul." Freud's swings between elation and depression were not so wide as they had been before. His personality was, by his account, closer knit, less vulnerable and sensitive. Freud felt he had overcome his dependency on Fliess. His relationships with other men, he believed, would be better balanced as a result.

IN SEPTEMBER 1899, in the farmhouse in Bavaria, Sigmund Freud completed *The Interpretation of Dreams*. He was exultant. Through his self-analysis and his work with patients, he had learned that dreams contained meanings, were capable of interpretation and could untangle neurotic conflict. The dream book was published that November with its quantity of self-disclosure so revealing of Freud's personal problems and character. A little over a year after its publication, Carl Jung would read Sigmund Freud's *The Interpretation of Dreams*. There he could catch glimpses of the inner life of a man he would come to love. Jung could see if he wished that Freud's relations with men were sometimes uneasy and complex. "As Caesar loved me, I weep for him . . . as he was valiant, I honour him; but as he was ambitious, I slew him," Freud had quoted in his dream book, remembering John. Jung did not know when he read those lines that one day he would be implicated in the drama as well. He would strew the pages of Freud's book with question marks, because he did not understand them.

CHAPTER SIX

THE BURGHÖLZLI Mental Hospital, where Jung began to work in December 1900, does not directly face the brilliant blue expanse of the Zürichsee in the valley below. Built high on a hill, the huge white structure angles awkwardly away from the lake out of consideration for its inhabitants, because it was feared a full view of the water might tempt them to suicide.

The well-intentioned gesture reflected a growing concern about the mentally ill in the years before the turn of the century. There was a desire to help, but the lack of medical knowledge thwarted most attempts at cure. For years the patients of the Burghölzli and their doctors had not understood each other. The hospital was staffed with German psychiatrists who did not know the lilting Swiss German spoken by their patients. And when the doctors spoke in their native High German, a language and more separated them from the people in their care. The lives of the Swiss peasants of Zollikon, Schmerikon and

Küsnacht, as in all the villages in the German sector, were steeped in local beliefs and in the subtleties of a dialect to which foreigners had not access. Nor in those days was access wished for. A doctor paid little attention to what his patients said, because their thoughts and fantasies played no role in treatment.

Peasants in the countryside were isolated as well, for distinctions of class forced sons to live as their fathers had. But by 1870, the rigid social patterns had begun to shift as powerful groups of villagers and farmers demanded their rights, among them that the University of Zürich be open to them. One of the first from his village to receive a college education was Paul Eugen Bleuler, whose father was a farmer in Zollikon. A rare fusion of ambition and humanity, Bleuler had known since high school that he wanted to become a psychiatrist and return to help his people. Unlike the German doctors, Bleuler spoke the softly cadenced Swiss German and knew the fanciful tales of the peasants, as well as the darker currents of their fears.

By 1900 Bleuler was the director of the Burghölzli Mental Hospital, where he fashioned from a deep compassion the attitudes that would inspire an entire staff, among them Carl Jung. Bleuler cared to an extraordinary degree about his patients. Before coming to the Burghölzli, he had been in charge of a large, dilapidated hospital at Rheinau. There, despite the differing needs of patients and staff, he had created an atmosphere that was more like that of a family than a hospital. He was unmarried then, and often a patient or two would come and live with him in his quarters at the hospital.

Because he listened carefully to his patients at a time when other doctors did not, Bleuler had been among the first to consider Freud's theories seriously. In 1896, while still at Rheinau, Bleuler had written a review of Breuer and Freud's *Studies on Hysteria*. "The fact that the book brings an entirely new view into the workings of the psyche makes this book one of the most important additions of past years in the field of normal or pathological psychology." It was a view Bleuler impressed upon his young residents when he reached the Burghölzli, a forward-looking, more important hospital than the one at Rheinau.

Bleuler was married with small children when he was the director of the Burghölzli. He did not like the separation from his patients that came from his increased administrative and family responsibilities. As it was, Bleuler left his office five and six times a day to visit his patients; when people wanted to find him, they usually looked first on the wards. There was among his patients one woman in particular whom Bleuler would have liked to help, but even their shared language was of no use. Bleuler often told his residents a story about her as proof that even the most resistant catatonic could be reached. One day he had found the woman in a state of mute agitation and decided it might help her to spend time in a different room. Bleuler was reluctant to remove her by force and tried to reason with her instead. Unperturbed by her lack of response, he talked on, and after many hours she finally followed him out of the room. Bleuler gave this example as evidence that catatonia could be penetrated, but what the young doctors heard was the compassion eloquent in Bleuler's hours of talk. One young doctor understood the troubled woman to be Bleuler's own sister, perhaps because she lived with Bleuler and his family in their apartment at the Burghölzli. She spent her days there in slow and ceaseless motion, walking to and fro while the children climbed upon her as they would a stick of furniture, because she never spoke.

FREUD WAS discouraged by the public reception of *The Interpretation of Dreams* during the early months of 1900. "Understanding for it is meager; praise is doled out like alms; to most people it is evidently distasteful. I have not yet seen a trace of anyone who has an inkling of what is significant in it." Only three hundred and fifty-one copies of *The Interpretation of Dreams* were sold in six years, and it would take eight years to sell them all. Freud received $209 for his efforts. He was often ridiculed after the publication of *The Interpretation of Dreams*. "In those days when one mentioned Freud's name," a friend remembered, "everyone would begin to laugh, as if someone had told a joke. Freud was the queer fellow who wrote a book about dreams and who imagined himself an interpreter of dreams. More than that, he was the man who saw sex in everything. It was considered bad taste to bring up Freud's name in the presence of ladies. They would blush when his name was mentioned. Those who were less sensitive spoke of Freud with a laugh, as if they were telling a dirty story. . . ." As Freud's colleague Hanns Sachs later wrote about Martha, "The attitude of friends and acquaintances in general was that of pity for the poor woman whose husband, formerly a clever scientist, had turned out to be a rather disgusting freak."

Freud understood. "I know that what I am doing is odious to the majority of people." He knew, too, that he had invited comment. "If you don't want the crows to circle," he would say, "don't be the vane on the steeple." Despite the ridicule and the limited sales, and despite Freud's contention that it was little reviewed, in fact his book attracted notice; and not all of it was unfavorable.

But it did not help matters that Freud was a Jew. Descriptions of Vienna at the turn of the century read like passages from historical novels: the ritual of the family gathering for the noonday meal; daily Sachertorte and coffee with friends in a favorite café, Viennese waltzes playing; horsedrawn carriages, and everywhere the soft glow of gaslight. But beneath the charming exterior lay a different reality. Vienna, after a quarter century of tolerance between gentile and Jew, had erupted into anti-Semitism. The Vienna State Opera rocked one night in 1899 in anti-Semitic fury such that the conductor Gustav Mahler was forced to pause for many moments, his head in his hands, until silence was restored and he could continue with Act Three of *Die Meistersinger*. Karl Lueger had years before recommended that all Jews should be packed on ships and sunk. Now he was the mayor of Vienna. *Schöner Karl* they called him: "handsome Karl." He had played cannily upon the issues of anti-Semitism in order to be elected, and the Emperor Franz Joseph had more than once disallowed him office on the basis of his rabid policies. But when he finally won, Lueger said, "*I' bestimm' wer a Jud' ist'* " (I'll decide who is a Jew). Lueger filled his municipal cabinet with Jews as well as gentiles, but he had gained office by articulating the anti-Semitic feelings of the day. Freud saw that white carnations had become an emblem of anti-Semitism in Vienna, and they proliferated.

During the early spring of 1900, Freud began to realize that his friendship with Wilhelm Fliess was not what it had been. He was aware that his feelings for Fliess were marked by ambivalence. An unconscious hostility had shown itself once when Fliess was ill in Munich and Freud was to travel to see him. Freud's "dream-thoughts," far from exhibiting concern over his sick friend, revealed to Freud the world of childhood and the irrepressible egotism of the young conquering hero. Such thoughts, Freud admitted in his dream book, "occurring to me at a moment at which I was afraid I might not find my friend alive if I made the journey to him, could only be construed as meaning that I was delighted because I had once more survived someone, because it was *he* and not I who had died, because I was left in possession of the field."

Freud's ambivalence was reflected in his demurral when Fliess suggested they meet at Eastertime in 1900. "There has never been a six-month period," Freud wrote him, "in which I so constantly and so ardently longed to be living in the same place with you . . . as the one that has just passed. You know that I have been going through a deep inner crisis; you would see how it has aged me. I was therefore deeply moved when I heard of your proposal that we meet again this Easter.

Anyone who did not understand the more subtle resolution of contradictions would think it incomprehensible that I am not rushing to assent to the proposal. In fact it is more likely that I shall avoid you—not only because of my almost childish yearning for spring and the beauties of nature. . . . But there are other, inner reasons, an accumulation of imponderables, which, however, weigh heavily on me (from the natural habitat of madness, you will perhaps say)." Freud stayed away from Fliess that Easter of 1900, saying cryptically, "During the summer or fall, no later, I shall see you, talk with you, and explain all the riddles of Count Oerindur to you." Freud was referring to a saying popular in Vienna, taken from the lines of a play: "Explain to me, Oerindur, this contradiction of nature." The contradiction was Count Oerindur's realization, and Freud's, that one could both love and hate someone at the same time.

Several months later Freud and Fliess met near Innsbruck, where they quarreled bitterly over the issues that dominated their intellectual lives: bisexuality, psychoanalysis and periodicity. It was perhaps on that visit that Freud subjected Fliess's belief in predetermined events and his elaborate numerical system to analysis. The fact that Wilhelm had seen his father die yet known he might have been saved, Freud said, had led Fliess to become a doctor. But then, "The sudden death of his only sister two years later, on the second day of a pneumonia for which he could not make the doctor responsible, led—as a consolation—to the fatalistic theory of predestined lethal dates." Freud's analysis stripped Fliess's theory of any scientific basis and lodged it in what Freud considered Fliess's neurosis. "This piece of analysis," Freud concluded, "very unwelcome to [Fliess], was the real reason for the break between us which he engineered in such a pathological (paranoic) fashion." After this meeting in August 1900, the men continued to correspond, but without their former warmth. Freud felt the loss acutely. "In my life, as you know, woman has never replaced the comrade, the friend," Freud would tell Fliess sadly a year later.

WHEN CARL JUNG first walked through the doors of the Burghölzli on a cold day in December 1900, his new chief, Eugen Bleuler, was there to greet him and with characteristic modesty to pick up the younger man's bags and show his new resident to his small room. Jung adjusted quickly to life at the hospital, but his friend Albert Oeri was stunned by his first visit to the wards. Jung moved genially among his patients, while Oeri gazed on in astonishment. The awkward shuffling, eccentric noises, disheveled dress and disordered speech of the mentally ill was unmodified by medication or modern hygienic practice in 1900, and Oeri was alarmed. But when a burly patient suddenly threatened to land a blow, Jung only laughed. Why, Oeri wanted to know, didn't patients actually strike him? "Because they know I'd hit back," Jung replied. The activity on the wards appealed to Jung. During his first years at the hospital, he organized dancing parties and an annual costume ball where doctors and patients waltzed amicably together, the patients' fantastic dress a particularly festive touch.

While Jung joked easily with his patients and danced with them at parties, he took the task of trying to understand them with infinite seriousness. Following Bleuler's example and his own inclination, Jung listened with great care to his patients, often for many hours at a time. Years later Jung would listen as the American psychiatrist John Rosen described a grueling sixteen hours he had spent with a patient; Jung replied with a smile, "Ah, I was like that once." After evening rounds the staff gathered for dinner. No wines or other alcoholic beverages were served because Bleuler thought it was important to set an example for the nurses and the attendants. Jung, like the rest of the doctors, abstained from alcohol not only within the Burghölzli but outside it too, in deference to Bleuler's wishes. He would not take a drink for nine years until, dared by Freud, he would break his vow of abstinence and drink a glass of wine with him.

After dinner the residents retired to write up their case histories, and in a day when other doctors wrote simply, "The patient does not speak," or "The patient cannot be understood," Jung's reports were meticulously detailed. Since the doctors on staff had no secretaries, Jung typed the pages himself. It was often late in the evening before he could turn to his own pursuits. Jung spent many of his free hours at the Burghölzli reading, for nothing he had yet experienced provided him with sufficient understanding of the suffering he encountered daily among his patients. During his first six months at the hospital, assuming the fault lay in himself and his lack of knowledge, Jung read through all of the fifty volumes of the *Allgemeine Zeitschrift für Psychiatrie* in an attempt "to know how the human mind reacted to the sight of its own destruction."

A few years later, looking back on his first months of confusion, Jung would recommend a different beginning. The young psychiatrist "would be better advised to abandon exact science, take off his scholar's gown, say farewell to his study, and then, strong in manly courage, set out to wander through the world; alike through the horrors of prisons, lunatic asylums and hospitals, through dreary outlying taverns, through brothels and gambling-hells, into elegant drawing-rooms, the Stock Exchanges, socialist meetings, churches, revival gatherings of strange religious sects, experiencing in his own person love and hate and every kind of suffering. He would return laden with richer knowledge than his yard-long text-books could ever have given him, and thus equipped, he can indeed be a physician to his patients, for he understands the soul of man." But now Jung understood little, and the realization disturbed him. His first exposure to the writings of Sigmund Freud was without effect. He read *The Interpretation of Dreams* when he first arrived at the Burghölzli, but the book did not inspire him. Even when Eugen Bleuler pressed him to report on Freud's pamphlet *On Dreams*, the brief outline of Freud's larger work appeared to interest Jung not at all.

Jung knew few people when he arrived at the Burghölzli in late 1900, and a friend of the family who lived near Zürich took him under her wing. She invited Carl to a festival in the town of Winterthur, and Jung saw again the girl he had played with as a little boy and always thought of as a fairy princess. Tall and slender now, with clear, steady eyes and dark brown hair wound up in braids, Emma Rauschenbach was lovely in her eighteenth year. A few months later her mother invited Jung to a ball in their village, and there at the Castle Munot, in a turreted courtyard high above Schaffhausen, Carl and Emma waltzed in a setting worthy of a fairy tale.

Jung was in love. The knowledge galvanized him and unnerved Emma. He drew her into the excitement of his intellectual world, pressed her to read his favorite philosophers, described the strange science of psychiatry, confessed his ambitions and his fears—the full magnitude of his genius unrestrained. Demure and shy, with an innocence born of a protected, wealthy childhood and limited schooling, Emma had never met anyone like Carl. His flights of ideas, his stories about the patients at the Burghölzli and the fire of his love—all bewildered her. And yet Jung endeared himself to her as well, writing her long letters and poems, often bringing books to discuss or even a little painting he had done, sometimes for Emma and sometimes for her mother. Berta Rauschenbach, who had known Carl as a child, approved of the young man with his fierce pride, offering her his painting and loving Emma so.

But when, after a visit to Schaffhausen in August 1901, Jung finally summoned his courage to write Emma and ask her to marry him, Emma was hesitant. She was already obliged, she told him, to a young man from Schaffhausen. Jung retreated to his journal, where he unburdened himself of his passion and sorrow. The next entry in it would be more than a decade later, in 1913, after his rupture with Freud.

Jung would always be a bit ashamed that he had been so sensitive to Emma's rebuff. His son, Franz, years later, understood. "You see, Father would never have asked her again. He was crushed. He was poor, and not on the same social level as Emma, and so he thought he didn't have a chance." Frau Rauschenbach intervened several months later. She asked Jung to meet her in a restaurant in Zürich, and there she reassured him that Emma was not promised to another. "My mother was very shy then, and introverted," Franz Jung explained. "She was afraid to move ahead, to say yes." Frau Rauschenbach invited Jung to come again to Schaffhausen, sending her horses and carriage to fetch him at the station. It was an elegant carriage, very dark green, decorated with red lines painted with a fine brush; and it carried Jung up the hill to Ölberg, the Rauschenbach estate. Emma's house looked out over the wide Rhine Valley surrounded by wooded hills, now ablaze in the October light. It is doubtful that Jung noticed. He asked Emma again if she would marry him, and this time she said yes. She would go and live with him in the Burghölzli, so different from the privileged, quiet, pastoral world of Ölberg.

JUNG ROSE quickly at the hospital. In addition to being the clinical director under Eugen Bleuler, he was put in charge of the outpatient department and would soon become the lecturer in psychiatry at Zürich University as well. Emma learned the extent of Jung's commitment to the hospital when he came down with the flu and she tried to keep him in bed. "The Burghölzli is much more important than a brood of second-rate bugs," Jung said, and went downstairs to the wards.

Late one evening in 1904, Eugen Bleuler knocked on the door of the Jungs' apartment at the Burghölzli. Waiting downstairs was Franz Riklin, a medical student just arrived from Germany. Despite the hour, Bleuler had been at the train station in Zürich to introduce himself to Riklin; the carriage ride back to the Burghölzli had been filled with talk of the work Riklin would find at the hospital and of Bleuler's enthusiasm for his clinical director, Carl Jung. When the three men sat down a few minutes later, young Riklin, then twenty-six, had news of his medical studies in Germany, in particular a scientific experiment in which a person is given a word such as *angel* and asked to make an association with it, using another word. Bleuler and Jung wondered whether the test might be used as a tool to make sense of the often confusing thoughts of their patients. The men were exhilarated by the possibilities and talked on for hours past midnight.

Jung began immediately to experiment with the word-association test. Together he, Bleuler and Riklin worked out the procedures and began testing. Sometimes, Jung noticed, the patients made mistakes. They stumbled over their answers or hesitated unduly long or gave responses that seemed to have no association with the word in question. Slowly Jung grew interested, not in his patients' "correct" answers but in these other, "wrong" ones, which were often accompanied by greater emotion. He had reread Freud's *The Interpretation of Dreams* and come away, finally, impressed. Now he began to wonder whether his patients' "wrong" answers sprang from the same source as their dreams, from unconscious processes in their minds. As Jung's work continued, his findings in large part confirmed Freud's belief that disturbances in sexuality lay at the heart of a conflict, what Jung chose to call a complex. Soon Jung and Riklin were able to say, "An overwhelming number of the complexes we have discovered . . . are erotic. In view of the great part played by love and sexuality in human life, this is not surprising." But while Jung was ready to admit that sexuality played a crucial role in most complexes, he was not sure that this was always so.

In gathering material for his article, "Reaction-time Ratio in the Association Experiment," Jung enlisted the help of one of his patients, a Russian girl who had been admitted to the Burghölzli in 1904. Unable to look anyone in the face, Sabina Spielrein had kept her head bowed, sticking out her tongue "with every sign of loathing" if anyone touched her. She was one of the first people Jung treated using Freud's methods. Now Sabina was well enough to help Jung in his work, and she went about the hospital in simple dresses, her dark hair in a long braid down her back. Sabina was only nineteen years old, but she impressed Jung. "Minds such as yours help advance science," she remembered that he told her. " You must become a psychiatrist." In a few years the warm relationship between Spielrein and Jung would explode suddenly in misunderstanding and passionate accusation, the painful details spilling out in letters from both of them to Sigmund Freud. In a few years more, Sabina, in correspondence with Freud and Jung at the time of their bitter quarrel, would record her horror at the destruction of the friendship between the two men. But now, in 1904, nothing was yet amiss as Sabina went about the wards working with Carl Jung.

With his natural, at times nearly uncanny talent for observation, his productive work with the word-association test and the new insights acquired from Freud's writings, Jung's ambition and creative drive were fully engaged. No one at the Burghölzli doubted that the handsome young physician was embarked on a brilliant career. But in 1904 Carl Jung was still unknown. In Vienna and elsewhere it was Eugen Bleuler's name the medical world recognized, not his.

IN VIENNA in spring the broad avenues are wreathed in pale leaves, and the city's parks are filled with flowers and the exuberance of children running coatless in the first warm days. In 1904, as always, Freud took pleasure in his swift walk around the cobbled Ringstrasse, marked by his children trailing along behind and by his stop at the tobacconist for his daily supply of twenty cigars. One day late in April he was particularly pleased. Just that month he had learned that a leading academic psychiatrist had written of his work with notable warmth. Eugen Bleuler, director of the Burghölzli Mental Hospital in Switzerland, had stated in a review, "Freud, in his studies on hysteria and on dreams, has shown us part of a new world, though by no means all of it. Our consciousness sees in its theater only the puppets; in the Freudian world, many of the strings that move the figures have been revealed."

Freud did not contain his joy. On April 26, 1904, he picked up his pen and wrote Wilhelm Fliess for the first time in over a year. "I recently found an absolutely stunning recognition of my point of view in a book review in the *Münchener medizinische Wochenschrift* by an official psychiatrist, Bleuler, in Zurich. Just imagine, a full professor of psychiatry and my + + + studies of hysteria and the dream, which so far have been labeled disgusting!" The little crosses, ordinarily painted inside the doors of peasant cottages to ward off evil, were drawn by Freud to mock the usual, wary response to his work. Freud hoped that Fliess might find his way back, if not to friendship then at least to join with him in the sudden bright promise of psychoanalysis. It was not to be.

Several months later, in July 1904, Freud and his family were in Bavaria near a lake high in the Alps where the mountains fall sheer into the cold blue-green water. The Freud children loved the Königsee and their villa, Sonnenfels. They rowed on the lake, fished with their father and went on excursions for mushrooms. Freud's son Martin recalled that his father once slipped while climbing thirty feet up a rock face in pursuit of an alpine flower. Falling dangerously, Freud recovered by lithely executing a perfect backward somersault, exploding with laughter as he did so and amazing his children. But Martin Freud remembered, too, that outings with his father had been few that summer because Freud had spent a great deal of time inside, writing.

The children did not know that on July 20, Wilhelm Fliess had written their father a letter putting an end to a friendship that had been uneasy for years. "Dear Sigmund," Fliess wrote, "I have come across a book by Weininger, in the first biological part of which I find, to my consternation, a description of my ideas on bisexuality and the nature of sexual attraction consequent upon it—feminine men attract masculine women and vice versa. . . . I have no doubt that Weininger obtained knowledge of my ideas via you and misused someone else's property."

Fliess was correct. Freud gradually revealed to him that he had confided to a patient, Hermann Swoboda, Fliess's theory of bisexuality. Swoboda had in turn disclosed these assertions to his friend Otto Weininger, who then described them as his own in the book Fliess referred to in his letter. Freud had been aware of his ambivalence toward Fliess; now, slowly recalling his full role in the Weininger matter, he admitted that his actions contained at bottom the wish to deprive Fliess of his "originality." Relations between Freud and Fliess were mired in distrust: in Freud's well-founded questions about the scientific validity of Fliess's periodicity theory; and now, in Fliess's suspicion that Freud had passed the substance of Fliess's bisexuality theory on to another man. The friendship, clogged with bitterness and resentment, was over.

In the fall of 1904 Freud resumed teaching his course on psychoanalysis at the old Psychiatric Clinic. For two hours on Saturday nights he stood quietly in the dimly lit auditorium articulating to six or seven people ideas that would soon pervade all of Western culture. There were only eight or ten chairs grouped close to the lecturer's table, and newcomers, taken aback by the intimacy of the little group, often stood indecisively in the doorway, eyeing the benches at the rear of the amphitheater. Did Freud hope that among the visitors might be one who would understand as Fliess once had? Freud would wave them down in a friendly way and say simply, "Won't you come nearer and be seated, gentlemen?"

OF THE men who taught at the Burghölzli, "it was C. G. Jung," one young student thought, "who turned out to be the greatest inspiration of those days. He kept his students spellbound by his temperament and the wealth of his ideas." By 1906 Jung was considerably impressed by the theories of Sigmund Freud, and his work on the word-association test had produced enough results for him to prepare a book on the subject. Jung's use of the association test as a diagnostic tool, in particular its emphasis on the patients' "mistakes," represented, he knew, an important contribution to the science of mental illness.

As Jung finished writing and editing his book, he was aware that he had been measurably helped in his work by the theories of Sigmund Freud. He did not want to admit it. For an ambitious man, the decision whether to give Freud his due was a difficult one. To align himself publicly with Freud would yield Jung little. "Freud was definitely persona non grata in the academic world at the time," Jung knew, "and any connection with him would have been damaging in scientific circles. 'Important people' at most mentioned him surreptitiously, and at congresses he was discussed only in the corridors, never on the floor."

Nor was Jung's chief fully won to Freud's views. Eugen Bleuler had taken to his bed one day in 1905 with an attack of rheumatism and read a book by Freud on his sexual theory. "This one," Bleuler wrote Freud courteously, "I cannot yet completely follow." Bleuler was bound to try to understand Freud's theory of dream interpretation. He described his dreams to his residents and his wife, gathered in discussion, but he could not agree with their explanations. He began to send Freud lengthy letters in which he tried to let his thoughts flow naturally about dreams he had had, but he failed miserably. "It seems idiotic that I with my paltry little experience should have doubts," he told Freud. "But it is also idiotic that I should succeed only in exceptional cases in interpreting a dream of my own. Hesitation, distraction by the sound of rain falling, thoughts of someone who was supposed to stop by."

But Freud's dream theory had begun to make sense to Jung. It reminded him "of the striking statue of Carnal Pleasure in Bâle Cathedral, which shows in front the sweet smile of archaic sculpture, but behind is covered with toads and serpents. Dream analysis," Jung had come to see, "reverses the figure and for once shows the other side." Jung's book on the word-association test was published in 1906. Included in it was his recent article, "Psychoanalysis and Association Experiments," generous in its praise of the theories of Sigmund Freud. In its closing lines Jung stated his position unequivocally: "It appears, from some recent publications, that Freud's theory . . . is still consistently ignored. It therefore gives me great satisfaction to draw attention to Freud's theories—at the risk of also becoming a victim of persistent amnesia." Jung wrapped up a copy of his little book and sent it to Vienna. On the eleventh of April, Freud replied:

Dear colleague,

Many thanks for sending me your *Diagnostic Association Studies*, which in my impatience I had already acquired. Of course your latest paper, "Psychoanalysis and Association Experiments," pleased me most, because in it you argue on the strength of your own experience that everything I have said about the hitherto unexplored fields of our discipline is true. I am confident that you will often be in a position to back me up, but I shall gladly accept correction.

Yours sincerely,
Dr. Freud

Jung saved Freud's reply for the rest of his life. One day he would take all of Freud's letters and place them between thick pieces of cardboard covered in a heavy linen cloth. He would keep the portfolio in his "secret cache," a small safe in his study in Küsnacht. But now he only set Freud's letter aside. There was no reason to take up the correspondence again until October, when Freud sent him a copy of his newly published *Collected Short Papers on the Theory of the Neuroses.* In Jung's reply to Freud, he stated his opinion on a subject that would one day be interpreted as the reason for their rupture: "it seems to me," Jung wrote, qualifying Freud's view, "that though the genesis of hysteria is predominantly, it is not exclusively, sexual." Freud, sanguine, replied, " Your writings have long led me to suspect that your appreciation of my psychology does not extend to all my views on hysteria and the problem of sexuality, but I venture to hope that in the course of the years you will come much closer to me than you now think possible."

Jung thought that, in order to secure a wider audience for Freud's theories, one should not emphasize publicly the disturbing issue of sexuality. But Freud was inflexible. "I beg of you, don't sacrifice anything essential for the sake of paedagogic tact and affability," he wrote Jung. "And don't deviate too far from me when you are really so close to me, for if you do, we may one day be played off against one another." Their correspondence warmed. Jung referred to "the lack of personal contact with you" as "that regrettable defect in my preparatory training." On the first of January 1907 Freud, speaking of his colleagues in Vienna, told Jung, "I know of only one who might be regarded as your equal in understanding, and of none who is able and willing to do so much for the cause as you." And in an elegant, offhand way, Freud invited Jung to Vienna: Jung had sent Freud an analysis of a dream he had had that contained a wish to travel to America; Freud replied simply, "Perhaps you will be coming to Vienna before you go to America (it's nearer)."

One day that same January in 1907, the young doctor Ludwig Binswanger approached Jung at the Burghölzli and asked him if he would sit for the word-association test. Several years of work on the experiment had yielded a set of procedures and analyses that seemed capable of great subtlety. But just how useful the test would be on a doctor who already knew the typical responses remained to be seen. Binswanger placed the electrodes on Jung's hands and began the test in the usual fashion. Jung responded to the fourth word, *prick*, with the word *knife*, a common response. Aware that the test word *angel* ordinarily followed, Jung was surprised to find it replaced by *devil*. Young Binswanger had changed the test, and Jung was on his own.

When Jung responded with *lie* to the test word *belly*, Binswanger noted that for the subject the word *belly* was "apprehended sexually and in the sense of 'crawling on one's belly' to some one; something very antagonistic to the subject, especially in scientific matters." Three quarters of the way through the test Binswanger had heard enough to observe, "We are here dealing with the complex of ambition, thirst for knowledge, 'will to power.' " Jung's last reactions pointed toward the future. On question ninety-eight he was asked to respond to the word *Vienna* and his answer was *Paris*. Binswanger's questioning revealed that Jung "is contemplating a journey to Vienna as soon as the vacation begins; he can hardly wait." The test was over and Binswanger removed the electrodes from his subject's hands. Proud, ambitious, eager for fame, thirsty for knowledge and unwilling to bow to another in scientific matters, Carl Jung was looking forward to Vienna.

TWO MONTHS later, on Sunday morning, March 3, 1907, Sigmund Freud left his house at Berggasse 19 shortly before ten o'clock and walked down the street to a nearby hotel. He entered the lobby carrying a bouquet of flowers to welcome Emma Jung, Ludwig Binswanger and Carl Jung. The walk had taken only a few minutes, but the journey had been long and for the most part solitary.

PART THREE

FRIENDSHIP

CHAPTER SEVEN

THE ENTRANCE to Berggasse 19 was being remodeled in March 1907. A chandelier hanging in the entryway was covered with old cloths to protect it from the work of replastering, but Freud's apartment looked much as it always had. Carl Jung was uncomfortable when the two men went into Freud's study on the ground floor. *Enfin seuls*, their wives teased. Finally alone. The study was a quiet place on Sundays and dim in the morning light. "Thick rich rugs," one visitor remembered. "Your feet sank like a camel's in the sand." Freud's books and small statues lined the room. Jung would feel at home. The spirit world personified by Freud's little figures was familiar to him, and some of the books on the shelves were on his own back at the Burghölzli, well-used like these.

Jung began to speak. He was an articulate man and now he was excited. Freud sat quietly behind his desk and listened. It is not difficult to imagine the scene: Jung, in whom laughter and anger were close to the surface, gesticulating broadly, his animated face vivid. And Freud with every sign of control: contained, self-deprecating, his face still and watchful as he took this first long look at Carl Jung. The young Swiss talked without pause for three hours. Finally Freud interrupted him calmly. They would spend the time more profitably, Freud said, if they proceeded in a more orderly fashion. He touched upon all the points Jung had raised and the questions he had asked, organizing them quickly under several topics. Jung was amazed. One of the subjects under discussion was Freud's sexual theory, and now it was Jung's turn to listen. What Freud said impressed Jung. "Nevertheless," Jung remembered years later, "his words could not remove my hesitations and doubts. I tried to advance these reservations of mine on several occasions, but each time he would attribute them to my lack of experience."

"For thirteen uninterrupted hours we talked and talked and talked. It was a *tour d'horizon*," Jung said. "Freud was the first man of real importance I had encountered; in my experience up to that time, no one else could compare with him. There was nothing the least trivial in his attitude. I found him extremely intelligent, shrewd, and altogether remarkable." Perhaps he noticed, as had another visitor, that Freud's "way of speaking was different from anything I had ever heard before or since: full of pictures; one could call it biblical." Later Jung would tell a friend he had been moved at times to tears when he found Freud's thoughts so closely matching his. "They were kindred spirits," Jung's colleague C. A. Meier said. "There was an attraction always."

Freud and his family were impressed with Jung. More than fifty years later, Freud's son Martin could still recall the cases Jung described at the dinner table. There was the story of a man who, shy and withdrawn in childhood and as a young adult, had matured into a strong and commanding presence; and another of a talented schizophrenic whose artwork displayed energy and promise. The stories were nothing in themselves, Martin realized, but Jung's striking portrayals fascinated the children and Freud as well. "Jung on these occasions did all the talking," Martin Freud remembered, "and father with unconcealed delight did all the listening." Unlike some of the other visitors at Berggasse 19, Jung was not interested in entertaining the Freud children, but they liked him best of all. Martin Freud was struck by Jung's soldierly bearing, "his liveliness, his ability to project his personality and to control those who listened to him." Years later and nearly seventy, Martin would confess modestly, "I cannot flatter myself that he ever noticed me."

For her part, Freud's eldest daughter, Mathilde, remembered Jung in all his boyish enthusiasm. She had taken Emma and Carl shopping, when suddenly soldiers were standing at attention along the Ringstrasse because the emperor was about to pass. "Excuse me, please," Jung said, and ran off to join the crowd. Jung loved parades all of his life, and even as an old man he would hurry to hear the drums. He had grown up in a city where the Swiss border fronts two countries and military readiness was critical; the sound of beating drums called up his childhood always.

The household Jung visited in March 1907 would be described by many in the years to come. It was of more than passing interest to observe in Sigmund Freud, father of psychoanalysis, the simple and unaffected father of six children. There was a singular lightness in his dealings with them, prompted by humor and affection and markedly different from the authoritarian rigidity found elsewhere. The Swiss pastor Oskar Pfister was particularly touched. "I, who grew up fatherless and suffered for a life-time under a soft, one-sided bringing up, was dazzled by the beauty of that family life, which in spite of the almost superhuman greatness of the father of the house and his deep seriousness, breathed freedom and cheerfulness."

Carl Jung, like other visitors to Berggasse 19, found no ritual observance of the fact that the Freud family was Jewish. Martha Freud came from a religious background and once confessed that a Friday evening early in her marriage must be counted among the saddest times in her life. Her husband would not allow her to light the candles that signaled the beginning of Sabbath, for in his house there would not be any religious ceremonies. Martha's mother was an orthodox Jew and her grandson Martin remembered her occasional visits to Vienna: "On Saturdays we used to hear her singing Jewish prayers in a small but firm and melodious voice. All of this, strangely enough in a Jewish family, seemed alien to us children who had been brought up without any instruction in Jewish ritual." Martha Freud would take the children on holidays to the home of Freud's mother. Dinner was always splendid, with roast goose, candied fruits and cakes; but it was served at Christmastime or on Easter, for Amalia ignored the Jewish feasts and so did her son.

Despite Freud's lifelong habit of nonobservance, he remained profoundly a Jew. The son of one of Freud's friends, Leopold Königstein, remembered meetings that his father and Freud attended at B'nai B'rith, a Jewish society in Vienna. "They came out in a very solemn mood," young Leopold recalled, and then went into the smoking room to play cards. Sometimes the boy sat and watched the men, but he didn't dare move. "If they saw that the one . . . looking on made the slightest movement there was hell!" The library at B'nai B'rith was important to both his father and Freud, he thought: on their visits they would borrow books from the thousand volumes of biblical and Jewish history. Freud's identity as a Jew was cultural rather than religious, but it was no less deep. As a child, Martin Freud saw his father's kindly face turn suddenly fierce as he strode waving his walking stick into a group of men jeering racial slurs. Freud's courage did not surprise his son, but the transformation of his mild and gentle father shocked him.

By 1907 Freud had experienced enough anti-Semitism to be wary of its potential effect on the psychoanalytic movement, which was then supported almost entirely by Jews. Freud, who had decided to go into medicine in part because the career was open to Jews, and who was for years denied an academic appointment for reasons of prejudice, was a realistic man. It would be a distortion to tie Freud's affection for Jung to political gain, and yet he knew what Jung's presence as a gentile would mean to the psychoanalytic movement. With Jung and Bleuler and the prestige of the Burghölzli behind them, Freud's theories might escape that part of the slander that would derive from anti-Semitism.

However much Freud's Viennese colleagues agreed with his assessment, they distrusted the Christian Jung from the first. Some eight or ten members of Freud's Wednesday Psychological Society had their first look at him on March 6, 1907. The little society had met once a week since 1902 in Freud's waiting room off the study, the members drifting in casually after their evening meals at home. When they had all gathered, Freud would appear. Martha Freud poured coffee while the men sat at a long table and talked, flicking their cigars into Freud's small collection of antique ashtrays. Martin Freud, returning home late one night from a dance, marveled that men could survive a room so thick with smoke.

Jung did not speak much on his first visit to the Wednesday Society in March 1907, explaining that he did not yet know Freud's theories well enough. He was not alone in this. Only the week before, one of the participants had suggested that "perhaps we may be inclined to overestimate the significance of the Freudian teachings for psychology; that is to say, the importance of the sexuality factor for psychology." The new concepts did not come easily to anyone, even the loyal Viennese. If Jung was quiet that evening, he also seemed slightly obtuse. In a discussion of a male patient who had dressed up as a girl and slept in his father's bed, one member described the patient as identifying with his mother. Alfred Adler, the Viennese analyst whose patient it appeared to be, pointed out a possible homosexual element; but Jung said only that the inclination to dress up in girl's clothes was a mystery to him.

Another young man would come to Vienna in 1907, but he would not pay a visit to Sigmund Freud. Eighteen-year-old Adolf Hitler, fresh from the provinces, walked through the doors of the Fine Arts Academy in the fall of 1907 to sit for the entrance exam. Hitler's test drawings showed an ability for line and detail, but despite this he was rejected twice. "Too few heads," was the comment, for Hitler demonstrated little talent for portraying the human form. He applied to the architecture school, but he lacked the necessary degree. For six years Hitler led a marginal existence in Vienna, sleeping on park benches and painting sentimental scenes of the city, which he sold to Jewish craftsmen to advertise their picture frames. Once he tried out for a part in the chorus of the Theater an der Wien, auditioning with a tenor part in a song from Franz Lehár's *Merry Widow*. The director was impressed enough to offer Hitler a place, but Hitler had to turn it down. He hadn't realized that he had to supply his own tuxedo, and he couldn't afford one. But Hitler would learn things in Vienna. When Karl Lueger died in 1910, Hitler came in from his men's hostel in northwest Vienna to see the funeral. Lueger's successful manipulation of anti-Semitic feelings had impressed the young man.

WHATEVER QUESTIONS Jung still harbored about Freud's theory of sexuality he kept to himself when he returned to the Burghölzli. "I am no longer plagued by doubts as to the rightness of your theory," Jung wrote Freud with seeming finality. "The last shreds were dispelled by my stay in Vienna, which was for me an event of the first importance." Binswanger had stayed on in Vienna, and Jung added that he "will already have told you of the tremendous impression you made on me. I shall say no more about it, but I hope my work for your cause will show you the depths of my gratitude and veneration."

While Jung now apparently agreed with Freud's theories, he persisted in believing that they should be made more palatable to the uninformed. "Is it not conceivable," Jung asked, "in view of the limited conception of sexuality that prevails nowadays, that the sexual terminology should be reserved only for the most extreme forms of your 'libido'?" Freud's reply was stately: "I appreciate your motives in trying to sweeten the sour apple, but I do not think you will be successful. . . . We are being asked neither more nor less than to abjure our belief in the sexual drive. The only answer is to profess it openly."

Although the men disagreed cordially over how best to serve up sexuality to the unenlightened, they had become allies in belief. "Often I have to transport myself back to the time before the reformation of my psychological thinking to re-experience the charges that were laid against you," Jung wrote. "I simply can't understand them any more." Jung did not hesitate to do battle on Freud's behalf and looked forward to representing his views at a medical congress in Amsterdam that fall. "Since I am not so deeply committed and am not defending my own brain-children," Jung said, "it sometimes tickles me to venture into the arena. The identification with you will later prove to be very flattering; now it is *honor cum onere*."

Jung's colleagues at the Burghölzli felt the force of his commitment. Dr. Abraham Brill was an American psychiatrist who had come to spend a few months working at the Burghölzli. "There I found an enthusiasm for psychiatry, which I never saw before nor since I left Zurich," Brill recalled. "The object was to determine whether there really was an unconscious, as Freud claimed, and whether Freud's views on sex in the neuroses were true." The young doctor was struck by Eugen Bleuler's scientific attitude: "There is more psychology in one page of Freud," Bleuler told him, "than in some voluminous textbooks. It is easy enough to make fun of him; but what we should do is to examine Freud's concepts and either confirm or disprove them scientifically." Jung did not share Bleuler's detachment. He "was the first assistant and at that time a very ardent and pugnacious Freudian," Brill remembered. " You could not express any doubt about Freud's views without arousing his ire." Allah and his prophet, they said at the Burghölzli: Freud and Jung.

Used to the newer and better-equipped hospitals back in the States, Brill was not immediately impressed by the Burghölzli. But his first staff meeting left him spellbound. "The way they looked at the patient, the way they examined him, was almost like a revelation. They did not simply classify the patient. They took his hallucinations, one by one, and tried to determine what each meant." This was very different from the attitude of Brill's colleagues back home in America. There the causes of mental illness were believed in large part to be genetic, owing to "degenerate stocks" and therefore incurable. The family physician was advised to proceed cautiously in the care of "nervous children": "Cold baths, frictions, exercise, hard beds," counseled one American neurologist, "cold sleeping rooms, wide open windows at night, develop the body's resistance to external stimuli. For these children country life is imperative, and the occupations chosen for later years should be outdoor and manual, never indoor and mental."

Brill was well aware that the sexual aspects of psychiatric cases were regarded with disgust in his hospital on Long Island. He told Jung that once in a meeting he had read aloud the case history of a patient who had made sexual advances toward his sister, and staff members had reacted in horror. "The trouble with you [Americans]," Jung replied, "is that you know nothing about Freud and his concepts on sex." Brill set out to learn. He honored the self-imposed rule of abstinence and submitted willingly to the monastic routine of the Burghölzli. Often after rising at six in the morning to begin his rounds, he saw Eugen Bleuler returning from the wards already having finished his. "It was inspiring," Brill remembered, "to be in a group of active and enthusiastic workers who were all toiling to master the Freudian principles and to apply them to the study of patients. Psychoanalysis seemed to pervade everything there."

In working with his patients, Brill found that their seemingly inexplicable behavior could often be traced to prior experiences in their normal lives. Suddenly the patients seemed not so very different from himself, and the realization alarmed him. "I feared lest there be something wrong with me; but I soon discovered that what I found in a patient, was only an exaggerated or distorted expression of that which exists in every normal person." Brill never forgot the relaxed late-afternoon discussions in the main office of the Burghölzli as the doctors finished their work; the topics ranged from the theories of Sigmund Freud to the mysteries of the occult.

It was one thing for Carl Jung to teach the sexuality theory to students like Abraham Brill within the walls of the Burghölzli. It was another to face a gathering of the medical community with the express intention of defending Sigmund Freud. At the end of August 1907 Jung traveled to Amsterdam, where he was to deliver a lecture before the First International Congress for Psychiatry, Psychology, and the Assistance to the Insane. When Jung first accepted the invitation, the challenge of presenting Freud's views appealed to him. Now he had the feeling things would not go well. "I have unpleasant presentiments," Jung told Freud in some alarm, "for it is no small thing to be defending *such* a position before *such* a public."

The men had been preoccupied with the Congress for several months. Freud was convinced that Jung's friendly and winning nature ("all hearts open to you," he told him) would succeed in drawing in the opposition. There was something in his own personality, Freud confessed, that people found strange and repellent. Jung, guided by an "unconditional devotion to the defence and propagation of your ideas, as well as my equally unconditional veneration of your personality," had one concern at the meeting: to present Freud's difficult and unpopular theories in a way that people might understand and accept them. As the time for the Congress drew near, Jung's frustration was complete. To simplify Freud's concept of sexuality, he realized, would be to rob the theory of its authentic power. To present it in all its complexity would leave the audience far behind. In the end Jung consoled himself that his paper, "this child of sorrow," would at least be a "demonstration, a confirmation, of the fact that in the year 1907 someone officially said something positive about Freud's theory of hysteria at an International Congress." Freud was more optimistic: "Your lecture in Amsterdam will be a milestone in history and after all it is largely for history that we work."

Jung arrived in Amsterdam and went to the Hôtel de l'Europe. Small and elegant, it was nestled on the bank of a busy canal within feet of the passing boats. A few days later he received a letter from Freud, who was spending a vacation with his family "hiking in the mountains and picking edelweiss." For nearly a month Freud had not touched the little notebook he carried to jot down notes and ideas, and he was feeling guilty at having left his young and inexperienced colleague to deal with the Congress alone. "Whether you have been or will be lucky or unlucky, I do not know," Freud wrote. "But now of all times I wish I were with you, taking pleasure in no longer being alone and, if you are in need of encouragement, telling you about my long years of honourable but painful solitude, which began after I cast my first glance into the new world, about the indifference and incomprehension of my closest friends, about the terrifying moments when I myself thought I had gone astray and was wondering how I might still make my misled life useful to my family, about my slowly growing conviction, which fastened itself to the interpretation of dreams as to a rock in a stormy sea, and about the serene certainty which finally took possession of me and bade me wait until a voice from the unknown multitude should answer mine. That voice was yours."

The meeting in Amsterdam began on the morning of August 4; when the German psychiatrist Gustav Aschaffenburg finished speaking, a gauntlet of sorts had been thrown down. Aschaffenburg had attacked Freud's theory of hysteria, predictably its emphasis on sexuality. Jung rose next to speak, outlined the principles of psychoanalytic technique and stated that his own clinical work confirmed Freud's theories. He continued talking beyond his allotted time and refused to stop until he was told to do so by the chairman. Flushed and angry, Jung strode from the room. A young Welsh neurologist sitting in the audience felt Jung had handled things badly. "I remember," said Ernest

Jones, "the unfortunate impression his behavior made on the impatient and already prejudiced audience."

Jung had lost his temper in his first important defense of Sigmund Freud. He thought the assembled group was "a gang of cut-throats" and "cowards, each man hanging on to the coat-tails of the fatter man in front. . . . A ghastly crowd," Jung wrote Freud that same afternoon, "a morass of nonsense and stupidity!" But he refrained from describing the role he had played in the morning's proceedings. A week later, back at the Burghölzli and still furious, Jung told Freud about the "reign of terror" one participant had proclaimed against Freud; the "benevolent neutrality" of others. The only bright spot Jung saw was the young Celt, Ernest Jones: "He is very intelligent and could do a lot of good." But even the appearance on the scene of young Jones was not enough to mollify Jung. "*One* thing that has filled me up to the neck at this Congress is a contempt bordering on nausea for the genus *Homo sapiens*." Freud dealt with his hotheaded young ally as diplomatically as he could. There was "nothing for it," Freud cautioned Jung, "but to go on working and to argue as little as possible." One day the confrontation in Amsterdam would be called one of the "great discussions" in the history of psychoanalysis. In the fall of 1907 the men were relieved simply to have it behind them.

As the months passed since Jung's first visit to Freud in March, something was troubling Jung. He was slow to write Freud at times, excusing himself on the basis of his many duties and fatigue or blaming an evil spirit for bedeviling his pen. But the real reason for his lapses in writing lay deep. A few months after Jung returned from Amsterdam, he finally explained himself: "Actually—and I confess this to you with a struggle—I have a boundless admiration for you both as a man and a researcher, and I bear you no conscious grudge . . . it is rather that my veneration for you has something of the character of a 'religious' crush. Though it does not really bother me, I still feel it is disgusting and ridiculous because of its undeniable erotic undertone. This abominable feeling comes from the fact that as a boy I was the victim of a sexual assault by a man I once worshipped. Even in Vienna the remarks of the ladies ('enfin seuls,' etc.) sickened me, although the reason for it was not clear to me at the time.

"This feeling, which I still have not quite got rid of, hampers me considerably. Another manifestation of it is that I find psychological insight makes relations with colleagues who have a strong transference to me downright disgusting. *I therefore fear your confidence.* I also fear the same reaction from you when I speak of my intimate affairs. Consequently, I skirt round such things as much as possible, for, to my feeling at any rate, every intimate relationship turns out after a while to be sentimental and banal. . . . I think I owe you this explanation. I would rather not have said it."

Freud's response was prophetic: "What you say of your inner developments sounds reassuring; a transference on a religious basis would strike me as most disastrous; it could end only in apostasy. . . . I shall do my best to show you that I am unfit to be an object of worship." If Jung was not to worship Freud, he would find another way to elevate him. "Let me enjoy your friendship not as one between equals," he would write Freud, "but as that of father and son."

Toward the end of November 1907, Ernest Jones set out for Zürich to spend a week at the Burghölzli. He was prepared to be busy, for Jung's cordial reply to his letter had contained a daunting schedule. Jung would meet Jones at the Hôtel Baur au Lac between eleven and midnight if Jones arrived in the evening. In any event Jones was expected to lunch at the Burghölzli the following day at eleven o'clock. Despite Jung's actions in Amsterdam, Jones had found him an attractive man, and the impression was reinforced during his stay at the Burghölzli. Jung could be courteous and even gallant: when Abraham Brill began in youthful enthusiasm to initiate Jones into the wonders of psychoanalysis, Jung quickly intervened. "We didn't invite Dr Jones here to teach him but to consult him."

During Jones's visit to the Burghölzli, the psychoanalytic cause was advanced a step further. Jung agreed to arrange the first Congress dedicated to Freud's psychoanalysis, to take place in Salzburg or Innsbruck the following spring. There, unencumbered by the opposition, they would enjoy the riches of Freud's theories. While he was in Zürich, Ernest Jones attended one of the first meetings of the Freudian Society of Physicians, a group that had begun to meet under Jung's leadership to discuss psychological issues. On that particular evening, Eugen Bleuler recited some verses he had prepared on the subject of Sigmund Freud and his obtuse critics:

A town once terrorized by Turks,
Finds within its walls there lurks
A dragon. With Libido's torch
He'd light humanity, and scorch
It into ashes with its searing,
Despite the rabble's angry jeering.

The "priceless doggerel," as Jung described Bleuler's verses, ended with:

Hence, Dr. Freud, respected Sir,
To chaster thinking now defer.
And do not mock our pieties
With public improprieties.

Jung laughed along with the rest, although, Jones noticed, "he could change his mood like a chameleon. One moment the big, vibrant, charming chairman of the group and the next a vociferous intervener who, when confronted by opposition, put his case with a vigour which some thought–well–pretty rough. I liked him at the time," Jones remembered. "He did not mince his words. He was forthright and–at that stage–neo-Freudian to the point where you wouldn't have known the difference." Abraham Brill, often present as well, agreed with Jones: "The meetings were, as a rule, very instructive and interesting, provided no one contradicted Freud's theories, for the chairman was at that time in no state of mind to tolerate such heresies."

Jones suspected Jung was struggling with some internal conflicts at the time, stresses of one kind or another that Jones could only guess at, but that, from time to time, he saw. Despite Jung's inner strain, his life at the Burghölzli was stable and satisfying. Emma Jung had won the affection of everyone at the hospital. Bleuler's young son, Manfred, remembered Frau Jung with particular fondness. He enjoyed going upstairs to visit her in the pleasant four-room apartment, now noisy with the Jungs' little daughters, Agathli and Grethe. As a boy, Manfred Bleuler thought of Jung as a kind of nobleman: "He had an intellectual background; he had wonderful manners; he was an elegant man." Manfred remembered, too, that Jung "was very nice with the children." Ernest Jones was impressed by Carl Jung's "breezy personality," his "restlessly active and quick brain." Jones would become Sigmund Freud's close colleague and official biographer, and he once stated what he thought had drawn Freud to Jung with such permanent force: "his unrestrained imagination. This was a quality that seldom failed to captivate Freud."

CHAPTER EIGHT

THE CONGRESS in Salzburg in spring 1908 would make me very proud; but I suppose I should be in the way and that you will not invite me," Freud wrote Jung, inexplicably diffident. Jung would have none of this: " You deceive yourself mightily if you think we are going to let you off coming to Innsbruck or Salzburg!" Moreover, Jung pressed Freud to assume the chairmanship. Freud had no interest in being chairman. He felt that under someone else's stewardship, this first gathering devoted solely to Freudian theory would seem less the arrogance of one man's vision and more the consensus of a growing science. He would rather Bleuler assumed the chair.

Salzburg was Freud's favorite city, a dark jewel, with cobbled, winding streets, delicate, baroque towers and narrow bridges gracefully spanning the swift waters of the Salzach River. In April the river flowed high with melted snow that came down from the Austrian Alps, and the ornate Mirabellgarten with its terraces and clipped hedges was bright with tulips and narcissi. Ernest Jones arrived in Salzburg April 26, 1908, the day before the Congress was to begin. When he entered the Hotel Bristol, he "felt distinctly nervous as a relative newcomer among so many people who already knew one another. . . . Especially of course I wanted to meet Freud and I kept scanning the lounge hopefully . . . until suddenly there he was." When Freud greeted Jones for the first time, he played a little trick on him: Freud told Jones that he knew him to be a Welshman by the shape of his head. Only years later did Jones learn that Jung had told Freud this before they ever met, that Freud had only teased him.

The Salzburg Congress began at eight o'clock in the morning on April 27, 1908. Some of the forty-two men seated at the long table in the Hotel Bristol would play critical roles in shaping and directing the analytic cause in the years to come. The correspondence of a few of them would chronicle, along with the early history of the psychoanalytic movement, the growing friendship between Freud and Jung and later, the details of its demise. They would consult with Freud and with each other when the rupture with Jung placed in jeopardy the future of the psychoanalytic movement.

Present at the Congress that morning in Salzburg was Ernest Jones, then twenty-nine years old, whom Jung had introduced to Freud the night before. Jones first read Freud in London, when he had just become a doctor. "I came away with a deep impression," Jones remembered, "of there being a man in Vienna who actually listened with attention to every word his patients said to him. . . . I had never heard of anyone else doing so." Freud's interest in his patients contrasted vividly with medical practice in England. As a young resident at University College Hospital in London, Jones had once received a phone call from an asylum director trying to fill a vacancy on his staff. "I don't expect him to be interested in insanity," Jones was told. "But he must be able to play cricket with the patients."

Jones sat that morning in Salzburg, a man with a secret. Early in 1906 he had been administering speech tests in a school for "mentally defective" children in London, and two of them had told their teacher that Jones had "behaved indecently." Jones maintained the accusation was false, but the case went to court. He was found innocent, but now two years later, there was more trouble. Jones had become interested in the sexual basis of nervous symptoms; knowing this, a colleague at the West End Hospital for Nervous Diseases had challenged him to find evidence of sexual trauma in one of his patients. Jones talked at length with the ten-year-old girl and found that a paralysis of her left arm had begun when she tried to ward off a boy's sexual advances. The young girl told her friends that Jones had been "talking to her about sexual topics." When her father learned of this, he complained to the hospital, and Jones was asked to resign. His reputation in London badly damaged, Jones had finally decided to leave for Canada and a post at the University of Toronto. The cold Canadian winters would give him pleasure, however, because he loved to ice-skate. It was "faster, more vivid, more exquisite," he would write, "than one expects anything in life to be." Jones would cause Freud many an anxious moment in the years to come. He was active and frank in sexual matters. Years into their friendship Freud would caution Jones to "be careful with those bad women," and he learned to expect the worst.

Also sitting at the table in Salzburg was thirty-one-year-old Karl Abraham, a German psychiatrist who had worked at the Burghölzli for three years under Bleuler and Jung and now had a psychoanalytic practice in Berlin. Abraham had begun to write Freud while still at the Burghölzli, and Freud had asked Jung about him. "I admit at once that I am 'jealous' of him," Jung replied, "because he corresponds with you." More than that, Jung suspected Abraham of taking other people's research ideas: "I once suggested that he collaborate on my writings, but he declined. Now he pricks up his ears whenever Bleuler and I talk about what we are investigating, etc. He then comes up with a publication."

However subtly, Freud fanned the fires of Jung's jealousy. "I was predisposed in Abraham's favour," he wrote Jung, "by the fact that he attacks the sexual problem head on"; something, he implied, he wished that Jung would do. When Freud finally met Abraham a few months before the Salzburg Congress, he found him inhibited and much as Jung described, but Freud knew why. "I believe he is prevented from unbending by preoccupations that I understand only too well: the fact of being a Jew and concern over his future." Abraham would become a close associate of Freud, but no love was ever lost between Abraham and Jung. Only recently, Jung had written Abraham a disturbing letter about a discussion in Berlin in which Freud's sexual theory had been attacked. "Freud was naturally moved by this discussion—he did get mentioned and a crumb even fell to him from the Lord's table," Jung told Abraham in apparent disdain. "A man of Freud's modest achievements can wax fat on that." Jung's words jolted the calm of his friendship with Freud, but Abraham was not surprised. He had observed his Swiss colleague closely during his stay at the Burghölzli and had drawn his conclusions early on.

Sándor Ferenczi had met Freud two months before the Salzburg Congress. The thirty-five-year-old Hungarian neurologist had found his way to Freud indirectly through Jung, through a colleague who had studied at the Burghölzli. Over the next twenty-five years he and Freud would exchange nearly a thousand letters, and Ferenczi would come to depend on Freud greatly. When the French psychoanalyst René Laforgue, vacationing in the Alps near the Freud family, told Ferenczi that he had tried to call on Freud without success, Ferenczi's solution was simple: "Why not do as I do every morning at eight o'clock and ring Freud's bell to ask him if he would be able to receive you during the day?"

Ferenczi was unnerved by the daunting figures of Carl Jung and Karl Abraham sitting with him in Salzburg. His fear of Abraham would one day lead him to misread a letter from Freud alerting him to the imminent visit of a colleague. "Apparently I was afraid that the guest would be Abraham," Ferenczi confessed to Freud in embarrassment. "He is the more important (perhaps the most important after Jung); to be able to measure myself against *him* is apparently my secret wish, not to be able to—the motif of fear and of antipathy!" As his maid stirred up the fire in his room, Ferenczi reread Freud's letter and was relieved to find it was Ludwig Binswanger who was to come to Budapest and not Karl Abraham.

Ferenczi would go home from Salzburg fully won to Freud's side and not without courage. "The colleagues behave disgustingly," he would report from Hungary. "They slander me and psychoanalysis at every turn." Ferenczi perceived great beauty in psychoanalysis. With typical, boyish enthusiasm, he wrote Freud one day, "I feel like that engineer I know who (retired after 50 years of service) stands in front of the locomotive stopped on the track and exclaims with naive admiration: 'It is indeed a beautiful invention!'—For years I have been preoccupied with psychoanalysis; from early morning til late at night I am a day-laborer of this method, it is my craft and my daily bread. And yet not a day goes by when I don't have to stop—often in the middle of work—to admire the phenomenal progress we have made in the understanding of sick and healthy mankind. 'It is indeed a beautiful invention!' "

The ever-modest Eugen Bleuler sat at the table in the Hotel Bristol along with the rest, though not at its head as Freud had wished; his thoroughgoing democratic spirit resisted the least effort to raise him above his peers. Bleuler's tolerance and even encouragement of diverse points of view on psychology was unalterably Swiss. Freud would call this Bleuler's "ambivalence" (a word that Bleuler had coined himself), would see it at times in Jung as well and despair of his theories ever sinking roots in such Swiss soil. Freud knew that Bleuler wished for a closer connection with him, and yet he was not sure of Bleuler; he did not know on what ground Bleuler actually stood. Other men in other years would contribute as much or more than these men to psychoanalysis. But Bleuler, Abraham, Ferenczi and Jones would be privy to the events that signaled the end of the collaboration between Freud and Jung. They would declare their allegiance to one or the other man, and their choices would determine the future course of psychoanalysis.

Abraham Brill was there as well in the Hotel Bristol that day. This was his first introduction to Sigmund Freud. Already impressed by Jung, Brill would quickly come to believe that the two men—Freud and Jung together—represented a powerful new science it was his task to bring to America. Brill had just finished translating into English Jung's book on schizophrenia, *The Psychology of Dementia Praecox*, and said of it that together with Freud's work it "forms the cornerstone of modern interpretive psychiatry."

When Freud began to speak at eight that morning in Salzburg, the men listened absorbed. "I had never before been so oblivious," Ernest Jones noted, "of the passage of time." As Freud talked on in a low, conversational tone, he drew his listeners into the strange tale of one man's obsession. The man was a patient of Freud's in whom ambivalence—the shift between love and hate—played desperate havoc. Among the points Freud emphasized, Jones remembered, "were the alternation of love and hate in respect of the same person, the early separation of the two attitudes usually resulting in repression of the hate. Then commonly follows a reaction to the hate in the form of unwonted tenderness, horror of bloodshed and so on." Freud thought he would only speak for an hour or so, but it was nearly eleven o'clock before he broke off, feeling the men had heard enough. They insisted he continue and it was almost one o'clock before Freud finally stopped, five hours after he had begun.

The topic of Karl Abraham's paper was schizophrenia, and it espoused a view that was in agreement with that of Freud: schizophrenia was psychically caused, the result of a massive blocking of the feeling processes. Jung, and particularly Bleuler, had spent years studying the problem of schizophrenia, the condition then commonly called dementia praecox; they were annoyed that Abraham made no mention of their work in his talk. When it came Jung's turn to speak, Freud already knew he would be disappointed in his paper. Jung had warned him by letter that it would place the cause of schizophrenia on toxins in the brain, hardly the stuff of psychoanalysis. The Salzburg Congress had two rivals, Jung and Abraham, both speaking on the same topic; but only one subscribed to Freud's view.

The gathering broke several times between papers. Ernest Jones was curious to meet the group from Vienna, whom Jung had described as "a 'degenerate and Bohemian crowd' who did [Freud] little credit." Freud himself was often critical of these men, telling Jung before the Salzburg Congress, "My eastern contingent will probably be inferior in personal merit to your western contingent." In a later letter Freud referred to the caliber of the Viennese group: "Here I must often content myself with very little. . . . I must ask you to do what you can to thwart my talkative Viennese; otherwise we shall all drown in the torrent of words." Jones had mixed feelings as he met them now for the first time: "They were all practising physicians, for the most part very sober ones, and if their cloaks were more flowing and their hats broader than what one saw in Zurich, London or Berlin . . . that was a general Viennese characteristic." But, Jones added, "they were decidedly middle-class, and lacked the social manners and distinction I had been accustomed to in London." As he chatted with them, Ernest Jones was aware of undercurrents of hostility. These men who had defended psychoanalysis, some of them since 1902, were wary of the Zürichers, late on the scene yet now pushed into prominence by Sigmund Freud.

Their resentment only intensified when a few members of the Congress made the decision to publish a journal, the *Jahrbuch für psychoanalytische und psychopathologische Forschungen*, to be edited by Jung. Jones heard predictions as the Viennese analysts relaxed over coffee "that Jung would not long remain in the psychoanalytic camp." Their suspicion of the Germanic, Christian Jung, a suspicion conditioned by years of anti-Semitism in Vienna, seemed to Jones in this instance to be unfounded. One morning in Salzburg as he walked the few steps from the Opera House to the Hotel Bristol, Jones was stopped by Karl Abraham. Abraham asked Jones "how far he thought that the touch of mysticism Jung brought to his thinking invalidated any genuine belief in . . . psycho-analysis." Jones was surprised and told Abraham that nothing Jung had said at the Congress warranted such a question. As the two men talked, Abraham lowered his voice when they reached the Bristol: "Do you think Jung can escape the anti-Semitism of a certain type of German?" Shocked, Jones asked Abraham in turn if he knew the words of Edmund Burke: "I do not know the method of indicting a whole nation." Just then they saw Jung approaching and fell silent.

In a letter to his wife, Freud called the Congress "a great success." But when he returned to Vienna, the tensions between Abraham and Jung continued. Jung's complaints focused on Abraham's Salzburg lecture, to be published in the new *Jahrbuch*. Not only was Jung angry that Abraham had neglected to mention his and Bleuler's contributions to the work on schizophrenia, he was sure Abraham had usurped Freud's theory about the cause of the disease. On this point Freud was clear: Abraham's "appropriation of it is perfectly acceptable to me, I only regret that *you* didn't appropriate it."

Freud felt the psychoanalytic movement was too small to withstand a rift between two of its major figures, and he asked Abraham and Jung to reconcile their differences. Abraham confessed his own part in the matter: "My Salzburg manuscript contained a sentence that would have gratified Bleuler and Jung, but following a sudden impulse I omitted it when delivering the paper. . . . That I did not mention Bleuler and Jung evidently signified 'Since you [two Swiss] are turning away from the sexual theory I won't cite you when I am dealing with it.' "

Freud cautioned Abraham to "be tolerant and don't forget that really it is easier for you to follow my thoughts than for Jung, since to begin with you are completely independent, and then racial relationship brings you closer to my intellectual constitution, whereas he, being a Christian and the son of a pastor, can only find his way to me against great inner resistances. His adherence is therefore all the more valuable. I was almost going to say it was only his emergence on the scene that has removed from psychoanalysis the danger of becoming a Jewish national affair."

The issue turned on the fact that Bleuler and Jung were not attributing sexual causes to schizophrenia, but were accounting for it by the presence of toxins in the brain. Freud did not press Jung to abandon his view, fearing that he might fail in the attempt and lose the young Swiss. He would wait a few months and talk to Jung in person. "I will do all I can," Freud told Abraham, "to put matters right when I go to Zurich in September. Do not misunderstand me: I have nothing to reproach you for. I surmise that the repressed anti-Semitism of the Swiss, from which I am to be spared, has been directed against you in increased force. But my opinion is that we Jews, if we want to cooperate with other people, have to develop a little masochism and be prepared to endure a certain amount of injustice. There is no other way of working together. . . . Why can't I pair you both together, with your keenness and Jung's enthusiasm?"

Freud was counting on a visit with Jung to straighten things out. He had good reason to think so. Soon after they had met for the first time in Vienna, Jung had written Freud, "I have the feeling of having made considerable inner progress since I got to know you personally; it seems to me that one can never quite understand your science unless one knows you in the flesh." The carrying power of their friendship seemed to rest on the sense of sureness each man gained in the other's presence. "I am quite certain," Freud told Jung after the Salzburg Congress, "that after having moved a few steps away from me you will find your way back, and then go far with me. I can't give you any reason for this certainty; it probably springs from a feeling I have when I look at you." He emphasized this again over a month later: "just seeing you in Salzburg, though there was hardly a chance of talking to you, I knew that our views would soon be reconciled."

"I HAVE a mountain of questions," Jung wrote in August 1908, looking forward to Freud's visit. He invited Freud to stay with him at the Burghölzli, or in a hotel if he preferred. "Please choose," Jung told him. Both men were tired and overworked, badly needing vacations. Before Freud arrived, Jung stole away for a few days to the "inaccessible solitude of a little Alpine cabin on Mount Säntis," forty miles from Zürich.

Jung made sure there was ample time to talk when they saw each other at the Burghölzli on September 18. "I shall banish all intrusions that might encroach upon our sessions, so we can count on being undisturbed." Freud would use those hours wisely. "My selfish purpose," he told Jung, "which I frankly confess, is to persuade you to continue and complete my work by applying to psychoses what I have begun with neuroses. With your strong and independent character, with your Germanic blood which enables you to command the sympathies of the public more readily than I, you seem better fitted than anyone else I know to carry out this mission. Besides," he added, referring to Jung's distrust of intimacy, "I'm fond of you; but I have learned to subordinate that factor."

For the first time, Freud saw Jung's world at the Burghölzli: the persistent, heedless excesses of psychosis and the work of the doctors, their refusal to capitulate to seemingly hopeless illness. Freud had treated such cases himself in Vienna, but rarely. One day when he and Jung were on the ward together, the Swiss stopped to chat amiably with an old woman patient. How, Freud asked him later, was he "able to bear spending hours and days with this phenomenally ugly female?" Jung was surprised. He was fond of the old woman and her lovely fantasies.

Freud was not distracted from the task that had brought him to

Zürich: he succeeded in convincing Jung to abandon the toxin theory of schizophrenia. Their theoretical differences were resolved amid more tangible concerns, when they visited the wards and discussed the patients in Jung's care and when they broke away from their tasks at the hospital to go mountain climbing.

Freud and Jung left the Burghölzli to hike on the Rigi, a string of mountains that sweeps down central Switzerland just south of Zürich. Inveterate walkers, the men covered ground quickly. They stood on mountaintops and gazed across shallow green valleys to other, higher peaks glazed with snow and luminous in the September sun. Freud and Jung loved mountains, the grueling work of psychoanalysis, strong peasant cheeses, the tough bite of wit. Freud liked to tell stories, and Jung could "laugh down to his shoes." They talked all day long. "Now that we can live, work, publish and enjoy a certain companionship, life is not at all bad," Freud would write Jung from Vienna, "and I should not want it to change too soon."

Freud and Jung shared an incomparable vision, at times almost an obsession. They were traveling a landscape unlike any other and struggled with fierce purpose to understand it. Psychoanalysis was not the only thing they thought about, nor was it the only thing that mattered. But it was what mattered most of all. The bond between them went deeper than friendship. It lay at the core of a passion that consumed them both: the nearly impossible dream of shaking loose the secrets of the psyche. Neither man ever abandoned the dream, but the fullness of their accord as they strode across the mountains that bright September would not stay.

SIX MONTHS later, on March 25, 1909, Carl Jung left the Hotel Regina in Vienna and walked over to Berggasse 19, where he found a warm welcome in the Freud household. "You have . . . built up an excellent reputation as a guest," Freud told him. Emma Jung had accompanied her husband to Vienna, and they dined that night in the familiar comfort of Freud's hospitality. Yet not everything was the same. When the men left the family to go and talk in Freud's study, it was not the room Jung knew. The study looked quite as it always had, but the actual room was different. Freud had taken over his sister Rosa's flat and moved his study upstairs. Rosa was Freud's favorite sister, a widow in her sixties who, according to her nephew Martin, "could still command love from young men, something about which she was very proud and not in the least discreet."

The men had much to discuss on Jung's second visit to Vienna.

Jung's trip was a celebration. He was finishing his work at the Burghölzli that month and was "house-building" in Küsnacht, a little village on the shore of the Zürichsee. It was to be a fine house, nearly grand, and Jung would live in it until he died. Freud was interested in the progress on the house and was looking forward to visiting the Jungs when they settled in Küsnacht.

Jung had decided several months before to leave the Burghölzli, and Freud had approved: it would give his Swiss colleague more time to devote to the growing demands of the psychoanalytic movement. Jung would also be less influenced now by Eugen Bleuler, whose espousal of Freud's sexuality theory had been less than wholehearted. It did not seem to have occurred to Freud that Jung might, freed from the Burghölzli, be more inclined than ever to find his own path: "The note of freedom in your letters since it is settled that you are to be your own master comes as an answer to my heartfelt wishes. You will see what a blessing it is," Freud had written Jung, "to have no master over you."

Just before coming to Vienna, Jung confessed to Freud that Sabina Spielrein, the young Russian girl who was his patient and had worked on the word-association experiment, was in love with him. Jung found himself caring about Sabina more than he should: "Until now I had a totally inadequate idea of my polygamous components despite all self-analysis," he told Freud. According to Jung, Sabina had "kicked up a vile scandal solely because I denied myself the pleasure of giving her a child. I have always acted the gentleman towards her, but before the bar of my rather too sensitive conscience I nevertheless don't feel clean."

Freud had comforted Jung by telling him, "To be slandered and scorched by the love with which we operate—such are the perils of our trade." But he noted uneasily that Jung's confession was dosed with biblical references to the devil and hell: "You definitely lapse into the theological style in relating this experience." Jung's religious tone disturbed Freud. He found himself in the role of father confessor and knew that one of the needs bound up in having a father was the need to overthrow him. Jung tried to reassure Freud. "You mustn't take on about my 'theological' style," he said, "I just felt that way."

As the men talked in Vienna, about Sabina and about Jung's future, their conversation would shift to family news as well. There would be talk of the recent marriage of Freud's eldest daughter, Mathilde, to Robert Hollitscher and of the birth of Jung's son, Franz. Nearly three years had passed since the men had started to correspond and now the ties were many and close. Freud had accepted an invitation to come to America and give a series of lectures; he was eager to explore with Jung what this first great journey might achieve for the psychoanalytic movement.

On the last evening in Freud's study an incident occurred that jarred both men. Jung had for years been interested in spiritualistic phenomena. His doctoral dissertation had been based on observations he made of his relative, Helene Preiswerk, who performed as a medium in séances. Jung, curious, asked Freud what he thought of occult phenomena. Freud rejected the possibility that they existed. Jung never forgot the scene that followed: "I had a curious sensation. It was as if my diaphragm were made of iron and were becoming red-hot—a glowing vault. And at that moment there was such a loud report in the bookcase, which stood right next to us, that we both started up in alarm, fearing the thing was going to topple over on us. I said to Freud: 'There, that is an example of a so-called catalytic exteriorisation phenomenon.'

" 'Oh come,' he exclaimed, 'that is sheer bosh.'

" 'It is not,' I replied. 'You are mistaken, Herr Professor. And to prove my point I now predict that in a moment there will be another loud report!' Sure enough, no sooner had I said the words than the same detonation went off in the bookcase. To this day I do not know what gave me this certainty. . . . Freud only stared aghast at me."

Jung knew he had profoundly upset Freud. Upon his return to Zürich he wrote, "When I left Vienna I was afflicted with some *sentiments d'incomplétude* because of the last evening I spent with you. It seemed to me that my spookery struck you as altogether too stupid and perhaps unpleasant." At first, Freud confessed, he had been tempted to accept the episode as proof that occult phenomena existed after all. But after Jung left, Freud told him, "my credulity, or at least my willingness to believe, vanished with the magic of your personal presence."

The evening's encounter produced the germ of an idea Jung would one day develop more fully. "I had the feeling," he told Freud, "that under it all there must be some quite special complex, a universal one having to do with the prospective tendencies in man. If there is a 'psychoanalysis' there must also be a 'psychosynthesis' which creates future events according to the same laws." Jung had taken a step out of Freud's orbit and had seen something of his own creative possibilities. It was a feeling heady enough to move Jung to declare, "That last evening with you has, most happily, freed me inwardly from the oppressive sense of your paternal authority." Just at the moment when Jung felt strong enough to cast off his need for Freud as a father, Freud availed himself of the position he had disdained: "It is strange that on the very same evening when I formally adopted you as eldest son and anointed you . . . as my successor and crown prince, you should have divested me of my paternal dignity, which divesting seems to have given you as much pleasure as I, on the contrary, derived from the investiture of your person."

During the next months, the spring of 1909, Freud was drawn into the passion of Sabina Spielrein for Carl Jung. She had turned to Freud in her despair. "My last hope of salvation was to speak with a person who deeply loves and respects him," Sabina wrote in reply to one of Freud's letters to her, "who possesses a profound knowledge of human nature, and when I received your last letter . . . tears came to my eyes: 'He loves him! What if he could understand all this!' "

Sabina's wish was to separate from Jung, a man she could not have, and so be free to find a young man whom one day she could love. Jung had succeeded in curing Sabina of a psychosis, and he had done so with his heart as well as his head. He had given her his friendship, and eventually his love as well. Sabina's mother, warned of the situation in an anonymous note, intervened. She wrote a letter to Jung and told him that he had made Sabina well and ought not risk a setback by going beyond the limits of friendship. Jung replied to Frau Spielrein in a letter he later regretted. "I moved from being her doctor to being her friend," he wrote, "when I ceased to push my own feelings into the background. I could drop my role as doctor the more easily because I did not feel professionally obligated, for I never charged a fee. . . . You do understand, of course, that a man and a girl cannot possibly continue indefinitely to have friendly dealing with one another without the likelihood that something more may enter the relationship. For what would restrain the two from drawing the consequences of their love? . . . Therefore I would suggest that if you wish me to adhere strictly to my role as doctor, you should pay me a fee as suitable recompense for my trouble."

Jung was upset by the letter he had written. He told Freud it was "too stupid that I of all people, your 'son and heir,' should squander your heritage so heedlessly." In a long explanation in his "theological style" Jung wrote, "I . . . deplore the sins I have committed, for I am largely to blame for the high-flying hopes of my former patient. . . . I imputed all the other wishes and hopes entirely to my patient without seeing the same thing in myself. . . . In view of the fact that the patient had shortly before been my friend and enjoyed my full confidence, my action was a piece of knavery which I very reluctantly confess to you as my father."

The intricate and exhausting tale of passion and betrayal was finally resolved by Sabina herself. Jung reported to Freud, she "has freed herself from the transference in the best and nicest way and has suffered no relapse (apart from a paroxysm of weeping after the separation)." Jung had erred in aspects of his treatment of Sabina, but he had accomplished much. She was cured.

Three dramas had unfolded in the lives of Freud and Jung that spring of 1909. In the first, the younger man had seen, in the strange occurrence in Freud's study, possibilities that encouraged him to assert his independence, while in the same instant Freud had crowned Jung his royal son. In the second drama, Jung begged Freud's fatherly forgiveness for indiscretions real and imagined toward Sabina Spielrein, but Freud did not want to hear the confessions of a penitential son. Beneath these surface tensions, yet a third, unspoken drama was playing all the while, involving two protagonists largely blind to fatal twists in the roles they had assumed. Imagine for a moment two men in darkened rooms with a closed door between them. The older man, knowing himself a king, knocks on the door and asks, "Are you my son?" The younger man says yes, and the king is relieved to have found his prince; the son is gratified to have found his father. But now the lights go on in the rooms; the king is revealed, resplendent in his royal dress and in his hopes. But on the other side of the closed door, the younger man is in monk's robes beseeching his father's forgiveness. Out of their own need, unknowing, Freud and Jung had chosen conflicting metaphors for the relations between a father and his son.

Unaware, for the most part, of this third and fateful drama, Freud and Jung wrote in their letters of news that excited them both. Jung had also been invited to America by Clark University to give a series of lectures on psychoanalysis in Worcester, Massachusetts. "Isn't it splendid about America?" Jung asked Freud. "I have already booked a cabin on the *G. Washington*—unfortunately only a very expensive one was left. I shall sail with you from Bremen. Now I am in for it —what am I to say?"

Freud was overjoyed. "Your being invited to America is the best thing that has happened to us since Salzburg." But like Jung, he worried. "Of course your joy is now beginning to be clouded by the same concerns as mine, culminating in the question: What am I to say to those people? On this score I have a saving idea, which I shall not keep secret from you. Here it is: we can think about it on shipboard, on our long walks round the deck." To his friend Oskar Pfister, Freud wrote, "You too must have been impressed by the great news that Jung is coming with me to Worcester. It changes my whole feeling about the trip and makes it important. I am very curious to see what will come of it all." Freud wrote Ferenczi in Budapest and invited him to join them.

G. Stanley Hall, president of Clark University, wrote Freud, "I hope you will be my guest as long as you can stay in this city. It would be well to take a carriage from the Worcester Station to my house, 94 Woodland Street, where you will find your rooms in readiness."

CHAPTER NINE

FREUD SPENT a short, sleepless night on the train coming in from Munich after a holiday with his family in the Bavarian Alps. When he arrived in Bremen at five-thirty in the morning on August 20, 1909, Jung and Ferenczi were already in the German city preparing for the voyage to America. Spirits were high at a luncheon Freud hosted in the Essighaus, a restaurant in a historic building in the port city. He and Ferenczi pressed Jung to have wine with his meal. Jung hesitated, mindful of his long-standing oath to abstain, yet aware of his newly acquired independence from Bleuler and the Burghölzli. After a heated discussion, he took up a glass of wine for the first time in nine years.

Freud saw something large in the gesture: he had won the young Swiss to his side. His elation faded when Jung began to talk about the legend of peat bog corpses found in northern Germany. The story of the mummified bodies of prehistoric man fascinated Jung. Acid in the peat had tanned and toughened their skin, preserving their hair yet disintegrating the bones. It was not known whether the men had drowned in the marshes or been buried, their bodies now flattened by the weight of the peat. Freud became angry and uncomfortable. "Why are you so concerned with these corpses?" he kept asking Jung, who continued to dwell on the fate of the bodies until suddenly Freud fainted.

The episode was puzzling to Jung. During the years of their friendship, he had often found Freud's self-assurance enviable, as yet beyond his own grasp. But now an altogether more human and complicated Freud had appeared. When Freud recovered, he seemed "convinced," Jung thought, "that all this chatter about corpses meant I had death wishes toward him." Jung did not think this was so, although one can imagine that Jung might unconsciously have wished the death of a man in whose shadow he seemed destined to stand.

Jung was host that night at dinner, and the next day the three men began the sail to America. Usually an enthusiastic traveler, Freud had displayed at moments an uncharacteristic reluctance about the trip. When Ferenczi plied him with books about America, Freud did not read them. He planned to work out his lectures while on board ship, but he did not. Freud had told people that he was going to America to see a porcupine and give some lectures: not wishing to face straight on the anxiety of what lay ahead in Worcester, he played a little game in which the search for a porcupine absorbed the tension of the trip.

Freud, Jung and Ferenczi, lulled by the long days at sea and far from the rigors of their professional lives, indulged themselves in the rare companionship of like-minded men. Left to the slow leisure of sea travel and the broad decks, they walked for hours around the ship analyzing each other's dreams. Ferenczi felt inadequate in the presence of Freud and Jung. "I had learned from your dream that with me it is only 'quarter to twelve,' " Ferenczi told Freud; he saw this as a symbol of the "not-quite-understanding" that he sensed between himself and Freud. Fond as Freud was of Ferenczi, he thought him childish and instructed him in how to overcome this trait. Ferenczi, in a long meditation on deck that he later described to Freud, rebelled at first. "I'd rather be the way I am," his meditation went. "I'm at least happy then, a happy child. But you," he told Freud, "are obviously (mentally) so old, explaining everything, dissolving all personal passions into thought, that you cannot be happy."

Ferenczi could be acute. And he was not afraid to tell Freud what he thought. In one of their sessions Freud expressed "dissatisfaction with the Vienna environment." In connection with the analysis of Freud's dreams, Ferenczi was sure that what dissatisfied and worried Freud was his family in Vienna. Moreover, Ferenczi said, repeating Freud's phrase, " 'the dissatisfaction of the soul' obviously has—in my thoughts—always sexual meaning as well."

Freud tolerated a free and easy exchange of dreams with Ferenczi, but with Jung it was different. Perhaps he realized the implications that attached to granting Jung access to his psyche. "When I analyzed Freud a bit further in 1909," Jung remembered, "on account of a neurotic symptom, I discovered traces which led me to infer a marked injury to his feeling life." Jung was convinced that one of Freud's dreams concerned his wife, Martha, and his sister-in-law, Minna. From something Minna had said on Jung's first visit to Vienna, he understood Freud to be involved in an unresolved relationship with her. It is unlikely that Freud had entered into a physical liaison with his sister-in-law. But Minna was an important part of Freud's life, and it was not surprising that she would figure in one of his dreams. "I interpreted it as best I could," Jung recalled, "but added that a great deal more could be said about it if he would supply me with some additional details from his private life." The topic, Jung told a friend years later, was "hot material."

Freud refused to give Jung more information. "I cannot risk my authority!" he said. Jung felt that "at that moment he lost it altogether. That sentence burned itself into my memory." More than seventy years later Franz Jung observed, "Father was very disappointed in his own father; and after that dream on the ship, he became very critical of everything Freud said. He had a negative father-complex, and he brought it to his relationship with Freud." Jung had his own view years later of his brief attempt to psychoanalyze Sigmund Freud. "I never thought," he told a friend, "of the great joke it is that the only analysis that Freud ever had was a Jungian one."

Freud fared little better in his attempt to analyze Jung. Among the many details of a long and complicated dream, Jung described to Freud two human skulls decaying on the floor of a cave. The dream captivated Jung in other aspects, but the skulls were what interested Freud. In Bremen, Jung's talk of peat bog corpses had caused Freud to believe his friend unconsciously wished his death. Now Freud wondered if this wish had surfaced again in Jung's dream of the two skulls. What wish was connected with these heads, Freud asked, as his hand grasped and shook an imaginary skull. Jung's view of the two skulls in the cave was the beginning of an idea that would occupy him for the rest of his life. Years later he would write, "In the cave, I discovered remains of a primitive culture, that is, the world of the primitive man within myself—a world which can scarcely be reached or illuminated by consciousness." For Jung, it was "my first inkling of a collective *a priori* beneath the personal psyche. This I first took to be the traces of earlier modes of functioning." Jung was convinced that Freud would not agree and knew as well that this delicate strain of discovery was not strong enough to survive Freud's criticism.

Jung did not reveal to Freud what he thought to be the true meaning behind the two skulls. He told Freud instead that the skulls were those of his wife, Emma, and his sister-in-law. Jung said this because he thought, "I would not have been able to present to Freud my own ideas on an interpretation of a dream without encountering incomprehension and vehement resistance. I did not feel up to quarrelling with him, and I also feared that I might lose his friendship if I insisted on my own point of view." By mentioning his own wife and sister-in-law, Jung had set up a mirror image between the dreams of the two men. Perhaps he hoped that Freud would reveal his own problems as he analyzed the wife and sister-in-law in Jung's dream. But Freud did not. Each man had sought distance from the other: one in a refusal and the other in a lie. Each man had retained a measure of independence from the other by refusing to disclose his feelings about a fragment of a dream.

Despite these moments of tension, the men enjoyed the trip. Freud was pleased one day to find his cabin steward reading a copy of his book *The Psychopathology of Everyday Life*. The late summer weather stayed warm and sunny until a fog rolled in. It was impenetrable and wet, causing Jung to think of primeval mists, the ship a prehistoric monster from the deep. He had the sense of slipping back into the ancient past as the ship sailed west through the dark day. Freud noticed that the world aboard ship had become strangely muffled and subdued, save for "the mating cry of the foghorns."

As the ship made its slow way from Europe to America in late August 1909, the news back in Germany was that Orville Wright, in Berlin without his brother, had decided to postpone his demonstration of flight until the Germans recovered from their "Zeppelin mania": thousands of people were flocking to Berlin on August 28 to see Count Ferdinand von Zeppelin fly to the capital in his dirigible. On that same day an Italian, Captain Spelterini, was flying across the Alps in a balloon fueled with some of Count Zeppelin's hydrogen. *Lâchez-tout*! had come the cry in Chamonix: let everything go. The gold ball lifted and spun gently over Mont Blanc, the pilot captivated by the "chaos of silver" below. The excitement of flight had gripped the world, but the implications were lost on the sea captains of the Atlantic in the summer of 1909. The *Mauretania* and the *Lusitania* were streaking back and forth across the ocean in nearly five days, competing for the swiftest crossing. It took the staid *George Washington* over a week to make the voyage to America.

ABRAHAM BRILL was standing on a pier when the *George Washington* docked in New York City on August 29. He had done what he could in the year since his return from the Burghölzli to introduce the theories of Sigmund Freud to America. He was up against prejudices that were strongly felt and deeply ingrained. The American psychiatrist Frederick Peterson would later say, "The theories of Freud and Jung are to psychology what cubism is to art, new, sensational and rather interesting. If they were not so pernicious in their application, as well as untrue in psychology, I should say nothing of them." The Swiss-born psychiatrist Adolf Meyer, now living in America, had written Jung only the year before, "On this side the abhorence [*sic*] of touching on the sexual problem is almost unsurmountable [*sic*], and it will take much tact and patience to put the whole matter into acceptable form."

Difficulties never dampened Brill's enthusiasm. In 1910 he would walk home across Central Park from his work at the New York Neurological Institute with a fellow physician, and he always managed to turn the conversation to the theories of Sigmund Freud. "And thus I became a convinced Freudian," recalled Brill's companion, Smith Ely Jelliffe, one of the first few dozen psychoanalysts to practice in America. But in 1909 such a "conversion" seemed unlikely. Jelliffe was spending the year abroad and writing a friend, "This whole Freud business is done to death. The lamp posts of Vienna will cast forth sexual rays pretty soon. . . . The poor unborn children cannot be told fairy tales any more because of their sexual significance. I suspect William Tell's apple must have been a pair of testicles and as for George Washington's cherry tree—well, perhaps you . . . can illuminate the dark places in my mind."

When Brill greeted Freud, Jung and Ferenczi walking toward him on the quay, the four men met as friends. Brill knew Jung well from his months at the Burghölzli and had met Freud and Ferenczi in Salzburg. Now he would show them New York, yet an innocent city; at least hindsight would have it so. William Taft was president in the summer of 1909, and his predecessor, Teddy Roosevelt, was off in Africa hunting game. America was at play in the August heat, camping on Staten Island in tent cities that stretched as far as the eye could see. Men in shirt-sleeves raised tent frames on platforms only feet apart, the rough canvas walls rolled up to let in the sea breezes, cots only inches from those of strangers. Women in long dresses waited for the grocery wagons to pass by with food to cook for dinner. There were pictures in the newspapers of a retreat E. H. Harriman was building on a fifty-thousand-acre tract of land in Orange County, New York. It was called the grandest summer residence in America, and it cost two million dollars to build. There were photographs in the papers, too, of elaborate "camps" in the Adirondack Mountains. The range of summer life styles was always great in America.

Brill installed the three men in the Hotel Manhattan and led them on a series of excursions around the city. They visited Chinatown, where Jung was served "an incredible dish with chopped meat, apparently smothered in earthworms." The men found themselves in museums as well, Freud losing himself happily in a collection of antiquities from Cyprus at the Metropolitan Museum of Art; in another, Jung enjoyed an exhibit of dinosaurs, "where all the old monsters, the Lord God's anxiety dreams of Creation, are to be seen," he wrote his wife. Freud and Jung spent several hours walking in Central Park and talking over the problems of psychoanalysis. "He is as clever as ever and extremely touchy," Jung confided to Emma in a letter. "He does not like other sorts of ideas to come up, and, I might add, he is usually right."

Ernest Jones, then living in Toronto, joined the four men on the next day to accompany them to Worcester, Massachusetts. They dined that evening at Hammerstein's Roof Garden, where a few weeks before, a trained monkey named Peter had been the main attraction, along with dancers and Italian singers. Freud, Jung and Ferenczi had not seen Jones since he had left London in disgrace the year before. His new life in Canada had not discouraged his interest in psychoanalysis. In fact, from his new vantage point, Jones surveyed all of North America and England as well with a proprietary eye. He would lead the psychoanalytic movement among these English-speaking peoples with only minimal direction from Freud. At least that was his private dream.

The psychotherapeutic movement in America was most vigorous in Boston, Massachusetts. Puritanical, hidebound and conservative, New England nevertheless contained several elements that made it particularly receptive to the psychoanalysis of Sigmund Freud. The transcendentalism and unitarianism peculiar to New England thought was not unsympathetic to hypnotism and the power of suggestion. Moral conflict and a host of unseen spirits were embedded in the harsh mental landscape of New England, and a rich rebellious strain of dissent was her pride. Intellectual liberty was a cause for which men had fought and died and was not taken lightly. Boston's interest in curing mental illness may have also sprung from greater need. New England was believed to spawn disproportionately large numbers of the mentally ill. The wife of Henry Adams complained that much of her time was taken up calling on relatives in asylums; she herself would one day commit suicide. Sexual taboos were more rigidly held here than elsewhere, and this had led a few influential Bostonians to take a closer look at the relationship between sexual disturbances and mental illness.

Ernest Jones had spent time in Boston trying to win the Harvard community to Freud's side. His greatest success was with James Jackson Putnam, a professor of neurology at Harvard. Putnam's mild manner and pale blue eyes belied a certain courage: his eminence and his genuine engagement in Freud's theories made him a valuable asset in the fledgling psychoanalytic movement. Where Jones had succeeded with Putnam, with others, he quickly found, the sexuality theory was unacceptable. A speech Jones had given before the American Therapeutic Association in February 1909 had fallen on deaf ears. Jones was sure that Americans would condemn Freud's theory in full when they realized it was inextricably rooted in sexuality. He decided it did no good to write continually about Freud's theories. "A man who writes always on the same subject is apt to be regarded here as a crank . . . and if the subject is sexual he is simply tabooed as a sexual [neurotic]. Hence," Jones announced to Freud, "I shall dilute my sex articles with articles on other subjects."

As Freud and Jung sat at dinner in Hammerstein's Roof Garden catching up on Jones's news while the supper show went on, there was little doubt they listened to him carefully. Neither Freud nor Jung quite trusted Jones. Jung thought Jones stopped short of believing in the sexuality theory. Freud wondered if Jones wanted the psychoanalytic movement in North America to belong only to him. He did not like to think that the growing friendship between Jones and Brill might one day lead Brill to disavow Freud's theories. "I find the racial mixture in our group most interesting," Freud had observed darkly to Jung. "[Jones] is a Celt and consequently not quite accessible to us, the Teuton and the Mediterranean man." Freud would watch Jones closely in the days ahead.

Several days later the men traveled to Worcester, where they met Stanley Hall, president of Clark University and one of the leading academic psychologists of the day. Freud would write a friend on his return to Vienna, "One of the most agreeable phantasies is that without our knowing it decent people are finding their way to our ideas and aspirations and then suddenly popping up all over the place. That is what happened in the case of Stanley Hall. Who would have imagined that over in America, an hour's train journey from Boston, a worthy old gentleman was sitting and waiting impatiently for the Year Book, reading and understanding everything, and then, as he himself put it, ringing the bell for us?" G. Stanley Hall was an innovative psychologist impressed by the theories of Sigmund Freud. He had come to believe that young children had sexual instincts, that disturbances in emotional development played a role in mental illness and that unconscious drives had a decisive effect on human behavior. At the age of nearly seventy, Hall was considerably more open to new ideas than many of his younger colleagues.

He greeted his visitors cordially. Everything had been done to make Freud and Jung feel at home. Cigars were everywhere; the men found them, to their surprise, in the bathrooms. Hall's wife served splendid meals. But even Jung's expansive nature was tested by the Hall household. "It was all but impossible to get five minutes alone," he complained. One day when he was trying to shave and brush his hair, each of his attempts to shut the door was immediately frustrated. The Halls simply opened it again. If the welcome at the Hall home on Woodland Street was warm, it remained to be seen what kind of reception would be given Freud and Jung on the following day a few blocks away at Clark University.

CHAPTER TEN

BY ANY ordinary standard, when Freud awoke in Worcester on the sixth of September he was a man with a problem. He did not know what he was going to say in his five lectures at Clark University, the first of which he would give at eleven o'clock that morning. It would not have helped him to know that Dr. Franz Boas, the renowned anthropologist, had given up one of his hours to speak so that Freud might lecture and that Boas was "enthusiastic over the sacrifice."

Deciding upon a brief outline of psychoanalysis, it remained for Freud to divide the material into five parts and organize each day's talk. An hour or so before his first lecture was to begin, Freud went for a walk with Ferenczi. They passed the frame houses, ponds and huge old trees of Worcester, flower gardens deepening into autumn color, purple asters blooming, the New England hills ripening in the late summer sun. At a suggestion from Ferenczi, the day's topic was chosen. They covered Freud's lecture briskly in half an hour, and Worcester. One of the most succinct of Freud's works—a little history of psychoanalysis—came from these walks. Each morning, sober and immaculate, his beard freshly trimmed, in a dark suit of the finest material, Freud walked swiftly through Worcester with Ferenczi. His lectures would be flawless, composed on American soil.

Freud spoke on the first morning without notes, as was his habit, and he spoke in German. This presented little difficulty, for among the several hundred people in the audience were many of America's leading academicians, whose education had included lengthy stays in Europe. "If it is a merit to have brought psycho-analysis into being," Freud began, "that merit is not mine. I had no share in its earliest beginnings. I was a student and working for my final examinations at the time when another Viennese physician, Dr. Josef Breuer, first . . . made use of this procedure on a girl who was suffering from hysteria."

Puritan New England opened her doors to listen in silence as a modest middle-aged Jew spoke earnestly in a foreign language on a subject that had met with scorn abroad. Slowly and carefully, Freud introduced his audience to the sad and bewildering story of Bertha Pappenheim, "Anna O.," who had fallen ill while caring for her dying father. Freud spoke of her symptoms, how in a waking dream while sitting beside the sickbed she had seen a black snake writhe from the wall to bite her father. She had tried to strike it but found herself unable to move her arm. When she looked down at her hand, Freud said quietly, "the fingers turned into little snakes with death's heads."

People said that Freud's case histories sounded like novels, and this was true in Worcester. The snake finally vanished, Freud continued, and "in her terror [Bertha] tried to pray. But language failed her: she could find no tongue in which to speak, 'till at last she thought of some children's verses in English." It became the only language she could speak. Then Freud explained how Breuer had cured her. "When she was put under hypnosis, it was possible, at the expense of a considerable amount of labour, to recall the scenes to her memory; and, through this work of recollecting, the symptoms were removed." Bertha lost her paralysis and regained her German. Freud finished to great applause. New England and Freud were at their best. "We are the men of the hour here," Jung wrote his wife with pride. Adolf Meyer, a lecturer himself at the conference, thought Freud had "front-page glamour."

After Freud's third lecture a woman in the audience went up to Ernest Jones and expressed her disappointment that Freud had not yet discussed his theory of sexuality. Would Jones, the woman asked, mention this to Freud? In light of all that had gone before, the question contained an irony. For years Freud had enjoined Jung not to dodge the sexuality issue, and he worried that Jones avoided it as well. Implicit in the woman's request was the same criticism, now leveled against Sigmund Freud. In his fourth lecture Freud did discuss sexuality, but by now he had his audience well in hand. "First and foremost," he began, "we have found out one thing. Psychoanalytic research traces back the symptoms of patients' illnesses with really surprising regularity to impressions from their *erotic life*. . . . I am aware that this assertion of mine will not be willingly believed. . . . There are among my present audience a few of my closest friends and followers, who have travelled with me here to Worcester. Enquire from them, and you will hear that they all began by completely disbelieving my assertion that sexual aetiology was of decisive importance, until their own analytic experiences compelled them to accept it."

It was not easy, Freud told the gathering, to get at the sexual disturbances of his patients. "People are in general not candid over sexual matters. They do not show their sexuality freely, but to conceal it they wear a heavy overcoat woven of a tissue of lies, as though the weather were bad in the world of sexuality." Nonetheless, Freud said, "the imperishable, repressed wishful impulses of childhood have alone provided the power for the construction of symptoms, and without them the reaction to later traumas would have taken a normal course. But these powerful wishful impulses of childhood may without exception be described as sexual."

For Freud, who had clung tenaciously to theories that had met with contempt and derision in Europe, Worcester was the realization of a dream. By day he gave lectures and listened while his friends expounded upon theories he had devised himself. At night he sat in the dining room of the Halls' house waited upon by footmen in dinner jackets and praised by his peers. People were impressed by Freud's clear, kind eyes, his beautiful hands gesturing expressively, his unassuming manner. They noticed that he never spoke of himself. "Again and again," one journalist observed, "he emphasizes the merits of his colleagues, particularly of his friend, Dr. Jung of Zürich."

One evening that September, as Freud sat with Jung in the Halls' house in Worcester, the American explorer Dr. Frederick Cook was in Copenhagen surrounded by explorers and correspondents in the gilded ballroom of the Tivoli Casino. He had secured the North Pole for America only months before. Cook was sitting at dinner, a garland of pink roses around his neck in the Scandinavian fashion of honoring heroes, when a whisper passed through the hall: Commander Robert Peary had just reached the North Pole as well. Cook covered his disappointment with stoicism. "We are rivals, of course," he said, "but the pole is good enough for two." Worcester would be electrified by the news of Peary's triumph: their own Donald B. McMillan of the Worcester Academy was with Peary at the Pole. TOP OF THE EARTH REACHED AT LAST, he cabled Worcester from Indian Harbor, Labrador. GREETINGS TO FACULTY AND BOYS.

Freud's accomplishments and his "glamour" justified his appearance on the front pages of newspapers, but he did not find himself there in abundance. It was Commander Peary the papers headlined with abandon, not Sigmund Freud. Said *The New York Times* of Peary, HE PLANTED AMERICAN FLAGS AT THE TOP OF THE WORLD, OVER A FATHOMLESS SEA. It would not be overreaching to accord Freud the metaphor. As American newspapers filled that September with the drama of two men fighting for supremacy at the Pole, distrusting the other's claim, diminishing the other's effort, did the possibility occur to Freud or Jung that they might one day stand in a similar relation? Certainly there was no hint of rivalry between them in Worcester, only the deep and satisfying pleasures of charting for the world a different, fathomless sea.

Perhaps Martha Freud and Emma Jung, their husbands also embarked on explorations and far from home as well, would have acknowledged a comparison with Commander Peary's wife: " You don't know," she told a reporter, "how hard it has been for me to have my husband spending year after year in the frozen north, when each time he left on an arctic exploration trip I did not know whether I should ever see him again or not, but now that he has been successful and has finally reached the pole, I believe he will settle down with me and enjoy home life for a while."

The day came for Jung to speak at Clark University. When he first met Emma, Jung had been a poor young doctor and worn a cardboard collar. Back home in Küsnacht he would go off to meetings in his old clothes and Emma would despair. "I couldn't make him put on his coat," she would complain to a friend. Emma always carried along a proper jacket in the hope he would get into it. But Jung was not without a sense of history. Emma would be pleased to learn that when her husband rose to address the gathering in Worcester, he was dressed impeccably.

Like Freud, Jung spoke in German. In his first lecture he talked about his work on the word-association tests; in his second, he traced repetitive family patterns. Only toward the very end of it did he mention for the first time the name of Sigmund Freud. His last lecture was charming and full of references to Freud's work. Jung described the conflicts of a young child as she came to grips with the birth of a baby brother. The child happened to be his daughter Agathli, the baby boy his son, Franz. Although Jung did not declare his paternity, the loving, slightly bemused father was in evidence nonetheless.

Jung told his audience how "Anna" was troubled by fears that had developed, he believed, from imperfect notions about birth and the sexual act. Bright, quick questions were in the air as the little four-year-old girl, having planted seeds in a garden and watched them sprout, turned to her mother (Emma) and asked her abruptly, "How did the eyes grow into the head?" "Anna" was thinking of her baby brother. Emma told her that she didn't know and suggested that Anna ask her father. The ensuing discussion one day after tea between a practical, curious girl and a father who was a gifted psychiatrist differed little from the wary efforts of quite ordinary parents:

ANNA: "Weren't the eyes planted?"
FATHER: "No, they just grew in the head like the nose."
ANNA: "But did the mouth and the ears grow like that? And the hair?"
FATHER: "Yes, they all grew the same way."

"The father," Jung said, "was now getting into a fix. He guessed where the little one was leading him, therefore he did not want to upset, on account of a single false application, the diplomatically introduced seed theory which she had most fortunately picked up from nature."

ANNA: "But how did Freddie [Franz] get into Mama? Did anybody plant him?"

"This extremely precise question," Jung told the gathering, "could no longer be evaded by the father. He explained to the child, who listened with the greatest attention, that the mother is like the soil and the father like the gardener; that the father provides the seed which grows in the mother and thus produces a baby. . . . The father of course was left with an uneasy feeling, for he was not altogether happy about having passed on to a four-and-a-half-year-old child a secret which other parents carefully guard. He was disquieted by the thought of what Anna might do with her knowledge." And yet, Jung concluded in his lecture, the knowledge had a beneficial effect on "Anna," for her fears disappeared.

The child was irresistible, the father fond. Jung's lectures were a success. Freud told Jung later that he "regretted that the scientist did not entirely overcome the father; it is a delicate relief when it might have been a vigorous statue." And he would write Ferenczi that "In [Jung's] personal essay about his Agathli he is too discreet and too inhibited." But James Putnam was struck by Jung's observations, "full of personality, fire, and life." For "the grand old man of Harvard," as Ferenczi called Putnam affectionately, the lectures by Freud and Jung were decisive. The men were "so kindly, unassuming, tolerant, earnest and sincere," Putnam wrote. He invited Freud, Jung and Ferenczi to visit him at his camp in the Adirondack Mountains.

Putnam realized that the sexuality theory would be hard for Americans to accept. In an article several months later he cautioned his readers to be open-minded and receptive. "This outcry against intolerance," Putnam wrote, "may seem overdone and out of place, but it is not so, and one evidence of the fact is that these remarkable researches of Freud and Jung, and their small band of followers, have met with such bitter opposition, even among physicians." Putnam's own wife was among the opposition. She "reacted with tragic bitterness," her daughter remembered, "feeling that [her husband] had been mistakenly lured into a false path which would ruin his professional standing."

When Freud and Jung rose at the end of the conference amid the rich pageantry of black and scarlet robes to accept the honorary degrees conferred upon them, Freud was unmistakably touched. "This is the first official recognition of our endeavors," he told the audience simply. In a little over a year, Freud had moved from a small gathering in Salzburg to a position of one among equals within the broad discipline of psychology. In a decade he had created, from the obscurities of childhood memory, theories that were accorded the same respect as the precise experiments of E. B. Titchener and the pioneering work of Franz Boas. Freud's views would survive theirs; their names, well known in 1909, would be lost to many. Freud and Jung did not know this yet at Worcester, but for the first time they sensed it might be so. "We are gaining ground here," Jung wrote his wife. "I was greatly surprised, since I had prepared myself for opposition."

"Freud is in seventh heaven," Jung told Emma, "and I am glad with all my heart to see him so." However pleased Freud was by his reception in America, he was also uneasy. An important part of the future of psychoanalysis lay in America, in the hands of Ernest Jones. He worried that Jones would break away from him and his sexual theory. The prospect of losing a continent of followers in America alarmed Freud. "He feared," Jones wrote years later, "that I might not become a close adherent." There was little Freud could do. Jones was called back suddenly to Toronto, and Freud went with him to the station. As they waited for the train, Freud told Jones they should keep together. His final words to the young Welshman were, "You will find it worth while." As the train pulled away, Freud felt a sudden warmth for Jones and hoped that the young man's energy and ambition would end in supporting his own. Meanwhile, he could only hope that Jung, on whose shoulders the future seemed more than ever to rest, was capable enough and loyal enough.

For his part, Jones was in a quandary. He wanted to lead, not follow. He admired Freud and his work, but the stubborn, rebellious desire to establish himself in his own right would not go away. Two months later, in November 1909, an article would appear written by Jones containing no reference to Freud or his sexual theories. Freud had every reason to worry.

PUTNAM CAMP lies at the head of the Keene Valley on its eastern side, tucked into the Adirondack Mountains. The three Europeans arriving there by boat across Lake Placid would notice the first touches of fall. The days were shorter, the nights chilly and the valley was brightening as the sugar maples among the spruce and balsam began to turn. Years before, four young doctors from Boston had bought up the land with its farmhouse, barn and shanty. James Putnam, his brother Charles and Henry Bowditch still brought their families and friends to the valley for weeks at a time. The fourth, William James, had sold his share in the camp but he visited often, accomplishing his daily fifty pages of solid reading beside a mountain brook.

The camp was an eccentric place, full of swift glints of humor and whimsical ritual, the efforts of gifted men, America's aristocrats. The old barn was turned into a workshop where Henry Bowditch and Charles Putnam built armchairs, tables, cribs and toys, the scene of endless activity and a child's delight. "I remember," said Elizabeth Putnam McIver, "a contraption of Dr. Bowditch's, beautifully made as everything he made was, for drawing the web from one of the big fat spiders found in the pasture and winding it onto a reel, operated by a little water wheel set in a tiny waterfall in the brook."

The pigsty of the old farm became a writing room, where pigs' tails painted onto the wall curled behind open books. The children were housed under the watchful eye of Mrs. James Putnam. There were fires on the hearths of their sleeping cabins, small tin bathtubs, "a lamp to read by and, on sunny days, a row of steamer chairs on the

. . . porch facing the mountains." "The Stoop" was the camp's parlor and library. In the afternoons Miss Annie Putnam made tea on a kerosene stove, cups hanging from the open shelves, and offered plates of gingersnaps, educator biscuits and chunks of chocolate. Freud and Jung stepped into this as into another world.

The patch of Putnam land carved out of the Adirondack wilderness amazed Freud more than anything he had encountered in America. "Everything is left very rough and primitive but it comes off," he wrote his family. He did not tell them there had been some confusion over the national identities of the three visitors: to welcome the Austrian, the Swiss and the Hungarian, their cabin had been decorated in black, red and gold, the colors of Imperial Germany. The spontaneous environment appealed to Jung. He sang German songs in the evening and loved the primitive living, the made-up games of childhood. Freud, more formal, hiked in the mountains with a gold-headed walking stick. He found the mountain climbing difficult. "We took trails and came down slopes which even my horns and hoofs were not equal," and he was happy that on the second day it rained. "Freud assumes a philosophical smile as he forges through this richly varied world," Jung noticed. "I trot along and enjoy it."

The trip, Freud wrote his daughter Mathilde, could "be described as a great success." He had enjoyed the company of Jung and Ferenczi. "My traveling companions were always very tender," he told her, "and also got along well with each other." But he was happy to be leaving. "America," he said, "was a crazy machine." Both Freud and Jung delighted in analyzing American life. Their critical, European-trained intellects displayed a nearly limitless capacity for intolerance when it came to the odd behavior of the American people. "In America the mother is decidedly the dominant member of the family," Jung thought. "American culture really is a bottomless abyss; the men have become a flock of sheep."

Jung would try to get to the bottom of the strange phenomenon that was America, and one day he thought he had found the answer in a book about America by Maurice Low. "Low thinks," Jung told Freud, "the colossal differences of temperature between summer and winter are to blame. Perhaps a harshly continental climate really is ill-suited to a race sprung from the sea. 'Something is wrong,' as Low says." America fascinated Jung, and at times he was genuinely fond of it. But Freud never overcame his initial distaste. "The Americans are really too bad," he would write Ernest Jones in 1921. "I think competition is much more pungent with them, not succeeding means civil death to everyone, and they have no private resources apart from their profession, no hobby, games, love or other interests of a cultured person."

The men left Putnam Camp on September 18, though not before Freud finally spotted a porcupine, unhappily quite dead. As a parting gift the Putnams gave Freud a small metal statue of the animal, which pleased him. He had accomplished both of his tasks, seen a porcupine and given some lectures. Years later Freud would repeat Schopenhauer's little story about porcupines in one of his books: it was very cold and several porcupines tried to huddle together for warmth, but they moved away from each other quickly when the sharp quills pricked and hurt them. But still it was cold, and so they once more drew close, only to retreat again from their neighbors' quills. It was a long time, Freud said, before the porcupines found a distance from which they could enjoy each other's warmth without harm.

Freud and Jung had come near in confessing their dreams, and drawn away in order to preserve their privacy. The warmth of friendship and a commitment to shared work encouraged them to intimacy, yet the possible consequences of such closeness threatened each man. But for the moment, it seemed they had, like the porcupines, found their proper distance.

H.D. in the 1920s (*The Beinecke Rare Book and Manuscript Library, Yale University*)

Anna Freud's consulting room, 1938 (*Courtesy of Edmund Engelman*)

Collection of figurines in Freud's study at Berggasse 19, 1938 (*Courtesy of Edmund Engelman*)

Figure carved by Jung (*Courtesy of Fritz Bernhard*)

Jung at Bollingen (*Erica Anderson, Courtesy of the Albert Schweitzer Center, Great Barrington, Massachusetts*)

Bollingen in 1955 (*Courtesy of the Jung Estate*)

Jung sailing on the Zürichsee, 1958 (*Courtesy of the Jung Estate*)

Freud and his daughter Mathilde on their arrival in London, June 6, 1938, with Dr. Ernest Jones (*Wide World Photo*)

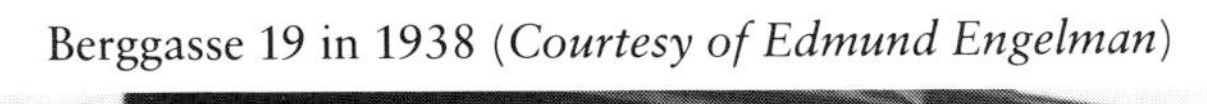

Berggasse 19 in 1938 (*Courtesy of Edmund Engelman*)

Sigmund Freud, about eight years old, with his father, Jacob Freud (*Mary Evans/Sigmund Freud Copyrights, Colchester*)

Freud and Martha Bernays, 1885 (*Mary Evans/Sigmund Freud Copyrights, Colchester*)

Freud with Wilhelm Fliess, August 1890 (*Sigmund Freud Copyrights, Colchester*)

Josef Breuer (1842–1925) (*Oster Nationalbibliothek, Vienna*)

Jung, six years old (*Courtesy of the Jung Estate*)

Jung (right) as a young man (*Courtesy of the Jung Estate*)

Jung in 1902 or 1903 (*Courtesy of the Jung Estate*)

Emma Rauschenbach as a bride (*Courtesy of the Jung Estate*)

Eugen Bleuler (1857–1939) (*Medizinhistorisches Institut, Zürich University*)

Burghölzli Mental Hospital, woodcut, 1867 (*Baugeschichtliches Archiv der Stadt Zürich*)

Freud in 1906, the photograph he sent to Jung (*Sigmund Freud Copyrights, Colchester*)

At Clark University in Worcester, Massachusetts, September 1909. Front row: Freud, Hall, Jung. Back row: Brill, Jones, Ferenczi (*Sigmund Freud Copyrights, Colchester*)

Küsnacht, detail of 19th-century engraving (*Graphische Sammlung, Zentral Bibliothek Zürich*)

Jung with his wife and children, 1918 (*Courtesy of the Jung Estate*)

The Weimar Congress, 1911 (*Courtesy of Paul Naeff*)

1 O. Rank
2 L. Binswanger
3 E. Bleuler
4 M. Moltzer
5 O. Pfister
6 A. A. Brill
7 A. Maeder
8 S. Ferenczi
9 L. Andreas-Salomé
10 S. Freud
11 C. G. Jung
12 E. Jung
13 K. Abraham
14 A. Wolff
15 J. Putnam
16 E. Jones
17 F. Riklin
18 W. Stekel

Lou Andreas-Salomé (*Mary Evans/Sigmund Freud Copyrights, Colchester*)

Freud with his daughter Anna in the Dolomites, 1913 (*Mary Evans/Sigmund Freud Copyrights, Colchester*)

Michelangelo's *Moses* in the Church of San Pietro in Vincoli, Rome (*Alinari/Art Resource*)

Toni Wolff (*Courtesy of Paul Naeff*)

Jung in his study, 1960 (*Henri Cartier-Bresson, Magnum*)

Freud in his study, 1938 (*Courtesy of Edmund Engelman*)

CHAPTER ELEVEN

"THE DAY after we separated," Freud wrote Jung from Vienna, "an incredible number of people looked amazingly like you; wherever I went . . . your light hat with the dark band kept turning up."

"Occasionally a spasm of homesickness for you comes over me," Jung returned, "but only occasionally; otherwise I am back in my stride."

The journey to America had transformed a warm exchange between scientific men into a friendship dense with shared interests. Implicit in the camaraderie was a sense of collusion: together Freud and Jung commiserated, questioned, formulated, doubted and joked. They gazed critically and with accord upon men and their surroundings, relishing the quick phrase sharp with truth. Mocking, irascible, they were not always kind. A streak of recklessness—allies storming the citadels of disbelief—bound the men as equals. In the fall of 1909, though Jung still paid obeisance to the older man and Freud's language was rich in delight at having found his heir, the enterprise was one of comrades in arms.

Freud and Jung took nearly childish pleasure in each new sign of interest in psychoanalysis. On Freud's return from America, he found that five letters had arrived from Switzerland alone; on the first day back at his desk he wrote nearly a dozen letters to foreign countries. He was pleased to note that scarcely two days passed without some sign that psychoanalysis was on the rise. Jung was exhilarated as well. "Your (that is, our) cause is *winning all along the line* . . . in fact we're on top of the world."

Dealing with the requests for advice, information and announcements of new patients was another matter. "In the end," Freud told Jung, "this will get to be monotonous and *a nuisance*." Where there had once been solitude for hours of theoretical thought, the press of patients, students and administrative work now resulted in numbing weeks of work. "I would invent the seventh day," Freud, exhausted, wrote Jung, "if the Lord hadn't done so long ago." Jung asked, "A damned sight too many patients seem to be demanding psychoanalytical treatment, don't you think?" Months later Freud would complain after a vacation, "Today I resumed my practice and saw my first batch of nuts again. . . . It always takes a week or two before they all turn up, and for a while there is enough resilience and alertness left for scientific work. Later on one is content with sheer survival."

Freud and Jung were gifted analysts, and moments of frustration aside, they cared about their patients. But the restless desire to discover, to part the curtain a bit further, was no longer fully satisfied by the insights they gleaned from their patients. "In my practice I come across little that is new," Freud complained, "little that was not already known to me." Jung one day would say that after the first shock of wonder, casework was monotonous. Theirs was the boredom of the born theorist. They were ready for something new.

Neither man liked the organizational details of psychoanalysis. Directing the work of conferences, sending out invitations, booking hotel rooms, soliciting and editing papers for the *Jahrbuch* was time-consuming. The diplomatic maneuvering that increasingly attached to the psychoanalytic movement frustrated both men. Freud contained a basic distaste for his Viennese colleagues only barely. Alfred Adler and Wilhelm Stekel, both Viennese analysts, needed constant supervision and appeasement; Freud did not trust them. Jung was experiencing difficulties in Zürich as well. Not enough men agreed unequivocally with Freud's theories, and Jung was constantly trying to persuade them to greater belief. Eugen Bleuler, an important force in academic psychiatry, would be a welcome addition to the psychoanalytic movement, and yet he hung back. His ambivalent behavior toward psychoanalysis frustrated Jung, but Freud advised patience. "There will be an opportunity for revenge," he said, "which tastes very good cold."

Freud and Jung, walking the tightrope of caution and restraint with their colleagues, found safe ground in each other. Freud sympathized with Jung's struggles to cope with his old chief at the Burghölzli: trying to understand Bleuler, Freud thought, was "like embracing a piece of linoleum." He described Bleuler another time as "a prickly eel, if there is such a thing." Jung agreed with Freud that Adler was paranoid and that Stekel, though brilliant, was a "swine." But, Freud conceded, "the pig finds truffles." Freud was often tempted to throw Stekel out but feared what he might do in retaliation. Besides, Freud thought Stekel was devoted to him, and "I am bound to put up with him as one does with an elderly cook who has been with the family for years." When Freud told Jung how he had rebuked an opponent of psychoanalysis for having lied, Jung replied, "Of course the slimy bastard was lying. I hope you roasted, flayed, and impaled the fellow with such genial ferocity that he got a lasting taste for once of the effectiveness of [psychoanalysis]. . . . Had I been in your shoes," Jung said stoutly, "I would have softened up his guttersnipe complex with a sound Swiss thrashing."

During the months after the trip to America, references to problems in their private lives slipped naturally into letters and conversations. Freud was fifty-three in 1909, yet he had thought of himself as an old man nearly always and had mentioned to Jung that his old-age complex had an erotic basis. The feeling may have been accompanied by vanity: an ornate mirror would hang for years on the window near Freud's desk, an odd juxtaposition for an unpretentious man. Freud's sexual life had been a subject for discussion between the two men. "Sexual excitement," he had written Wilhelm Fliess in 1897, "is no longer of use for someone like me." The condition had plagued Freud intermittently, and now he wrote Jung sadly, "My Indian summer of eroticism that we spoke of on our trip has withered lamentably under the pressure of work. I am resigned to being old and no longer even think continually of growing old."

For Jung, nineteen years younger, the problems were different. His analysis with Freud coming home from America had done him, he thought, a lot of good. He was much more reasonable now than Freud might suppose. In a burst of optimism Jung had even undertaken to analyze his wife, Emma. But he confessed that he was troubled by the ethical problem of sexual freedom and told Freud that it "really is enormous and worth the sweat of all noble souls." The dilemma of sexual freedom haunted Jung. First Sabina Spielrein and then other women would take refuge in his warmth and stay to love him. Years later, many people would tell what they knew of Jung; in some aspects the accounts would differ. But on one point their recollections reliably converged: Jung's effect on women was overwhelming. For a young man of thirty-four, sensing this, the realization must have been confusing. Jung told Freud he was suffering from the nuptial complex and said finally, "The prerequisite for a good marriage, it seems to me, is the license to be unfaithful."

THE MOOD of the friendship that fall of 1909, in addition to sharing the work of the psychoanalytic movement, news of family life and the occasional, introspective moment, had all the savor of life at the edge of the frontier. The first solitary ax swings had opened up new vistas; now Freud and Jung together would clear and extend the view. Each new effort met with generous, spontaneous praise from the other. For Freud who had worked so long alone, and for Jung with the insecurities of youth, approval meant much. Freud returned to work on his lecture on the Rat Man he had delivered to acclaim at the Salzburg Congress the year before; clarifying and honing its basic concepts, he sent the paper on to Jung. " Your Rat Man has filled me with delight," Jung told him. "It is written with awesome intelligence and full of the most subtle reality. Most people, though, will be too dumb to understand it in depth. Splendid ingenuities! I regret from the bottom of my heart that I didn't write it." Freud, who had waited anxiously in Vienna, replied simply, "I am overjoyed at your praise."

When Freud reorganized his university lectures into a seminar, one of his first topics was based on a paper by Jung. He was pleased to report that discussion of Jung's work had been so productive that he had decided to extend it another week. And when Jung in a book review discussed the philosophical implications of psychoanalysis, Freud was moved. " Your remarks . . . are supremely wise—a programme that seems to well from deep layers of my soul. We understand each other." For Jung, there was satisfaction to be found in the work of elaborating Freud's views, finding them structurally and philosophically sound. But there was not the joy of conquest. Part of the greatness of Freud and Jung lay in their immediate grasp of the essential: mindless categories of belief fell before the swift certainty of their intuition. Both men used the metaphor of exploration in describing psychoanalysis, and they were eager now to raise the flag in a new land.

They found it that fall in mythology. "Archaeology or rather mythology has got me in its grip," Jung told Freud two weeks after their return from America. "I was delighted to learn that you are going into mythology," Freud returned. "A little less loneliness. . . . I hope you will soon come to agree with me that in all likelihood mythology centers on the same nuclear complex as the neuroses." At Freud's stroke of insight the whole of mythology was freed from the dry conventions of history and infused with new wonder. Four days later Jung replied, "For me there is no longer any doubt what the oldest and most natural myths are trying to say. They speak quite 'naturally' of the nuclear complex of neurosis."

It was as if each man wore seven-league boots. Ranging down the sides of ancient myths, they sought the source, the wellspring of the first telling. Night after night, month after month, Jung immersed himself in tales of pagan rites and vengeful and angry gods, the age-old attempts of the human spirit to find order and meaning. "I have the most marvellous visions," Jung wrote Freud. "Glimpses of far-ranging interconnections which I am at present incapable of grasping." But one thing had become clear to him: "We shall not solve the ultimate secrets of neurosis and psychosis without mythology and the history of civilization."

Freud was surprised by Jung's fervor, slightly taken aback by the power mythology seemed to exercise over his friend. But he was used to reining Jung in, used to his zeal. After all, Jung's enthusiasm was one of the reasons Freud liked him so well. Yet on one occasion at least, when Freud asked a simple, seemingly unrelated question, he wondered at the full force of Jung's passion for mythology. "I should like to bring up an idea of mine," Freud said to Jung, "that has not yet fully ripened: couldn't our supporters affiliate with a larger group working for a practical ideal? An International Fraternity for Ethics and Culture is being organized in pursuit of such ideals."

"I imagine a far finer and more comprehensive task for [psychoanalysis] than alliance with an ethical fraternity," Jung answered reasonably enough. And then he continued, "I think we must give it time to infiltrate into people from many centres, to revivify among intellectuals a feeling for symbol and myth, ever so gently to transform Christ back into the soothsaying god of the vine, which he was, and in this way absorb those ecstatic instinctual forces of Christianity for the *one* purpose of making the cult and the sacred myth what they once were—a drunken feast of joy where man regained the ethos and holiness of an animal." There was more, but that was enough.

"Yes, in you the tempest rages," Freud replied mildly. "It comes to me as distant thunder. . . . But you mustn't regard me as the founder of a religion. My intentions are not so far-reaching. . . . I am not thinking of a substitute for religion; this need must be sublimated. I did not expect the Fraternity to become a religious organization any more than I would expect a volunteer fire department to do so!" Freud's words of caution were couched in affection. The Viennese Jew who had devoted his life to a belief in reason only gazed with fond indulgence upon the excesses of his brilliant Christian friend. Jung's vision of psychoanalysis, transformed into a vessel for restoring to Christianity the "drunken feast of joy" and to man the "holiness of an animal," seemed to leave Freud curiously undismayed.

The warmth of friendship absorbed Jung's fervent outburst. Little more was said, the matter was dropped. It had become part of a pattern. For despite the nameless fit of friendship and sweeping areas of agreement, problems recurred. Freud and Jung met them with humor and the civility of understatement, but the issues were serious. One source of disagreement was the matter of the libido. Among the most basic of Freud's concepts, libido was the energy that motivated a person to act. According to Freud, the energy was sexual in nature and present even in infancy. The child's earliest experiences were shaped by his desire to possess one parent and do away with the other. In adulthood the individual's unconscious was composed of these childhood wishes, the fruit of his libidinous and incestuous desires, the source of his guilt.

This aspect of Freud's theory had troubled Jung from the first, and he had accepted it only hesitantly. Now Jung wrote, "I often wish I had you near me. So many things to ask you. For instance I should like to pump you sometime for a definition of libido. So far I haven't come up with anything satisfactory." Freud, who must have been shocked by Jung's statement, maintained a tolerant silence. A few weeks later Jung expressed doubt that neurosis was sexually caused. "The question of the original sexual constitution seems to me particularly difficult," Jung said. "Would it not be simplest, for the time being, to start with sensitivity as the general foundation of neurosis?"

As Jung well knew, the sexual basis of neurosis, like the concept of libido, was central to Freud's work. This time Freud replied quickly. He did not think, he told Jung, that the young men coming along in the field of psychoanalysis would try to preserve the work of Sigmund Freud. In fact they would tear it down. He was sure, Freud said with an irony greater than he knew, that Jung was "likely to play a prominent part in this work of liquidation." Nonetheless, Freud continued with humor, "I shall try to place certain of my endangered ideas in your safekeeping." Chief among them was libido. "In the first sentence of the *Theory of Sexuality*," Freud told Jung, "there is a clear definition in which I see nothing to change." Jung was sorry. "My attempt at criticism, though it looked like an attack, was actually a defence." He had felt, he said, that Freud did not consider him knowledgeable enough in the field of mythology to make a genuine contribution; and so he had lashed out. But his apology was not a full concession. "I note," Jung added, "that my difficulties regarding the question of libido . . . are obviously due to the fact that I have not yet adjusted my attitude sufficiently to yours."

One other subject disturbed them both, and that was personal. Freud felt Jung did not answer his letters soon enough. "It probably isn't nice of you," Freud told him, "to keep me waiting 25 days . . . for an answer—as though the promptness and length of my last letter had frightened you away." "Pater, Peccavi," Jung answered, quoting Luke. "Father, I have sinned." Two years before, he had confessed that such lapses in writing were attempts to keep his distance, that a homosexual assault on him as a boy had made him wary of friendships with men. It had been a confession upsetting to make and it would be embarrassing to repeat. Jung resorted now to other explanations. He had been busy, he said; and this was undeniably true. In addition to seeing patients and teaching twelve hours a week, four foreigners had come that fall to work with him. Jung's excuses were various and novel as days would slip by between letters. He had a mighty hangover from the Carnival, he would write. But even Jung could tolerate such excuses only so long. Predictably, he would pull himself together and say honestly, "[I] still have resistances to writing you at the right time. . . . The reason for the resistance is my father-complex, my inability to come up to expectations, (one's own work is garbage, says the devil)."

Freud did his best not to pressure Jung. He tried not to write too often or too soon. He would save a letter and mail it after a safe interval. Or send it right away and explain that psychoanalytic business had made the letter necessary. But once in a while he would chastise Jung. "I am merely irritated now and then—I may say that much, I trust—that you have not yet disposed of the resistances arising from your father-complex, and consequently limit our correspondence so much more than you would otherwise. Just rest easy, dear son Alexander," Freud told him, probably referring to Alexander the Great. "I will leave you more to conquer than I myself have managed, all psychiatry and the approval of the civilized world, which regards me as a savage!" But after each flare-up there was calm again. Disagreements over definitions of the libido and the frequency of their correspondence were tempered with humor, mild reproach and the inevitable apology, and quickly lost among other, more immediate concerns.

Freud was well pleased in his choice of successor. It was Jung who found his position trying at times. He told Freud, "like Herakles of old, you are a human hero and demi-god," and complained, "It is a hard lot to have to work alongside the father creator." Freud assured the younger man many times that the future of psychoanalysis was his, but privately Jung was troubled. He unburdened himself in December 1909 to Sándor Ferenczi, who had accompanied Freud and Jung to America three months before. Jung's letter began modestly, but it ended altogether differently.

"Whether I am recognized or not recognized as the 'crown prince' can at times annoy me or please me," Jung confessed to Ferenczi. "Since I gave up my academic career my interest in science and knowledge has become purer and amply compensates for the pleasures of outward esteem, so that it is really of greater importance to me to see clearly in scientific matters and work ahead for the future than to measure myself against Freud . . .

"What does one want actually?" Jung wondered to Ferenczi, and suddenly his formidable wish was plain. "In the end it is always the one who really is or was the strongest that remains king, even if only posthumously. As always, we have to submit trustingly to this natural law, since nothing avails against it anyway." A dark image of two great rivals awaiting the judgment of history flickered for a moment in the light of Jung's ambition, and was gone. But the light had lasted long enough to see that the penitential son now wished to assume a throne.

ARRANGEMENTS WERE made early in 1910 for a congress to be held in Nürnberg on March 30 and 31. Freud and Jung had not seen each other in six months. "Won't mythology . . . be represented on the programme?" Freud asked Jung as they organized the schedule. Suddenly and unaccountably, in the midst of the last-minute details, Jung sailed for America to see a patient he had treated in Zürich. Freud learned that another Swiss friend, Oskar Pfister, would not be able to attend the Congress. "I still have not got over your not coming to Nuremburg," Freud told Pfister in alarm. "Bleuler is not coming either, and Jung is in America, so that I am trembling about his return. What will happen if my Zurichers desert me?" Jung arrived at the eleventh hour at the Grand Hotel (his speech was rescheduled, which gave him time to rest), and the Congress numbered between fifty and sixty participants. The afternoon session, which began at five o'clock, was stormy. At one point the chairman was forced to interrupt the proceedings in order to give various groups the opportunity to meet privately, for under Freud's direction, Ferenczi dropped something of a bombshell. Freud's Viennese colleagues listened in disbelief as Ferenczi asked them to form the International Psychoanalytical Association with Carl Jung as its lifetime president. Moreover, Ferenczi proposed that Jung should have the power of veto over all articles on psychoanalysis written by members of the Association.

Months before, Freud had confided to Ferenczi his dream that Jung should lead the psychoanalytic movement. Ferenczi was a generous and good-hearted man, and loyal to Freud; but he was aware of an element of rivalry in his relationship with Jung. "I am not jealous of Jung," Ferenczi told Freud, and he tried hard not to be. He tried to outgrow his conception of the relationship among the three men—that of Freud with his two sons, Ferenczi and Jung. He had even sought the advice of a psychic on the matter.

Frau Jelinek lived in Budapest in the dingy rooms of what Ferenczi referred to as a "coffeehouse for very poor people." Thin and frail, often ill, Frau Jelinek had been told by one of her doctors that she must tell people's fortunes: otherwise she would die. Her husband hypnotized her by drawing lines in the air. "*What is to be recommended regarding my relationship with Jung?*" Ferenczi asked Frau Jelinek. Her answer was, Ferenczi recalled, "It will work out all right. He is, to be sure, irritable and violent." (Ferenczi was not certain he remembered this last word accurately.) "But in the end," Frau Jelinek said, "you will come together in collaborative work."

Frau Jelinek's description of Jung touched upon an aspect of his character that concerned Freud and Ferenczi as they evaluated his ability to lead the psychoanalytic movement. "Obviously," Ferenczi told Freud, "as a full-blooded human being [Jung] also has to struggle with his temperament and especially with his hunger for power and ambition. Most likely, this will be the last thing he will overcome. But these affects are very well suited to the work we expect from him, provided that he does not let himself be dominated by them." Ferenczi compared Jung with the Viennese, admitting the inescapable value that attached to their "constant contact" with Freud. "But what the Viennese lack," Ferenczi thought, "and Jung possesses in ever greater measure, is the insight that psychoanalysis has to begin with self-criticism, without which any analysis will acquire a paranoic tinge." Ferenczi had concluded to Freud that "after careful deliberation I have to concur with you absolutely about Jung's future role in psychoanalysis. His two great achievements: his courageous and independent stand in acknowledging your ideas, as well as the first experiments in psychoanalysis, secure this role for him, even if he were to accomplish nothing more." It is striking that in this lengthy appraisal of Carl Jung, Ferenczi did not place on the scales the weighty fact that Jung was a Christian. In Ferenczi's view Jung had won the position on individual merit; the fact that he was a gentile went unmentioned.

Now as Ferenczi stood before the gathering at Nürnberg, he was simply implementing his decision and Freud's that Jung represented the best leadership for the psychoanalytic movement. Just why Ferenczi had taken upon himself the unpleasant task of confronting the Viennese was a question. Freud had asked him once to assume the position as "wise counselor" at Jung's side, and Ferenczi had accepted. "It would be childish defiance of fate, were I to rebel against this." Moreover, Ferenczi believed Freud needed him. He had asked Frau Jelinek about his "Viennese friend" as well, and she had replied, "*You should stay true to him. . . . Not only is he useful to you, you are to him, too; therefore never let go of him.*"

Ferenczi's proposal at Nürnberg that Jung be appointed lifetime president of the International Association inflamed the Viennese. All of their jealousy and pent-up distrust of Jung rose to the surface. Their response disappointed Ferenczi. He knew his own envy of Jung and had struggled to overcome it. "I was not prepared, however, for an uncultivated, unanalyzed brother-complex such as with Adler and Stekel against Jung," he told Freud later. "It saddened me very much to discover this in people who have been living near you for almost a decade." On the way home from Nürnberg, Ferenczi would carefully suggest to the Viennese that they analyze each other on this issue, but his comment only invited derision. "We have no time," they told him. "Something the Zürich people certainly do have."

The Viennese contingent gathered in the Grand Hotel behind closed doors to plot their next move. When Freud learned of the protest meeting, he went at once to Stekel's room. Accounts differed over what happened next; Franz Wittels' was the most restrained. "Most of you are Jews," Wittels remembered Freud saying, "and therefore you are incompetent to win friends for the new teaching. Jews must be content with the modest role of preparing the ground. It is absolutely essential that I should form ties in the world of general science. I am getting on in years, and am weary of being perpetually attacked. We are all in danger. . . . They won't even leave me a coat to my back. The Swiss will save us—will save me, and all of you as well."

Not for just a year, or even two years, had Freud gambled the presidency on Carl Jung, a man who questioned the very essence of his sexual theory. On Jung, Freud gambled for a lifetime. He was risking the future of psychoanalysis on one who would have it revivify Christianity and bring to "fruition its hymn of love, the agony and ecstasy over the dying and resurgent god, the mystic power of the wine, the awesome anthropophagy of the Last Supper." No one could say that reason alone was Freud's guide.

CHAPTER TWELVE

On CHRISTMAS Day in 1910, nine months after the Nürnberg Congress, Freud was sitting in the Park Hotel in Munich waiting for Eugen Bleuler to arrive from Zürich. Germans that Christmas season were delighting in the news that the American Navy would not brave the winter waters of the North Sea to visit German ports. Their own sailors endured them daily, and Germans scoffed that "the American fleet is not of particularly tough fibre." In the news across the Atlantic on December 25 was a different, somber story of military might. "When Count Zeppelin, the German inventor, introduced to the civilized world his dirigible *Zeppelin I*," *The New York Times* reported, "he added to the already overloaded art of war another problem." It was an altogether new and chilling possibility: "The story of the fields below with their massed troops will be . . . plain to the trained observer overhead."

A light drizzle fell on Germany on Christmas Day, on Munich's medieval square, on the horse-drawn carriages in the cobbled streets and on the carved figures of knights and peasants moving mechanically around the Glockenspiel in the tower above. "There is hardly a flake of snow anywhere in the empire," a reporter noted, but it had not affected the German love of Christmas. The country had experienced a year of great prosperity, and Christmas shopping had been on such a lavish scale that the big department stores had been closed at times to prevent overcrowding. A visitor to Germany reported that on Christmas Eve, families had gathered around the tree, sung the Teutonic yuletide song of "Stille Nacht" and participated in elaborate exchanges of presents.

It was not for pleasure that Freud had made the long journey to Bavaria at Christmastime in 1910. The psychoanalytic movement had suffered serious setbacks since the Nürnberg Congress, particularly in Switzerland. Bleuler, who had been among the first to acknowledge Freud's theories, now refused, along with most of the Swiss, to join the new organization dedicated to Freud's psychoanalysis. Bleuler's influence over his Swiss colleagues was significant, and his stature in academic psychology would have lent Freud's association an austere luster. Here in Munich, amid the robust festivities of the German Christmas, Freud would do his best to win him back.

The actions of the Nürnberg Congress had left Freud exhausted but satisfied. One outcome of the meeting had been the decision to found a second journal. The new *Zentralblatt*, Freud felt, was "a double-edged weapon." It was to be published in Vienna, as the *Jahrbuch* was published in Zürich; Ferenczi agreed that it was good "to keep two irons in the fire and the competition between Vienna and Zürich can benefit the cause." More important, Jung had been elected president of the new International Psychoanalytic Association, though only for a two-year term and not with the power Freud had wished. Nonetheless, Freud had been pleased. For the moment the future of psychoanalysis lay securely to the west in Switzerland, in the capable hands of Carl Jung. "I hope you agree with the Nuremberg decisions and will stand loyally by our Jung," Freud had written his Swiss friend Oskar Pfister. "I want him to acquire an authority that will later qualify him for leadership of the whole movement."

But problems in Switzerland had arisen almost immediately. Swiss analysts questioned the requirement that local groups be limited to members of the International Association. They decided to open the Swiss society to all who were interested. Their action incensed Freud: to leave the door of the Swiss society ajar would be to say that one could be called a psychoanalyst without subscribing to Freud's sexual theory. Referring to the Swiss as "blockheads," Freud had written Jung bluntly. "The goings-on in Zürich strike me as stupid. I am amazed that you could not summon up the authority to forestall a decision which is quite untenable. . . . In your place I should never have given in."

But even among the Swiss, Jung's influence seemed slight. He was unable to convince Bleuler to join the International Association. "The break with Bleuler has not left me unscathed," Jung confessed to Freud. "Once again I underestimated my father complex." Nor had it left him kind. One day when Bleuler asked him to interpret one of his dreams, Jung told Freud later in disgust: "He dreamt he was *suckling his child himself*. . . . At last he holds *me*, his child, to his breast again. . . . He does not feel in the least homosexual. Consequently, from love of me, he is turning himself into a woman." Years later Jung's colleague C. A. Meier would say, "Jung was very critical of men. It was frightening, almost. There was something odd about it."

Freud thought some of Jung's difficulties in courting the independent-minded Swiss had developed because Jung was otherwise infatuated, by his "coy new love, mythology." Organizing the psychoanalytic movement required close attention to detail; yet Jung had let his correspondence pile up and left things undone. The business of psychoanalysis for Jung seemed only to obscure the sheer beauty of the work. "Seclusion is like a warm rain," he told Freud. "One should therefore barricade this territory against the ambitions of the public for a long time to come. So I am not in the least worried by this period of depression; it is a guarantee of unsullied enjoyment, like a beautiful valley high in the mountains not yet discovered by Thos. Cook & Co."

Jung did not seem to wish to rule so much as he wished to reign. Yet the theories of psychoanalysis, Freud felt, were not so firmly established that leadership was unnecessary. Events were proving him to be right. Sándor Ferenczi reported a meeting in Hamburg, Germany, in 1910, where Freud's theories were debated. A professor of medicine, Wilhelm Weygandt, brought down his fist and shouted, "This is not a topic for discussion at a scientific meeting; it is a matter for the police." Freud, in correspondence with some of the Hamburg doctors, read between the lines of their letters "that we Viennese are not only pigs but Jews as well." Ferenczi, giving a paper in Budapest that same year, was told that "Freud's work was nothing but pornography and that the proper place for psychoanalysts was prison."

Freud was counting on Jung to coordinate the international effort to spread his theories. He had passed over for leadership the loyal

Karl Abraham. In his support of Jung, Freud had invoked the lasting bitterness of his Viennese colleagues. He was more alone than he knew. Ernest Jones, whose vacillations Freud had observed on his trip to America, had finally come to accept Freud's leadership in the psychoanalytic movement. " You are right," Jones had written Freud, "in surmising that I had at one time hoped to play a more important part in the movement in England and America than I now see is possible: it should and must be directed by you and I am content to be of any service in my power along the lines you advise." But Jones would soon get into fresh trouble. In his capacity as a medical doctor in Toronto, Jones would treat a woman who would then accuse him of having sexual intercourse with her. She would even try to shoot him. Astonishingly, though he protested his innocence, Jones would pay the woman five hundred dollars in blackmail money, in order, as he said, to prevent a scandal. He would have to leave Canada, thereby jeopardizing Freud's position in America.

The precarious future of the analytic movement now depended, through attrition and by design, on one man: Carl Jung. Yet Jung had offended Freud's Viennese colleagues, and now he had proved no more successful with his own in Switzerland. "I wish," Freud thought, "I lived nearer to Jung, so that I could support him in his young authority, on which part of my future seems to depend." Finally, Freud wrote Jung affectionately, "As it is, the first months of your reign, my dear son and successor, have not turned out brilliantly. Sometimes I have the impression that you yourself have not taken your functions seriously enough and have not yet begun to act in a manner appropriate to your new dignity."

Jung was chastened. "I realize now that my debut as regent has turned out less than brilliantly. . . . It is a grim pleasure to be God knows how many decades ahead of these duffers." In an attempt to begin to repair the damage of the past months, Freud decided to see Bleuler himself. A trip to Switzerland would allow him to clear up the problems there and to visit Jung in his new house in Küsnacht. But when Bleuler offered to put him up at the Burghölzli, Freud and Jung were in a quandary. Neither man wished to be in the same city unable to see the other freely. "This would be so miserable for us," Jung said. It was decided that Freud and Bleuler would meet in Munich. Jung would then travel there himself and appear after Bleuler had gone. The "little intrigue" delighted Freud. He booked rooms at the Park Hotel in Munich and so did Jung. "Please leave me a note at the hotel," Jung wrote, "saying when you wish to see me and how I have to conduct myself so as not to bump into Bleuler."

MUNICH LIES just north of the Alps in southern Germany, about halfway between Vienna and Zürich. Freud and Bleuler greeted each other there early on Christmas morning, and they walked around Munich for hours, "with breaks, however," Freud remembered. "The glorious meals at the Park Hotel." Freud refrained from mentioning his wish that Bleuler should join the International Association, but otherwise the men spoke frankly. Bleuler's admiration for Freud warmed into friendship. As Freud told Ferenczi later, "he is just a poor devil like us and wants people to love him a little bit, which is something," Freud said, referring to Jung, "that has perhaps been neglected by an important party." When Bleuler left the next day, Freud felt they parted as friends. "So it looks as though Zürich will flourish," Freud thought, "which is so crucial for us."

Jung arrived at the Park Hotel in time for dinner on the twenty-sixth of December a few hours after Bleuler had gone. He had spent a traditional Christmas at home dining formally in black tie, the huge dark fir in his living room laden with cookies and candied quinces for his children. He greeted Freud in high spirits. Though the men spoke about Bleuler and mythology as they had planned, Freud said later, "I poured out my heart about many things, about the Adler movement, my own difficulties. . . ."

Alfred Adler was a source of pain to Freud, in part because he reminded him of Wilhelm Fliess. "The same paranoia," Freud told Jung; and to Sándor Ferenczi he wrote, "Adler is a little Fliess come to life again." Freud had brought a paper to Munich he had just written on paranoia. It had given him much trouble because, Freud admitted to Jung, "I have had to fight off complexes within myself (Fliess)." As Freud handed Jung the paper that had stirred up memories of a complicated friendship, there was yet another reason to be reminded of Fliess. For in the dining room of the Park Hotel, Freud had fainted on two occasions, precipitated by his difficulties with Wilhelm Fliess. He could not know that one day soon he would faint again, in the same room of the Park Hotel.

Freud thought he had overcome his complexes—his need to confess his weaknesses, his hesitations and doubts about himself: "since Fliess's case . . . ," he had written Sándor Ferenczi a few months before, "that need has been extinguished. A part of homosexual cathexis has been withdrawn and made use of to enlarge my ego." Just a few days before coming to Munich, Freud had said again to Ferenczi, "I have now overcome Fliess, about whom you were so curious." Ferenczi had wondered about Fliess, had wondered at times whether Freud held back some greater sorrow over the loss of this friend, but Freud said no.

When Freud and Jung turned to mythology that day in December 1910, Freud found himself impressed by Jung's "significant researches." But he detected some hesitancy in Jung as he spoke about his work, and Freud did not know why. When he returned to Vienna, he would write, "I don't know why you are so afraid of my criticism in matters of mythology. I shall be very happy when you plant the flag of the libido . . . in that field and return as a victorious conqueror to our medical motherland." They discussed whether to explore the possibility of thought transference, using the tools of psychoanalysis. Freud did not want to do so. The subject disturbed him; yet he knew it fascinated Jung, and Ferenczi as well. Jung laughed at Freud's fears, but commended him for his caution and agreed to wait two years before writing on occult matters. "I am glad," Freud told Ferenczi later, "that he has such broad shoulders. I found this burden to be almost too much for me."

The conversations between Freud and Jung during their visit in Germany had a powerful effect on both men. Always, it seemed, the magic of the other's presence worked its wonders and resolved all problems. On his return to Vienna, Freud told a friend that Jung "was entirely splendid again and did me a lot of good." Freud had gained assurance enough to last another day. "I am more than ever convinced that [Jung] is the man of the future."

JUNG HAD good news when he wrote Freud from Küsnacht. "Bleuler has now joined the Society. I bow to your arts!" But as soon as the situation seemed to stabilize in Zürich, conditions worsened in Vienna. Alfred Adler, chairman of the Vienna Society, and its vice-chairman, Wilhelm Stekel, resigned their positions because their views were no longer compatible with Freud's. They chose to remain members of the group, however, and Freud kept them on a tight rein. Freud worried that Adler was devaluing sexual libido. "He has created for himself," Freud wrote, "a world system without love, and I am in the process of carrying out on him the revenge of the offended goddess Libido."

Troubling though it was, Freud tolerated the disaffection of Adler and Stekel because it cleared the path for Jung. "If the kingdom established by me is orphaned," Freud told Ludwig Binswanger early in 1911, a few months after his visit with Jung in Munich, "none other than Jung must inherit the whole thing. You see, my policy is solely directed toward this goal, and my comportment toward Stekel and Adler forms part of the same system." Several weeks later he wrote Binswanger again on the same theme. "The difficulties in Vienna could probably be eliminated only through a rapprochement with Stekel and abandonment of Jung."

For Freud, having constantly to deal with the insurgencies of the "palace revolution in Vienna," the summer of 1911 passed with little time for scientific work. But for Jung, in his love of mythology and the occult, it was "a time full of marvels." For nearly two years Jung's search had driven him down through the historical layers of man's past and swept him across continents in pursuit of the parallels of myth. To discern pattern in the many and varied historical references Jung had found had been enormous work. His "Transformations and Symbols of the Libido, Part I" was published in the *Jahrbuch* that summer of 1911. In it, Jung had succeeded in showing that at the core of myth lay Freud's theory of infantile sexuality in all its guises. Freud seemed anxious to read it. "I have been working in a field where you will be surprised to meet me," Freud wrote Jung. "I have unearthed strange and uncanny things and will almost feel obliged *not* to discuss them with you. But you are too shrewd not to guess what I am up to when I add that I am dying to read your 'Transformations and [Symbols of the Libido].' "

Jung was beside himself. He could not make out what Freud meant. Ten days later Freud explained. He had been working for several weeks on the origin of religion, the same area covered by Jung's paper, and he hadn't wanted to confuse Jung with his own thoughts on the subject. Now, Freud saw with relief, Jung's conclusions were the same as his. "So you too are aware that the Oedipus complex is at the root of religious feeling. Bravo!" Freud's relief was not Jung's. Two months later Jung would complain that "the outlook for me is very gloomy if you too get into the psychology of religion. You are a dangerous rival—if one has to speak of rivalry." But now he let Freud's letter pass in silence unanswered. Freud was coming to Zürich in a few weeks before going on to the Weimar Congress at the end of September 1911. They would talk things over then.

EARLY IN the morning on September 16, 1911, Jung was at the Zürich railroad station to greet Freud. The men rode in the carriage along the Seestrasse into Küsnacht and down the long drive, Swiss-straight, to Jung's door. Freud did not know, had no reason to think, it would be the only time he would ever visit Jung's home.

"Invoked or not invoked the God will be present." The words carved in Latin above Jung's door would not surprise Freud, nor would Jung's explanation: "I wanted to express the fact that I always feel unsafe, as if I'm in the presence of superior possibilities." Though the house was large, this was the only door. "We Swiss live in the centre of Europe," Jung was fond of saying, "and lots of things may happen." Once inside, the old-fashioned comfort of dark paneling, parquet floors, oriental rugs, the round stand by the door full of walking sticks and the polish of meticulous housekeeping belied Jung's feelings of insecurity. Possibly Jung's two daughters and his little boy came running to meet them, as they often ran to meet the friends and patients who came to the door. Freud had been looking forward to seeing the children, particularly Agathli, the spirited young girl whose sexual curiosity had inspired one of Jung's lectures in America.

Emma Jung would greet Freud with warmth. She was very fond of him. He had sent her a package of books once, and they had exchanged notes on the details of a congress. She had enjoyed their conversations. But Emma would see to it that Freud and Jung had time to talk undisturbed. It seemed to her that Carl had difficulties in his relationships with men, and she would do her best to help him. Besides, she knew that her husband was anxious to know more of what Freud had thought of his latest work, the first part of his "Transformations and Symbols of the Libido." They needed time alone.

There would be a tour of the new house. It had been designed by an architect cousin, but Jung was not a man to have things done for him. And so, despite the conventions of rugs and prints, the house bore the unique stamp of its owner and the inevitable mistakes of the amateur. Emma thought the linen closet was awkwardly placed, too near the room where Carl saw his patients. The formal brown marble mantel in the living room did not at all suit the black and white tiles on the hearth below. One day many years later, tapping the marble mantel, Jung's son, Franz, gave one reason why he had become an architect: "This, I think, is wrong. My father was at times uncertain about architecture. That's why I thought there might be some possibilities here for me."

In the little study upstairs just off the library, Jung had made no mistakes, although he called it his "chamber of horrors." It was a square room lined with ancient texts and bathed in a milky light that filtered through the amber-green panes of the small windows. On the desk that had once belonged to Jung's grandfather lay stacks of unread letters, handwritten notes, books on arcane subjects open to Jung's investigation and small exotic objects. Hanging on the wall behind his desk was a picture draped in cloth. It was a photograph of the Shroud of Turin, whose image, it was believed, bore the impress of Christ's face. "Even if it were not the face of Jesus," Franz Jung said, "it was a face of such pain, such inspiration. For my father it was a mystery." And so Jung kept it covered.

The room was a part of Jung's world that troubled Emma Jung. It was where her husband saw his patients; and although Franz later recalled that "my father always kept her in the play," Emma often felt isolated. "The women are all in love with him," she would confide to Freud. Here her husband worked with his patients, giving them his strength until they found their own. Women would say that in his presence, often in the first visit, they would feel whole again. They responded to Jung with emotions that sometimes lasted all their lives. Many years later Jung's son would understand: "It was not so much what he did, so much as what he was." But a young wife is not a son fully grown and in 1911 Emma Jung did not understand. Sabina Spielrein, the Russian girl whom Jung had treated at the Burghölzli, had come many times to this little room in Küsnacht. And now there was another. Antonia Wolff, a deeply troubled girl from a wealthy Zürich family, saw Jung here as well, loved him as well.

Despite Emma's concerns, the household was generous and free. When the weather was fine, the family took tea outside at a table filled with sweets and cookies Emma had made herself. Dogs ran about on the lawn, and while the children fed the ducks and played in the reeds at the water's edge, their father sat smoking cigars and reading the afternoon paper. But there was little time for such domestic moments that September. Freud's visit was crowded with receptions, seminars with Jung's students and last-minute details for the Congress. James Putnam had come from America to accompany the group to Weimar and was having a few hours of analysis with Freud.

Jung was fascinated by a conversation he had with Freud on the mythology of brothers. They discussed pairs of famous men in mythology, and Freud found a common thread. There was inevitably, Freud told Jung, one who was weaker and fated to die. Emma took pleasure in Freud's visit, but she thought something was wrong. She found Freud depressed and resigned. He was worried about his children and told her on the first morning that his marriage "had long been 'amortized,' now there was nothing more to do except—die." As the days went by, Emma noticed that Freud did not mention her husband's new work. She knew Carl was eager to know Freud's opinion of "Transformations and Symbols of the Libido." But Freud said nothing at all.

Among the visitors to Küsnacht was Alphons Maeder, a young Swiss doctor who had worked with Jung at the Burghölzli. As he sat in Jung's home in September 1911, Maeder watched Jung and Freud together. Jung "was a man of great stature, surely a highly gifted, ingenious personality. But he also was strongly and a bit massively Swiss-German compared to Freud. Freud had something noble about him." Maeder was troubled. Like Emma Jung, he sensed strain between the two men. "They must have had heavy controversies," he said, remembering. "I think already then the relation was broken inwardly. But Jung never said a word about that." When the group left by train for the Weimar Congress, Maeder found himself in the same compartment with Freud and Jung. "Hang it all, they have a lot of difficulties," Maeder thought to himself, and the realization saddened him.

THE THIRD Psychoanalytic Congress began on September 21, 1911, in Weimar's finest hotel, the Erbprinz. Freud's paper, his "Postscript" to the Schreber case, was remembered for its elegance and its use of myth. The audience was impressed by Freud's cautionary tale of the eagle and the sun, symbol of the father. The eagle, Freud said, always forced its young to look at the sun without blinking and rejected those who failed. Stark and unforgiving, the message was plain. Each son must confront his father, must risk his very life, in order to prove he is his father's legitimate heir.

Freud had been guided into his use of myth by Jung's example. He was influenced by Jung as well in a comment Ernest Jones remembered, that the "unconscious contains not only infantile material but also relics from primitive man." Freud was conceding that the unconscious might contain more than memories of childhood experiences. It might come already equipped with patterns of behavior. Freud paid a debt to Jung that day at the Weimar Congress: "[These remarks] may serve to show that Jung had excellent grounds for his assertion that the mythopoeic forces of mankind are not extinct." Jung spoke next on his work on mythology; sitting in the audience were Emma Jung, Toni Wolff and Sigmund Freud. When Jung was acclaimed as president of the Association for another term, he stood at the center of each of their very different dreams.

One other besides Emma Jung and Alphons Maeder noticed something amiss between Freud and Jung that September. Jones never forgot the Weimar Congress and a disturbing conversation he had there with Carl Jung. Fifteen years would pass before he was forced to mention it to Freud. One day in 1926, Freud wrote to correct something Jones had written about the end of the friendship between Freud and Jung. "On page 7 there is a mistake," Freud told Jones: Jones had written that his own "opposition against Jung dates from the Weimar Congress."

Jones replied in sorrow that Weimar was where he had begun to distrust Jung. "At the end of the Weimar Congress," Jones told Freud, "Jung talked to me about the time when he would stand higher than you. I was very astonished and naturally asked him why he did not analyze his father complex instead of trying to live it out in such an inappropriate way. His mystical answer 'it is my fate' showed me which way things were moving. . . . My opposition really began from Weimar."

Freud did not know this in September 1911. Several days after he returned to Vienna he wrote Jung, "The days in Zürich and Weimar seem even more splendid in retrospect. Toothache and strain sink into oblivion, the exchange of ideas, the hopes and satisfactions that were the substance of those days stand out in all their purity."

PART FOUR

LOSS

CHAPTER THIRTEEN

ONE DAY in October 1911 when Freud opened a letter from Sándor Ferenczi, he found enclosed a second letter written by Emma Jung. In it, Emma confessed to Ferenczi her fear that something was wrong between Freud and her husband. She sensed in Freud an aversion to giving himself "fully as a friend" and thought this was owing to Freud's need to maintain his "authority." Emma also felt that Freud did not approve of her husband's latest work.

Emma asked Ferenczi not to mention her fears to Freud. But Ferenczi was anxious to straighten out the misunderstanding. He attributed Freud's aloofness to "the profound after-effects of the Breuer-Fliess experiences" and was sure Freud's reserve was not personally directed toward Jung. He thought Emma might have sensed that Freud was disturbed by Jung's interest in occultism and by his work on the libido. "My proposal would be," Ferenczi wrote Freud on October 19, 1911, "to write a letter to Frau Jung reassuring her (and I can do this with a good conscience), that I have *not* noticed *any* opposition from you and, at the same time, encouraging her to turn to you directly without any risk of a misunderstanding."

Freud answered Ferenczi quickly and told him what to write to Frau Jung, expressly asking him not to mention "occultism or libido." Ferenczi misread Freud's instructions. On October 23, 1911, he reported to Freud: "I touched on occultism and libido transformation." It is not possible to know how much harm Ferenczi caused by this mistake. Freud had asked him to "strike" any mention of occultism or libido because these were matters which Frau Jung believed were creating friction between Freud and Jung. " You can imagine my unpleasant surprise," Ferenczi wrote Freud in deep shame, "when now, *naturally* after sending the letter to Frau Jung, I reread your letter and noticed that . . . I had mistakenly read *to strike*, for *to touch upon*!" (In German, the words are *streichen* and *streifen* respectively.) The letter that Emma received from Ferenczi had mistakenly confirmed her fears.

With a heavy heart, Emma Jung wrote a series of four letters to Freud that fall of 1911, letters she kept secret from Carl for several weeks. "Dear Professor Freud, I don't really know how I am summoning the courage to write you this letter," Emma Jung began. "Since your visit I have been tormented by the idea that your relation with my husband is not altogether as it should be." She could not bear, she said, to see Freud so resigned. It was true that Freud was depressed that fall. His new work on religion was not going well. Where once he had depended upon intuition to cut through the tedium of research, his studies on religion demanded the slow buttressing of careful scholarship. Freud felt at times, he told Ferenczi, "as if I wanted to start a little liaison and I discovered, at my age, that I have to marry a new woman." Moreover, it bothered Freud that he had moved into territory belonging to Jung. It was nearly poaching. "Why in God's name did I allow myself to follow you into this field?" he asked Jung in despair.

Freud's resigned mood was real, and Emma's concern was well founded. But her worry about Freud's reaction to her husband's "Transformations and Symbols of the Libido, Part I," intensified by Ferenczi's letter, was misplaced. "I knew how eagerly Carl was waiting for your opinion," Emma wrote in her second letter to Freud. "He had often said he was sure you would not approve of it, and for that reason was awaiting your verdict with some trepidation." Freud was confused by Emma's insistence that something was amiss between himself and Jung. He and Ferenczi had worried that she was really voicing her husband's concerns, but they dismissed the idea. Emma had traveled to Schaffhausen right after the Weimar Congress, and Carl had gone to St. Gallen: "The couple," Freud told Ferenczi, "probably has not talked in weeks." But now Freud began to understand. He had neglected to mention Jung's new, published work for nearly three months. With Emma's letters before him, Freud realized that his silence over Jung's work had been badly misconstrued. "Comprehension is dawning on me only now," Freud admitted to Ferenczi as he looked over Emma's letter, "since the not mentioning of 'Transformations' appears in the foreground. . . . Because I am now working on the same subject, I might have aroused suspicion with certain peculiarities having to do with the roots of my work." Possibly Freud's silence reflected a dilemma he had lately recognized in himself: he found it difficult to accept another's thoughts, and yet he knew that the work of others was important to the future of psychoanalysis. Jung's work, he knew, was the most important of all.

When it finally came, Freud's praise of Jung was generous. "One of the nicest works I have read (again)," he wrote Jung on November 12, 1911, "is that of a well-known author on the 'Transformations and Symbols of the Libido.' . . . It is the best thing this promising author has written, up to now. . . . Not least, I am delighted by the many points of agreement with things I have already said or would *like* to say." But Freud did not explain why he had kept such praise to himself for so long.

Emma was mistaken in her belief that Freud disapproved of her husband's findings in the fall of 1911. But when in her letters she turned to his relationship with her husband, Emma's troubled words seemed to ring true. "Do not think of Carl with a father's feeling: 'He will grow, but I must dwindle,' " she wrote Freud, "but rather as one human being thinks of another, who like you has his own law to fulfill." Freud had been witness as no one else to Jung's swift rise. Their correspondence overflowed with innovative ideas, not least from Jung. Freud found Jung's latest work distinguished, had even followed him into the field of religion. He had placed Jung higher than himself in the psychoanalytic organization. "The President of the International Association and his mentor," Freud had called them once.

Now Emma Jung was implying that in her husband's growth Freud saw his own demise. Diminished by the younger man's energy and the raw power of Jung's new work, in name no longer the leader of the movement he had founded, did Freud now gaze after Jung as Breuer had once gazed after Freud himself: as a hen after a hawk? For a moment that autumn it seemed so. It was as if Freud, immobile and depressed, stood watching Jung—whom he would one day call a young eagle—face the sun, take flight and soar. The moment would not last. Freud would gather his strength again. Yet Jung had grown in intellectual stature, and Freud had paused to take his measure.

Emma Jung had done her best. She loved Freud, and she had intervened because she believed in honest discussion. She did not understand the reluctance of her husband and Freud to deal directly with each other. At considerable risk to herself and her marriage, she had tried to bring matters into the open. But Emma's hand could not sustain the complex ephemera that was the friendship between Freud and Jung. Within a year, it would slip through everyone's fingers and be gone.

IF FREUD thought there was something wrong between himself and Jung in the weeks after the Weimar Congress, he gave no sign. He had enjoyed his days in Küsnacht, he said. He thought the Congress had been a success. His letters to Jung in the fall of 1911 continued with the same warmth as before, and he made no allusion in them to Frau Jung's disturbing questions. Freud even allowed Jung to disagree with him on a problem that had plagued them for years—the libido theory. Freud believed that from infancy, two basic drives fueled all behavior: the hunger drive and the sexual drive, which he called libido. The child's earliest experiences, shaped by these drives, were unique; they were determined by his relationship with his parents. The individual's unconscious was composed of personal childhood experiences.

Jung had never agreed completely that the sexual drive thoroughly pervaded the life of childhood. Now he was considering an adjustment to Freud's theory that came from his studies in mythology. Jung had found patterns among myths that seemed to bear out Freud's theory of infantile sexuality: countless tales in all their guises and symbols told the same ancient oedipal story of a father slain by his son in order to gain possession of his mother. But Jung had begun to believe that these universal patterns were part of one's genetic inheritance and not the sole result of a child's struggles with his parents. The unconscious, Jung felt, was not simply the repository of early experiences; it already contained genetic patterns of behavior.

Despite Freud's reservations about tampering with the libido theory, he did his best to be open-minded. When Jung wrote him, "The essential point is that I try to replace the descriptive concept of libido by a *genetic* one," Freud had a ready answer. "I am all in favour of your attacking the libido question and I myself am expecting much light from your efforts. Often, it seems, I can go for a long while without feeling the need to clarify an obscure point, and then one day I am compelled to by the pressure of facts or by the influence of someone else's ideas." Freud was aware that not all of the premises upon which psychoanalysis depended were in complete agreement. More than that, Jung's work drew them into the future and was full of promise. "Your demonstration of unconscious heredity in symbolism . . . ," Freud told him, "lead[s] us far beyond the original limits of [psychoanalysis] and . . . we . . . should follow."

BUT A disturbing sense of resentment lay beneath the cordial scientific exchange in the early months of 1912. Jung's letters were arriving in Vienna less and less often. Sometimes weeks would go by with no word from Switzerland. Over the years, Freud had come to understand why Jung was slow to write: he was afraid of intimacy with Freud. "Man should not wish to extirpate his complexes," Freud had told Ferenczi once, "but to come to terms with them, they are the rightful conductors of his behavior in the world." It troubled Freud that Jung had not come to terms with his complexes; and more than that, it hurt him.

Freud had begun to think Jung no longer cared about him. He felt he had given much and received little. Freud now regretted that he had responded so gently to Emma's letters. Her fear that Freud was aloof and unyielding in friendship, he now believed, was actually something quite different. "You can see now," he wrote to Ferenczi, "that his wife's letter to you was really nothing but a projection of ill will toward me." Freud was upset that he had been "once more very warm out of foolish devotion, and that I communicated all the results of the inquiry into religion to him as well as to you. He who has the makings of a sentimental ass will not even cease in gray-haired age to make a fool of himself."

It seemed to Freud that he had reached the end of a rope. "I certainly knew about his ambition," he conceded to Ferenczi, "but I hoped to have pressed this power into my service through the position I created for him and [am] still [preparing]. The prospect of doing everything myself as long as I live and then failing to leave behind a worthy successor to carry on, is not very comforting." Sándor Ferenczi took Freud's distress seriously, but he thought that Freud's experiences with friends in the past were distorting his relations with Jung. Although he agreed with Freud in large part, Ferenczi had his own view of Carl

Jung. "I suspect in him . . . a boundless and unbridled ambition, which is expressed to you, who are so very superior to him, in petty hatred and envy. Perhaps his unsatisfied ambition makes him *dangerous*." Yet Ferenczi did not believe Freud should bear Jung a grudge on the evidence of his ambition. Ferenczi wished Jung would go to Freud for analytic treatment; he thought Jung needed it. And he advised caution regarding Jung. But, Ferenczi said firmly, "In my view he does not deserve the transference of the Fliess-*distrust*." Ferenczi's final words were disheartening, however: "There is nothing else for it," Ferenczi told Freud soberly. "All through life you have to do everything yourself. Your successsor has not yet arrived."

Freud finally confronted Jung with his concerns, but the younger man defended himself with vehemence. Perhaps, Jung said, Freud did not trust him. "Of course I have opinions which are not yours about the ultimate truths of [psychoanalysis]—" Jung wrote, "though even this is not certain, for one cannot discuss everything under the sun by letter—but you won't, I suppose, take umbrage on that account." Jung then quoted Nietzsche: "One repays a teacher badly if one remains only a pupil." Freud's kindness was evident in his reply, and his pain. "The indestructible foundation of our personal relationship is our involvement in [psychoanalysis]; but on this foundation it seemed tempting to build something finer though more labile, a reciprocal intimate friendship. Shouldn't we go on building?" But then Freud's pen slipped. "You speak of the need for intellectual independence and quote Nietzsche in support of your view," Freud continued. "If a third party were to read this passage, he would ask me why I had tried to tyrannize you intellectually." Freud had not meant to say "why." He had meant to say "when."

Jung's increasing restlessness, Freud's distress over their dwindling correspondence and Jung's conduct of the psychoanalytic organization had been grist for recrimination on both sides. Now, over the problem of the libido, there was disagreement yet again. Jung was struggling in the early months of 1912 to finish the second half of his "Transformations and Symbols of the Libido." Part of his difficulty lay in the fact that he had begun to differ with Freud over the meaning of incest. The full force of Freud's libido theory lay in his belief that each child desired the parent of the opposite sex. This was not, according to Freud, an idle wish or daydream, but charged sexual feeling. Jung, however, had come to believe that incest was not actually desired, but rather a matter of fantasy.

The strains between Freud and Jung were many, but they receded for a moment in May 1912 as Freud faced another, more immediate concern. His friend Ludwig Binswanger, a Swiss who lived in the little village of Kreuzlingen on Lake Constance some forty miles from Zürich, had undergone an appendix operation during which a malignant tumor was discovered and removed. It was thought Binswanger would not live much longer. Freud wrote Jung, "On the evening of the 24th I shall be leaving for Constance to see Binswanger. I am planning to be back on the following Tuesday. The time is so short that I shall not be able to do more." Freud's note was written in haste in the unspoken hope that Jung would join him. It made no mention of the reason for his trip.

Misunderstandings would grow from this small incident and over time engulf it. Freud left for the village of Kreuzlingen, traveling a day and a half by train to spend two days with Binswanger. On his journey through the Alps that spring to visit a man whose friendship he might lose in death, did Freud fear as well the loss of yet another? Freud's train crossed the Rhine where it flows into Lake Constance and then steamed north on the flat green plain toward Kreuzlingen. There was every reason for Freud to seek Jung's face as he got off the train from St. Margrethen. But only Binswanger was at the village station at noon that Saturday, and Jung never came to Kreuzlingen; nor did he send word that he would not.

"The fact that you felt no need to see me," Jung surprised Freud by writing a few days later, "must, I suppose, be attributed to your displeasure at my development of the libido theory." Jung had taken Freud's brief note not as invitation but as dismissal. Freud was upset. He told his Swiss friend Oskar Pfister, "It is a pity that you did not meet or speak to Jung. You could have told him from me that he is at perfect liberty to develop views divergent from mine, and that I ask him to do so without a bad conscience." To Jung himself he wrote in apparent calm, "Even if we cannot come to terms immediately, there is no reason to suppose that this scientific difference will detract from our personal relations."

Freud explained his trip to Kreuzlingen, although he remained discreet on the subject of Binswanger's illness. "I had a special reason, unknown to you, for wanting to talk with Binswanger at that time," Freud told Jung. "But if you had come and spent half a day in Constance, it would have been a great pleasure for us all." It would have meant more than pleasure. Upon occasion the fitful rhythm of their correspondence—written words no longer sufficient to the task of explanation and renewal—had jeopardized the friendship. Each time, the simple comfort of the other's presence had meant much. A tone of voice, a now familiar gesture as Jung warmed to his subject, circling the air with his hand; Freud, economical, more restrained, his intensity in his eyes as the hours passed in friendship: there had not been this at Kreuzlingen.

Nothing that had gone before prepared Freud for Jung's next letter with its cryptic words. "Now I can only say: I understand the Kreuzlingen gesture. Whether your policy is the right one will become apparent from the success or failure of my future work." Freud was at a loss. What, he wondered, could Jung possibly mean by the "Kreuzlingen gesture"? He sent Jung's letter on to Ludwig Binswanger and asked, "For all its unintelligibility, isn't this an outright breaking-off of relations?" There was no news, Freud wrote Ernest Jones in vast understatement from Karlsbad, where he had gone for treatment in the hot thermal springs. "The most interesting may be that I got yesterday a letter from Jung which cannot but be construed into a formal disavowal of our hitherto friendly relations."

Other people in other years would not find in Jung's letter the decision to sever a friendship, but Freud had, and so did Ferenczi: "After everything that I already knew about Jung's behavior, his open declaration of war could only sadden me but not surprise me," Ferenczi wrote Freud on August 6, 1912. "Apparently, the 'Kreuzlingen gesture' . . . which Jung reproaches you with [is] part of the fantasies which Jung uses to justify his behavior to his conscience. He treats psychoanalysis as if it were a personal matter between the two of you, not something objective and scientific." Ferenczi was relieved to find Freud detached. "I am very glad you take Jung's defection so well. It proves to me that you have finally given up the forced effort to create a successor and leave the cause of analysis, for which you have done everything in your power, to its fate." Perhaps Freud was detached. Certainly he was depressed that summer and not well.

CHAPTER FOURTEEN

DURING THE past months, various, related actions, however well-meant, had made of the balky, prideful exchange between Freud and Jung something so tangible it could not be gotten around. Each act had made the disagreement more real and given it greater depth. Emma Jung had expressed her unease, involving first Ferenczi and then Freud. Ferenczi had added fuel to the fire by mistakenly confirming Emma's fears. Freud began to circulate Jung's bitter letters among his friends. Jung offered to table his presidency until matters could be discussed at the next congress. The quarrel between Freud and Jung had moved beyond themselves. "There is no lack of others," Freud wrote Sabina Spielrein acutely, "who are at pains to widen these chinks into a breach."

As signs of trouble increased during the summer of 1912, Jones and Ferenczi discussed the possibility of a secret committee to be formed among those loyal to psychoanalysis. Jones offered the thought to

Freud, who replied, "What took hold of my imagination immediately is your idea of a secret council composed of the best and most trustworthy among our men. . . . You say it was Ferenczi who expressed this idea, yet it may be mine own shaped in better times," Freud added sadly, "when I hoped Jung would collect such a circle around himself. . . . Now I am sorry to say such a union had to be formed independently of Jung." Ernest Jones's suggestion might well have been premature, sharpening unnecessarily the dull edge of resentment. Perhaps it was also self-serving; Jones would stand nearer Freud if Jung were left outside the circle.

Ludwig Binswanger's response to the troubling situation was more conciliatory. He excused Jung's behavior on the basis of his recent, great creative effort, but Freud would have none of it. When Binswanger wondered whether Jung's actions might have hurt Freud, the reply from Vienna was brusque: "Fortunately you are completely mistaken in assuming I am at all hurt by his behavior. I am completely detached." But Freud understood Binswanger's concern well enough. "Do not fear," he wrote. "I shall do nothing that might bring about a rupture." To that end, Freud struggled to keep the issues in hand. He did not believe that Jung's new ideas conflicted impossibly with his own nor did Jung himself. "Nothing," Freud told Ferenczi on August 8, 1912, just after receiving a letter from Jung, "justified the assumption that his modifications involved any break with our fundamentals. . . . The question as to why such changes should come about with stormy emotions . . . and the loss of human relations, would be reserved for a later date."

On September 7, 1912, Freud was on a train to Italy with Ferenczi after taking the cure in the hot springs of Karlsbad. He had planned to visit Ernest Jones in London during the next weeks, but illness in the Freud family and his own depressed mood made him decide against it. "I felt increasing fatigue and inactivity since Karlsbad, sleeping badly and spirits rather low. . . . unfit to produce myself in clever society," Freud wrote Jones now in apology, his handwriting shaky with the rhythm of the speeding train. "Even Ferenczi kind as he is who would not leave me for his own pleasure and recreation, is sometimes too much for me. He is reading in the next compartment and must not know it. I cannot remember a similar condition which I am prone to ascribe to the long action of the hot waters."

Ernest Jones had lately been in Zürich and had read Part II of Jung's "Transformations and Symbols of the Libido." Jones had sent Freud a full account of the work, and Freud had hurried to get a copy. Now, sitting alone on the train, Freud looked Jung's paper over quickly. He would read it at leisure with Ferenczi, but just a glance satisfied him. Freud noted the page where Jung had made his mistake. Jung had interpreted one of Freud's papers as offering up the possibility of a nonsexual libido and he had used the idea to advantage in his "Transformations and Symbols of the Libido, Part II." Freud was sure he could straighten out the misunderstanding.

Freud arrived in Rome after several weeks of ill health. His heart, he felt, could suddenly tolerate neither tobacco nor wine. He realized that everyone would attribute psychic factors to his recent illness. "All I ask," he wrote Ludwig Binswanger, "is that not too much blame be placed on Jung." Freud craved solitude. When Ferenczi left him and went to Naples, Freud spent hours alone walking among the ruins of the Palatine. Each day he went to a quiet church, a respite from the Roman sun. But it was not for comfort that Freud sought San Pietro in Vincoli. In its dim recesses stood the statue of Michelangelo's *Moses*. The angry prophet embodied emotions Freud knew well. Freud was a different kind of prophet and this was another time, but he sensed there were lessons to be learned from standing at Moses' knee. "Bring my deepest devotion to Moses," he would say when Ernest Jones visited Rome a few months later, "and write me about him."

There was time in Rome to read over Jung's new work. "To be sure it is all discutable [sic] and highly interesting and there is no germ of enmity in it," Freud told Jones, and he said much the same thing to Binswanger. "I have finally received the paper; it is perfectly respectable, and would not provide any pretext for a personal conflict, any more than his previous mistakes." Freud hoped Jung would continue to be his friend, as he had at other times when there had been disagreement over points of theory. Certainly he saw no great danger of a separation between himself and Jung.

Freud also had time to think over Jones's visit to Zürich, where the air had been filled with talk of Freud and Jung. Jones felt that Jung thought himself "great." His character, Jones told Freud, quoting his Zürich sources, was considered "really too bad" for association. But the Swiss also thought, Jones said, that Freud had provoked Jung needlessly. Freud defended himself against charges that his behavior might have contributed to the quarrel. "I am quite sure [Jung's] friends are mistaken about my provoking his sensibility in some points," Freud told Jones. "I never but spoiled him and he behaved in details, which are not known to you quite odiously against me. He wanted a dissension and he produced it. . . . If he thinks himself so great as you describe him he will not be fit for working with us and will become a danger for our work." Freud would not stand in the way of a reconciliation, but he wavered over the possibility of friendship. He did not know whether his previous feelings could be restored.

Freud's walks among the ruins, his daily visit to *Moses* and the warm sunny weather worked upon him as Rome always would. Despite Jones's criticisms of Jung, in the end Freud himself had not found cause enough for a rupture, had found at moments even, hope for friendship still. He took to wearing a gardenia in his lapel every day. He was feeling better.

THERE WOULD be no congress that year. While Freud was in Italy with Ferenczi in September 1912, Jung was in America giving a series of lectures. Since he was to be gone for some time, Freud and Jung had decided to postpone the Congress until the following year. Freud had not considered chairing the meeting himself. The possibility never occurred to him, Freud told Ferenczi; and besides, "such a suggestion could only have come from Jung." At first Jung's trip to America had seemed a good idea. It would allow him to assess the strength of psychoanalysis there and to renew acquaintance with his American colleagues. But with the quarrel had come reassessment. Freud no longer thought much of the invitation. "A small, unknown catholic [*sic*] university run by Jesuits, which Jones had turned down," he told Ferenczi. Jung would end by giving nine lectures and more than a dozen seminars at Fordham University in New York.

In May 1912, the New York Psychoanalytic Society with Abraham Brill as its chairman had voted to hold a formal dinner in the fall in Jung's honor. The members of the Society did not know that under their auspices Jung would turn decisively against Freud's theories. "I do not think I am going astray," Jung told a gathering of over ninety people in September 1912, "if I see the real value of the concept of libido not in its sexual definition but in its energic view." Jung's stark new definition of the libido, stripped of the intensity of sexual emphasis, was certain to please many in his audience. "Libido," Jung said, "is intended simply as a name for the energy which manifests itself in the life-process."

When Freud learned of Jung's change in the libido theory, he moved quickly. He arranged for a critique to be published, telling Ferenczi grimly, "So we're opening up the hostilities." Ernest Jones had showed Freud essays by Bleuler, Maeder and Adler, and in Freud's view they represented "three regrettable misunderstandings . . . about our psychoanalysis." Freud had spoken earlier of "Jung's rebellion"; now he began to develop a "war plan." Since Jung had been publishing in the

Jahrbuch, Freud would use the *Zentralblatt* as the "mouthpiece" for his views. Although Freud would not write the articles himself, he told Ferenczi in early October 1912 that "It should not be a secret that I am behind this. But I count on you as my general staff in this internal campaign." Freud thought Jung's personality, in particular his obsessiveness, would put off many who might follow him. He felt that they would win through Jung's mistakes. "If he were clever," he would tell Ernest Jones, "there would be no chance." Jung was not Freud's only concern in the fall of 1912. Stekel, who edited the *Zentralblatt*, was "creating new and impudent difficulties." Freud thought he was up to something: "Maybe he wants to provoke a show of strength at the *Zentralblatt*, which I will certainly not evade. Few sacrifices would be too great for me to get rid of him."

Jung had been too busy to write Freud during his two-month trip to America nor had he felt inclined, and his words were provocative in the letter he wrote upon his return. After describing the effect of his adjustment of Freud's theory on his American audience, Jung ended his letter with the now familiar glancing blow: "Your Kreuzlingen gesture has dealt me a lasting wound." When Freud replied on November 14, 1912, he dropped for the first time the habit of addressing him as "Dear friend." Now he wrote, "Dear Dr. Jung, I greet you on your return from America, no longer as affectionately as on the last occasion. . . . I still hold that personal variations are quite justified and I still feel the same need to continue our collaboration. . . . I must own that I find your harping on the 'Kreuzlingen gesture' both incomprehensible and insulting, but there are things that cannot be straightened out in writing."

19 November 1912

Dear Sir: It is unanimously agreed that the conference will be held in Munich. The meeting will take place at 9 a.m., November 24th, at the Park Hotel. . . .

Very truly yours,

President:
Dr. Jung

Freud was one of several men to receive Jung's formal typewritten letter. The meeting was called to approve Freud's decision to let the Viennese analyst Wilhelm Stekel go and to let the *Zentralblatt* he edited go with him. "We left each other in a friendly way," Freud said of Stekel, "but Hell knows what his dark designs are." Stekel's defection was just one more chapter in the tempestuous young history of the Vienna Psychoanalytic Society. The meeting began at nine o'clock in the morning in the Park Hotel, and it was quickly agreed that Freud's wishes regarding Stekel be observed. The gathering in Munich provided Freud and Jung with the first opportunity to see each other in many months, and at the end of the meeting they set off on a walk.

During the past year Jung had made public his own definition of the libido. Freud and a silent few, Jones and Ferenczi among them, had set up a secret council that deliberately excluded Jung. Letters between Freud and Jung had been strained, particularly Jung's, with their references to the "Kreuzlingen gesture." There had been no moment in recent months that had recaptured the vitality of their friendship, nor was the moment auspicious now. Freud addressed himself to the task of unraveling the mystery of Kreuzlingen. It took some time. Why, Freud asked, had Jung taken such offense at his visit to Binswanger? Because, Jung said at first, he had felt slighted by it. Jung thought that Freud had not wanted him at Kreuzlingen, that Freud had sent the invitation so late it made Jung's going there impossible. Jung said he suspected Freud of conspiring with his "*enemies*." Freud was shocked. "He brought out the complaint," Freud told Ferenczi later, "that I had visited his enemies, Binsw[anger] and Häberlin, and had prevented him from seeing me by informing him about the visit only after I had already come back." Ludwig Binswanger was a long-time colleague of Jung. They had worked on the word-association test years before and had traveled to Vienna together in 1907 to make the acquaintance of Sigmund Freud.

Jung's suspicions may have been reinforced by Freud's cryptic explanation after the fact: "I had a special reason, unknown to you, for wanting to talk with Binswanger. . . ." What was in Freud's heart as he reproached Jung for his lack of trust can only be guessed at, for Freud's secret committee was conspiracy of a kind, a circle that ranged itself against the likes of Jung. Jung's hostility arose from his fear that Freud was conspiring against him. Did the irony escape Freud that he was?

"What would you say, if I wrote you after the fact that I had been in Wiener Neustadt [a town near Vienna]?" Jung asked Freud. "That would be beastly," Freud answered. "But this was not the case with me." Freud had sent the note to Jung on the same day he had written to Binswanger, who had received his in time to be at the train station. Suddenly Jung remembered. "I was away Saturday and Sunday, sailing," he said. He hadn't returned to Küsnacht and opened his mail until the Monday Freud left Kreuzlingen. Why had Jung not checked the postmark? Freud pressed. Why had he not asked his wife when the letter had arrived? Jung had no good answers.

Freud told Ferenczi later that Jung was "absolutely beaten" and "ashamed" when he realized there was no reason to mistrust him. Then, Freud reported, Jung "admitted everything: he had been afraid for a long time that intimacy with me or others would harm his independence and he had therefore decided to withdraw; he had seen me according to the father-complex and had been afraid of what I might say about his modifications." One day in later years, Jung would listen in silence as a friend, the analyst Jolande Jacobi, described a patient who had dreamed that he and Jung were swimming in the Zürichsee and that Jung had helped him. Jacobi explained that the man was a homosexual and asked Jung if he would see him. "No," Jung replied. "I don't want to." He told Jacobi of the time when a family friend had made a homosexual advance. "You see," Jung said, "that's also the reason why I was afraid of Freud's approaches." Jung had the same feeling, he said, when Freud had wanted to make him his heir and successor. "No, no, no, I don't want to belong to anybody."

Freud did not let Jung off lightly as they talked together in Munich on the morning of November 24, 1912. He told Jung that it was not possible to maintain a friendship with him, that Jung "had conjured up the intimacy" only to break it off "abruptly." It was, Freud thought, what Jung did with his male friends. "He pushes all of them away after a time," Freud wrote Ferenczi later. It had been a difficult discussion, and Freud drew from it difficult conclusions. "I have been wrong about him on one point," Freud conceded: "Namely in thinking him a born ruler who, through his authority, could spare others many mistakes, but he was not." Freud felt the conversation had done Jung good, but Freud was still disturbed. "If [Jung] were someone on whom one could make a real impression, I would believe in a lasting change," he told Ferenczi. "But there is a core of disingenuousness in his being which will allow him to shake off these impressions again."

Despite all, Freud allowed himself to be hopeful. "Jung was very affable," he reported to Binswanger, "and in an hour of private conversation he allowed himself to be persuaded that his charges against me were hardly justified. The 'Kreuzlingen gesture' with which he always reproached me was based on an incredible neurotic reaction on his part. . . . I think that everything will go well now. Let the theoretical differences remain in force until they can be worked out in scholarly papers and at the Congress." To James Putnam he wrote much the same thing. "Everybody was charming to me, including Jung. A talk between us swept away a number of unnecessary personal irritations. I hope for further successful cooperation. Theoretical differences need not interfere."

When Freud and Jung met the others in the dining room of the Park

Hotel, Freud was in high spirits. He had won Jung around again. Just as Freud's victory once before had been symbolized by a glass of wine Jung had raised in Bremen, the lunch at the Park Hotel was a celebration. But as in Bremen, Freud began to grow uncomfortable. He accused the Zürich men, Jung among them, of neglecting to mention his name in their papers. The discussion then moved to a paper Karl Abraham had written about the son of the Egyptian king Amenhotep. Freud had already made it known in a letter to Abraham that "I have misgivings about presenting the King so definitely as a neurotic. It stands in sharp contrast with his extraordinary energy and achievement. . . . We all have these complexes and must be careful not to call everybody neurotic. When we have fought against our complexes we ought to be spared the name."

But now Freud appeared to feel differently. Ernest Jones noticed that Freud seemed to be taking the matter rather personally. Amenhotep IV, Freud remembered aloud, had scratched out his father's name on monuments. " Yes, he did," Jung replied. "But you cannot dismiss him with that. He was the first monotheist among the Egyptians. He was a great genius, very human, very individual. That he scratched out his father's name is not the main thing at all." For Freud in November 1912 it was an important one. Months before, Jung had warned Freud, quoting Nietzsche, "Take care that a falling statue does not strike you dead!" Now Jung was defending the king who had symbolically killed his father by effacing his name from statues erected in his honor. To Freud, Jung's actions seemed to mirror those of the ancient and rebellious Egyptian son.

Perhaps only Ferenczi, who had predicted it, would not be surprised when he learned that in the midst of a heated discussion about maligned fathers and their disrespectful sons, Freud had fallen to the terrazzo floor of the dining room in a faint.

CHAPTER FIFTEEN

ERNEST JONES, sitting at the table with the others in the Park Hotel in Munich on November 24, 1912, heard a slight rustle as Freud began to fall to the floor; but it was Jung who moved quickly to Freud's side. Jung had drawn close to Freud on their long walk before lunch. He had the feeling he had never really understood Freud until then, and he apologized for the mistakes he had made. Jung loved Freud, but his love was often mute, obscured by difficulties within himself. Now for a brief moment he allowed his deep feeling for Freud to express itself in worry and concern. He would brush aside offers of help as he picked Freud up in his arms. Carrying him from the room, Jung thought Freud looked up at him as if Jung were his father. In the lounge where Jung took Freud to rest, Ernest Jones heard Freud exclaim, "How sweet it must be to die!" Freud lay on a sofa in the Park Hotel, nauseated; his head would ache, and he was aware as no one else of the significance of his latest fainting attack. Contrary to everyone's expectations, the gathering in Munich ended in greater understanding between Freud and Jung. They parted at five o'clock in the evening with Jung saying, "You will find me completely on the side of the cause."

Freud slept well on the night train back to Vienna. The meeting in Munich had hardly been restful, Freud reported to his daughter Anna in Italy, with hours of discussion from nine in the morning until nearly midnight. He said nothing of his talks with Jung, nor did he mention his fainting attack. But he was in good humor as he sent his best wishes for her seventeenth birthday. He promised a surprise package of books and wrote of refurnishing her room: "Writing table and carpet are in any case assured." But with others, Freud could not avoid an explanation of what had happened in Munich.

To acquaintances, he tossed off Mark Twain's quote, "Reports of my death grossly exaggerated." But to Ludwig Binswanger, Freud admitted that memories evoked by the Park Hotel were involved, and that "repressed feelings, this time directed against Jung, as previously against a predecessor of his, naturally play the main part." Freud told Ernest Jones, "I saw Munich first when I visited Fliess during his illness, and this town seems to have acquired a strong connection with my relation to this man." Freud was frank. "I cannot forget that 6 and 4 years ago I have suffered from very similar though not so intense symptoms in the *same* room of the Parkhotel; in every case I had to leave the table."

Despite his honesty there were mysteries in Freud's statements. He maintained that four and six years before, he had fainted in the Park Hotel, or nearly so, and he implied that the cause had been his relationship with Fliess. Yet six years before, 1906, was long past Freud's last meeting anywhere with Fliess, and four years before, 1908, only longer. Moreover, while sometimes one cannot with precision fix Freud in a particular place at a given time, one thing seems clear: Freud appears not to have been in Munich in either 1906 or 1908. To complicate matters further, Freud never made it entirely plain in whose company he had fainted in the Park Hotel on those two prior occasions. Ernest Jones thought Freud had collapsed once in the presence of Wilhelm Fliess in the midst of a quarrel. Another attack, Jones felt, had occurred during a painful scene with Oscar Rie, Fliess's brother-in-law and Freud's good friend.

But, however obscure the other figures in these episodes and however uncertain the dates, Freud was clear about his feelings when he fainted. He attributed the fainting spell to an "unruly homosexual feeling." He told Ernest Jones that he was right "in supposing that I had transferred to Jung homosex. feelings from another part." Freud confessed to Jones that his childhood wish for the death of his baby brother Julius and his guilt at having it come true had been the psychological cause of his fainting. His guilt over surviving a brother who died had been transferred to guilt at his triumph in winning Jung back to the cause. Ernest Jones thought Freud was a little like those patients Freud himself described "who are wrecked by success." Freud's success lay in defeating an opponent, the earliest example being the death of his little brother Julius, the latest his victory over Jung. The fact that Freud had fainted again troubled his colleagues. Ferenczi hoped that Freud was capable of analyzing the reasons for it, but Ferenczi's uncertainty was only thinly disguised when he told Freud, "In spite of all the shortcomings of self-analysis (which is surely more protracted and difficult than being analyzed), we have to assume you have the ability to keep your symptoms in check."

Freud was a man in whom passion was held in strict control. He had fainted, or nearly so, four times in the midst of heated discussions with men he cared about deeply. On two of those occasions he sensed that Jung unconsciously wished his death. Perhaps Freud felt that to respond to this man he loved and whom he thought wished him ill would unleash the measureless passion he feared in himself. He would not explode in anger or expose his pain. He would not shake his fist or walk away. His feelings would engulf him because they had found no release, and he would faint.

LOU ANDREAS-SALOME did not know what to think when Freud returned from Munich and announced at the Vienna Psychoanalytic Society his rapprochement with Carl Jung. She had met Freud at the Congress in Weimar in 1911, and she was now in Vienna attending Freud's lectures and the gatherings of the Psychoanalytic Society. The indulged only daughter of a former general in the Imperial Russian Army, Lou Salomé was captivated by the intellectual life of Europe and drawn to Freud. Perceptive and quick, she felt she understood him. Noticing the way Freud entered a room, stepping a little to one side, Salomé saw in his gesture "a will to solitude, a concealment of himself within his own purposes." Salomé found Freud changed since Weimar, older and more harassed. She wondered at the good news he had brought from Germany. On November 27, 1912, in the small red loose-leaf notebook that was her diary, Salomé wrote, "Freud has returned almost too refreshed and content from the trip to Munich. Is the understanding with Jung really such a certainty as it officially sounded on Wednesday?"

It was not. On returning to Küsnacht, Jung was quickly solicitous of Freud. "I have been very worried about how you got back to Vienna," Jung wrote, "and whether the night journey may not have been too much of a strain for you. Please let me know how you are, if only a few words on a postcard." Freud replied promptly, but he was not so open as he had been with Jones about the psychological reasons for his fainting. "According to my private diagnosis, it was migraine . . . not without a psychic factor which unfortunately I haven't time to track down now. The dining-room of the Park Hotel seems to hold a fatality for me. Six years ago I had a first attack of the same kind there, and four years ago a second. A bit of neurosis that I ought really to look into."

Jung told Freud that his "bit" of neurosis should be taken very seriously indeed because it had resulted in "the semblance of a voluntary death." He remembered that Freud had collapsed in Bremen during Jung's animated discussion of mummified corpses. Jung believed the fantasy of father-murder was common to both cases: Freud thought that Jung harbored death wishes against him and had participated in Jung's fantasies in a brief moment of psychic death. This neurosis, Jung contended, had affected their relationship and had led Freud to underestimate Jung's work. With "Helvetic bluntness," Jung moved into a new style in his letter to Freud. "I am writing to you now," Jung said, the pages slashed with angry underlines, "as I would write *to a friend*—this is *our* style." Jung reminded Freud that he had begun writing *The Interpretation of Dreams* with "the mournful admission of your own neurosis . . . identification with the neurotic in need of treatment. Very significant," Jung said, and repeated the reason Freud had given for refusing to continue his analysis with Jung on board ship in 1909: "You 'could not submit to analysis *without losing your authority*.' " Freud's words, Jung wrote, "are engraved on my memory as a symbol of everything to come."

Freud confined his reply to other, less volatile topics. He contented himself with a word of caution. "Let each of us pay more attention to his own than to his neighbour's neurosis." But while Freud's letter remained coolly indifferent, his comments to Ernest Jones about Carl Jung told another story. "He behaves like a perfect fool, he seems to be Christ himself," Freud said. "The letters I get from him are remarkably changing from tenderness to overbearing insolence. He wants treatment, unfortunately by my last attack I have lost position of my authority." But Freud resolved not to react too strongly. "After all I think we have to be kind and patient with Jung and as old Oliver said keep our powder dry," he told Jones. Jung was worth it, Freud thought; he was at least an *Aiglon*, an eaglet, Freud said. Perhaps Freud was referring to the myth he had told at the Weimar Congress the year before: the young eagle must dare to gaze at the sun in order to prove himself his father's legitimate heir.

Letters between Freud and Jung now followed in swift succession, with each man answering a letter nearly on the day it arrived, until Jung made a slip. "Even Adler's cronies," Jung told Freud, "do not regard me as one of yours." Jung had not meant to say that. In German, the difference between *yours* and *theirs* is very slight, the difference between the capital letter *I* and the lowercase *i*: *Ihrigen* and *ihrigen*. Jung had wanted to say that Adler's followers did not consider him one of theirs. Insignificant as it seemed in the writing, Jung's mistake spoke volumes. Freud could not resist calling it to Jung's attention: "But are you 'objective' enough to consider the . . . slip without anger?"

Jung's storm of protest tore at the last remnants of friendship. "Your technique of treating your pupils like patients is a *blunder*," Jung wrote bitterly. "You go around sniffing out all the symptomatic actions in your vicinity, thus reducing everyone to the level of sons and daughters who blushingly admit the existence of their faults. Meanwhile you remain on top as the father, sitting pretty. . . . You see, my dear Professor, so long as you hand out this stuff I don't give a damn for my symptomatic actions; they shrink to nothing in comparison with the formidable beam in my brother Freud's eye. I am not in the least neurotic—touch wood! I have submitted *lege artis et tout humblement* to analysis and am much the better for it. You know, of course, how far a patient gets with self-analysis: *not* out of his neurosis—just like you."

Jung's letter produced such feelings of shame in Freud that at first he hesitated to send it on to Jones as he had sent several others. He wrote, "As regards Jung he seems all out of his wits, he is behaving quite crazy. After some tender letters he wrote me one of the utter insolence, showing that his experience at Munich has left no trace with him." He told Ferenczi that Jung had already forgotten the lesson he had learned in Munich and that he was behaving like a "florid fool and a brutal fellow, which he certainly is." But in his reply to Jung, Freud simply said he was sorry that noting Jung's slip had been the cause of so much irritation. Then, uneasy, Freud set the letter aside. Jung, Freud told Jones, "could take so meek a reaction as a sign of cowardice and feel his importance the more."

Freud was not sure how to respond to Jung's letter. "The reaction to it is difficult," he told Ferenczi. "[It] is obviously calculated to provoke me so that the blame for the break-up will fall on me and he can say that I cannot tolerate analysis." Freud blamed Jung's provocative letter on the fact that Jung himself was undergoing an analysis.

"The master who analyzed him," Freud wrote Ferenczi, "can only have been Fräulein Moltzer. . . . It was she in all likelihood," Freud concluded darkly, "who stirred him up immediately upon his return to Zürich." Freud refrained from venting his anger upon Jung. "I cannot suffer myself to be provoked as much as the letter deserves, our common interests standing in the way of an official separation." But he was provoked. "The letter to Jung was not mailed," Freud announced to Ferenczi, "and will not be replaced by another. To hell with him, I need neither him . . . nor his falsehoods."

The indecision over how to reply to Jung was resolved slowly. "I'm in the process of forming a completely reserved attitude toward Zürich," Freud wrote Ferenczi, "but there will be no more trace of wooing." And to Binswanger he declared ominously on New Year's Day in 1913, "The harmony established in Munich can hardly be expected to last long." Freud used large sheets of paper when he wrote his letters. He liked the measure of freedom it gave him in a life that was otherwise restricted. On January 3, nearly two weeks after the first draft of his letter to Jung, Freud wrote a second. "Your letter," he told Jung, "cannot be answered. It creates a situation that would be difficult to deal with in a personal talk and totally impossible in correspondence. It is a convention among us analysts that none of us need feel ashamed of his own bit of neurosis. But one who while behaving abnormally keeps shouting that he is normal gives ground for the suspicion that he lacks insight into his illness. Accordingly, I propose that we abandon our personal relations entirely."

As Freud put down his black pen with its broad nib, the large sheets covered with gothic German script that told Jung he no longer wished to be his friend, did he hesitate? Did he wonder which draft to send? "I'm letting you know," Freud told Ferenczi, "that I have found a few good, polite but unequivocal phrases to stop the private discourse with Jung. . . . His behavior is neurotic, childish. If he were in treatment with me and paid for it, I would obviously have to put up with his utterances, but this way I can spare myself and use my strength for other things." Several days later Freud received Jung's reply. "I accede to your wish that we abandon our personal relations, for I never thrust my friendship on anyone. You yourself are the best judge of what this moment means to you. 'The rest,'" Jung concluded gravely, "'is silence.'"

SIGNS OF a rupture between Jung and Freud had been evident to Americans since September 1912. "It is quite unfortunate that a little (and as I think quite unnecessary) split has taken place between [Jung] and Freud, fortunately not a serious one, it seems," James Putnam wrote Fanny Bowditch in Switzerland that December. Fanny was a daughter of Henry Pickering Bowditch, Putnam's colleague and close friend. The Putnam and Bowditch families had shared a camp in the Adirondacks for many years. During the winter of 1911, Fanny had suffered a breakdown at the death of her father; in a desperate effort to save her, Putnam had sent Fanny to Jung for treatment and she was still in Zürich in the early months of 1913.

Putnam's humanity and optimism were unfailing, and his many letters to Fanny in Switzerland were a gentle record of love and concern. Cousin Jim, as Fanny called him, kept the image of home and Boston alive in her mind. "This is a cold Sunday morning, with a blue sky and bright sun," he would write, "and we are all scratching round after breakfast, getting into our various employments. . . . This is just a bit of a picture of New England life, the interior of an American family as it were, to make you feel as if you were at home. . . . The rest of the family is busied in clearing off the table, except poor Molly who is upstairs with an acute cold, without which no self-respecting New England family can long get on."

But he also tried to allay Fanny's fears, among them that she would become like Ethel, her near relation in a hospital in Boston who relieved her restless fits by tearing bits of cloth and paper. " 'Manic-depressive insanity' you can tell Dr. Jung," Putnam wrote Fanny describing Ethel, adding, "I do not believe that you are threatened in the least by any such attack as she has had. . . . Your temperament and hers are very different. I hope that Dr. Jung's judgment on these points will coincide with mine."

Increasingly, Putnam worried that the vulnerable, suicidal and depressed Fanny was not strong enough to stand up to Jung. "It is a fault in Dr. Jung (*entre nous*)," Putnam told Fanny, "that he is too self-assertive, and I suspect that he is lacking in some needful kinds of imagination and that he is, indeed, a strong but vain person who might and does do much good but might also tend to crush a patient." Putnam tried to be reassuring when he learned that Maria Moltzer, a colleague of Jung's, was also analyzing Fanny. "I think perhaps you take the analysis and Dr. Jung and Schwester M. [Maria Moltzer] and all, too seriously, and feel yourself far too much of a helpless fly on sticky paper," he wrote. "After all, they are only humans, with limitations and failings, like you and me." But Putnam was uneasy. It would not have helped him to know that Jung was in a state of disorientation as he treated Fanny Bowditch during the early months of 1913.

"After the parting of the ways with Freud," Jung wrote years later, "a period of inner uncertainty began for me." Jung felt under increasing pressure, strong enough at times to make him believe he was emotionally disturbed. He did not know where to turn or what to do. Even careful analysis of his dreams did little to relieve him. Finally Jung decided, "Since I know nothing at all, I shall simply do whatever occurs to me." Jung found himself turning to a game that had occupied him as a child. Down by the lake, which receded during the winter months, he began to gather little stones and fit them carefully together into houses. The lake bed was filled with stones several inches in size, and slowly Jung finished several constructions. "I went on with my building game after the noon meal every day, whenever the weather permitted. As soon as I was through eating, I began playing, and continued to do so until the patients arrived; and if I was finished with my work early enough in the evening, I went back to building." It was an occupation Jung was to indulge in for years, and sometimes Jung's son, Franz, would help. "Father would be down there fitting rocks together," Franz said. "He was a genius at that. He would build towers and houses and churches, until he had whole villages. I would cut reeds for the roof beams and fill the little houses with sand so they wouldn't fall down. In the spring when the lake rose, the little villages all disappeared."

The little boy's joy was not his father's. As the huge, bearlike Jung and his small son bent seriously over their work on the dried shore of the Zürichsee, Jung remembered, "It was a painfully humiliating experience to realise that there was nothing to be done except play childish games." Jung was saddened and disoriented by the realization that his friendship with Freud was no more. He greeted his patients in 1913, Fanny Bowditch among them, with an inner uncertainty he was unable to overcome.

CHAPTER SIXTEEN

FREUD KNEW nothing of Jung's private strains during the early months of 1913. He knew only there was much work to be done in Vienna. Jung represented a fatal threat to the life of Freud's theories. He offered escape from Freud's emphasis on sexuality, he was a commanding figure with many loyal adherents and he was not a Jew. Freud found the directions Zürich and Vienna were taking so different that he believed they would not understand each other in two or three years. He would put their theoretical differences plainly when he wrote in his brief autobiography: "Jung attempted to give to the facts of analysis a fresh interpretation of an abstract, impersonal and non-historical character, and thus hoped to escape the need for recognizing the importance of infantile sexuality and of the Oedipus complex as well as the necessity for any analysis of childhood."

There was a concerted effort in Vienna not to expose the quarrel between Freud and Jung to the opponents of psychoanalysis, who would benefit from evidence of a schism. The members of the Vienna Psychoanalytic Society, Lou Andreas-Salomé noted in her diary, had been asked "to behave 'diplomatically' on the Jung affair; but actually Munich was already a rupture." Returning to her hotel in Vienna after seeing Freud one cold winter's day in 1913, Lou Salomé looked through the plate glass windows of the Alsergof to see a group of analysts gathered in heated discussion. When she walked in to listen to the voices raised in debate over Jung's conceptual shift, she thought, "It is beginning to be plain that any purely factual deliberation about Jung gets very complicated on account of the need to overlook differences in the interest of unity. A dangerous question."

Emotions ran high. It was no simple matter for an analyst loyal to Freud to tolerate Jung's change in views without comment. "I recollect vividly," Jones wrote years later, "the moment when Freud told me that Jung had expressed his disbelief in the existence of childhood sexuality, one of the main factors of psycho-analytical theory. I was astounded and said: 'How is that possible? Why, it is not long since he published an analytic study of his own child depicting as discerningly as possible the stages in the development of her infantile sexual life.' "

There were those who did not find in Jung's new ideas reason enough for rupture. Lou Andreas-Salomé had seen Freud change theoretical ground without apology, had observed that for Freud, "Theory is by no means hidebound, but is adjusted to further findings." Once when she had drawn Freud's attention to a discrepancy between what he had written and what he had just said in a lecture, Freud said simply, "My latest formulation." Loyal as she was to Freud, Salomé noted in her diary that "Jung is right in claiming that the character of the libido is too narrowly construed as sexual in the interpretation given to incest." Salomé liked Jung's new concept of incest. She also felt that Jung "is the one to whom we are most indebted for the discovery of the relationship between libido . . . and archaic thought." She observed sadly, "One is sometimes led to suspect that a quarrel over terms results when the real issue is much deeper and not a terminological one at all." In April 1913 Lou Andreas-Salomé attended her last meeting of the Psychoanalytic Society. As she had for some months, Salomé sat listening to the sharp disputes and arguments of the men around her and to the low, quiet voice of Sigmund Freud. The Society's commitment to the principle of honesty had impressed her deeply. "As long as it abides by the ideal of the honest community then it is also a beautiful thing and a joy, at least in a woman's eyes, to see men opposing one another in struggle."

Lou Andreas-Salomé was beautiful, with an open face and soft curls piled high. The poet Rainer Maria Rilke loved her, and Friedrich Nietzsche once said he had never known a more gifted or more understanding creature. She was a complex mixture of brilliance and seduction. "Her interests are really of a purely intellectual nature," Freud told Ferenczi, "she is a highly eminent woman, even if all tracks lead to the lion's den with her, in and out." Anna Freud would visit Lou in the years to come and tell her father, " 'My new friend' as you write, is truly magnificent and actually I find it uncanny that I should be with her. . . . One lives so easily with her, so simply and naturally as with few other human beings." Anna would read Lou parts of a paper she was writing and report to Freud, "She claims that I am writing it all on my own, but I think she inspires me in a strange, occult-like fashion, for when I am alone I know nothing at all about such things."

Freud had been wary of Lou Salomé at first, describing her to Ferenczi as "a female of dangerous intelligence." But he had grown fond of her. When she failed to come to one of his lectures at the Psychiatric Clinic, he "stared as if spellbound" at her vacant chair. When she was absent on another occasion, he told her later that he had spoken "falteringly." Salomé and Freud met often at Berggasse 19 and sometimes talked on until very late at night, but Freud always saw her safely back to her hotel. On Lou's last day in Vienna, Freud invited her to tea and sent her home with roses. When they next saw each other, the intellectual struggle Salomé had admired at the Wednesday meetings would be played out in a larger arena: she was to join Freud in Munich for the Fourth International Psychoanalytic Congress in September 1913.

THERE WAS little doubt that Jung seriously endangered Freud's position. "I am deeply impressed by the success of Jung's campaign," Ernest Jones told Freud in April of 1913. "He appeals to formidable prejudices. It is in my opinion the most critical period that psychoanalysis will ever go through." When Freud told Sándor Ferenczi that Jung had gone to America to treat a member of the Rockefeller family, Ferenczi replied, "I would rather you had been called to Rockefeller's, but the Americans don't deserve better." The outlook was gloomy. Freud wrote, "Naturally everything that tries to get away from our truth will find approbation among the general public. It is quite possible," he said in sorrow, "that this time they will really bury us, after having so often sung the funeral song for us in vain."

The issue of gentile and Jew rose abruptly. Alphons Maeder, a man who described himself as venerating Freud, wrote that the recent scientific disagreements were the inevitable result of the differences between "Aryan" and Jew. "Certainly," Ferenczi replied to Maeder, guided by advice from Freud, "there are great differences between the Jewish and the Aryan spirit. We can observe that every day. . . . But there should not be such a thing as Aryan or Jewish science. Results in science must be identical." Freud approved of Ferenczi's reply: "It is very dignified and appropriate." But he did not think much would be gained by it. "Certainly no diplomacy will help against the unleashed anti-Semitism of our Zürichers," he said. "Not to woo, stand fast." Freud was philosophical. "These fights . . . are good," he had consoled Ferenczi the year before. "They keep one tense."

The discussion of Christian versus Jew was not confined to rationalizations of scientific differences. It touched upon whether Freud would keep those of his closest followers who were not Jews. Ferenczi had written to Freud months before, "Putnam . . . may easily desert us; you must keep Jones constantly under your eye and cut off his line of retreat." Freud agreed. In a letter to Sabina Spielrein, herself a Jew, Freud wrote, "We are and remain Jews. The others will only exploit us and will never understand or appreciate us."

In the spring of 1913, it was by no means certain who in the end would stand at the side of Freud and at the side of Jung. The question included not only such people as Oskar Pfister and Ludwig Binswanger, men who were expected as Swiss to be torn in their loyalties between their countryman Carl Jung and the man they loved and admired, Sigmund Freud. Questions of loyalty surrounded even the members of Freud's secret council. Only three years before, Ernest Jones had vacillated over Freud's theory of sexuality. Now, under Jung's leadership, he and others were offered a strong alternative. Jones appeared to have been won completely to the cause, but Freud was uneasy at times. "I am not at all contented," he would complain to Jones, "that you bear Jung's insolence without remonstrating." Freud was even briefly unsure of Karl Abraham: "Abraham has been here for three days," Freud wrote on one occasion. "I am not informed how far Rank [a colleague of Freud] succeeded in gaining him to join our band." (Freud would give gold rings to the members of his secret committee, symbols of loyalty, and Karl Abraham would receive one of them.)

Both Freud and Jung wanted to avoid any outward appearance of a quarrel, and arrangements were made for the Congress in September 1913 in the understanding that both men would attend. Freud went so far as to recommend to his colleagues that they vote for Jung's reelection as president of the International Association. To preserve the illusion of unity, the Viennese and the Swiss would stay at the same hotel in Munich. "I think it is right to avoid a personal duel between Jung and me," Freud told Ferenczi in May. But there were limits beyond which Freud would not go. "I shall not present my compliments to Jung in Munich," he told Sabina Spielrein, "as you know perfectly well."

The unity was fragile at best. Freud and Jung confessed their unease in letters to Sabina Spielrein. Jung described the rupture, saying, "I was completely discouraged, since at that time everyone attacked me, and in addition I gained certainty that Freud would never understand me and would break off his personal relations with me. He wants to give me love, while I want understanding. *I want to be a friend on an equal footing, while he wants to have me as a son.* For that reason he ascribes to a complex everything I do that does not fit the framework of his life." Freud was bitter, too, when he wrote Sabina, "I am sorry to hear that you are consumed with longing for [Jung], and this at a time when I am on such bad terms with him, having almost reached the conclusion that he is unworthy of all the interested concern I have bestowed on him. I feel that he is about to destroy the work that we have built up so laboriously, and achieve nothing better himself."

During the months before the Congress, Freud struggled to maintain an atmosphere of reason and objectivity among his colleagues. His task was not an easy one. After Jung had traveled to the United States early in 1913, Jones reported to Freud, "His recent conduct in America makes me think more than [ever] that he does not react like a normal man, and that he is mentally deranged to a serious extent; he produced quite a paranoiac impression on some of the psycho-analytic psychiatrists on Ward's Island." Freud indulged in similar descriptions upon occasion: "Jung is crazy," he told Karl Abraham, "but I have no desire for a separation and should like to let him wreck himself first."

The need for unity remained paramount. Freud tried to confine such expressions to his own circle and to remain objective about new developments in Jung's theories. He knew Jung had felt for some time that the unconscious fantasies of patients were of considerable therapeutic importance. Freud had been skeptical, but in August 1913, amid the tensions of warring factions and the uncertainties of the Congress to come, he told Jones dispassionately, "As regards . . . the importance of the unconscious fancies I see no reason why we should submit to the arbitrary judgment of Jung instead of the necessary one of the patient himself. If the latter values those productions as his most precious secrets . . . we have to accept this position and must ascribe to them a most important role in the treatment."

The summer of 1913 was filled with difficulties. Freud had somehow to bear the loss of his closest friend, had constantly to appease his angered colleagues and yet had at the same time to retain his integrity over the scientific truths he had sacrificed much to serve. "It is like a shower of bad weather," he would tell Ernest Jones. "You have to wait [to see] who will hold out better, you or the evil genius of this time." That summer was the only time in Freud's life Anna recalled seeing her father depressed.

THEY WOULD not stay, this time, at the Park Hotel in Munich. "Don't forget," Freud wrote Ernest Jones on August 29, 1913, "it is the Bayerisch. Hof and we hope to arrive Friday 5th in the evening (9 h)." Lou Salomé arrived at the small, thirty-room hotel a day later and spent the evening in the lounge with Freud, Abraham and a few others. Elsewhere in the hotel the atmosphere was tense. There were many private meetings as the eighty-seven participants gathered in groups to discuss the schism and sound out each other's loyalties. One morning Alphons Maeder paced up and down the hall rehearsing the lecture he was to give on dreams when he saw Freud open a glass door into the corridor. "Good morning, Herr Professor!" Maeder said and offered his hand; but Freud refused to take it.

In the conference hall, Jung sat at a table with the rest of the Swiss. "Two years ago," Lou Salomé wrote, remembering the Weimar Congress, "Jung's booming laughter gave voice to a kind of robust gaiety and exuberant vitality, but now his earnestness is composed of pure aggression, ambition, and intellectual brutality." Salomé sat with Freud at a table opposite that of Jung. "One glance at the two of them," she felt, "tells which is the more dogmatic, the more in love with power." She noticed that Freud controlled himself with the greatest effort. Yet after the long months of struggle and maneuvering, Salomé thought, "one could, one ought, one had the right to thunder." Freud, she knew, had maintained a lifetime of deliberate calm. It was to Victor Tausk, the brilliant and abrasive analyst sitting at Freud's other side, that would fall the task of angrily defending Freud's cause. Tausk was Salomé's lover, "a blond fellow with a big head"; Freud was glad to have him there. "Clever and dangerous," Freud said. "He can bark and bite."

Salomé's perception of Jung and her loyalty to Freud moved her to write, "I have never felt so close to Freud as here; not only on account of this break with his 'son' Jung, whom he had loved and for whom he had practically transferred his cause to Zürich, but on account of the manner of the break—as though Freud had caused it by his narrow-minded obstinacy." For his part, Alphons Maeder found his colleague Jung strangely silent during the long hours of discussion. When Maeder gave his lecture, which diverged in theory from both Freud and Jung, Maeder resented the fact that Jung said little. "Then I saw he was a bit similar to Freud," Maeder said. "He could not really bear the independence of his collaborators; basically he had the same faults for which he reproached Freud."

The behavior of the Swiss offended Freud and his colleagues. Salomé thought Jung improperly shortened the time for papers. One Swiss report was so filled with statistics that Freud was moved to say, "All sorts of criticisms have been brought against psychoanalysis, but this is the first time anyone could have called it boring." Freud's followers had intended to vote for Jung; it had been much discussed in Vienna and finally agreed upon. But when the time came to count the vote, a number of cards were found blank. Although some ten participants had registered their protest against Jung by abstaining, he was reelected president by a vote of 52–22. The Congress pleased no one. One of Salomé's friends went so far as to say, "The best thing now would be for the whole association to blow up; in that way like minds could find one another honestly, and Freud would not be forced to go to war against attacks from his own camp or to protect those who stand with him."

The day after the Congress, Freud spent some quiet hours with Salomé in the Hofgarten, the palace gardens of Munich etched in careful patterns with precise, gravel paths lined with shrubs. Talk of events of the days before turned to a conversation about thought transference, "which," Salomé noticed, "certainly torment[s] him." The subject of mental telepathy had been a source of tension between Freud and Jung and had occasioned a scene between them years before in Vienna. It was a subject Freud had tried to dissuade Jung from exploring, a phenomenon that Freud both believed in and feared. Thought transference was "a point," Salomé saw, "which he hopes need never again be touched in his lifetime."

For her part, Salomé would remember a story Freud told her during the Munich Congress. It suited the air of finality that surrounded those days. When his son Ernst was a young boy, Freud said, at the end of a holiday with his family, he had "looked back to the sea from the stagecoach as the family was leaving Italy and declared over and over again all the while the coach was carrying him away: 'I'm staying here, I'm staying here, I'm staying here!' Only when a bend in the road hid the sea from his sight did he realize his helplessness, and now pale and quiet murmured countless times, 'Good-by sea, good-by sea, good-by sea!' "

The Congress was over. The ordeal of the preceding months was at an end. "We dispersed," Freud said, "without any desire to meet again." Nor did Freud and Jung ever see each other again in the long years that were left them. "If the real facts were more familiar to you," Freud would write Stanley Hall, who had been his and Jung's host in America in brighter days, "you would very likely not have thought that there was again a case where a father did not let his sons develop, but you would have seen that the sons wished to eliminate their father, as in ancient times." Freud could not pronounce Jung's name, after the Congress. He kept saying Jones, by mistake.

Jung returned to Zürich while Freud went on to Rome. "I have visited old Moses again," Freud wrote. His words conveyed nothing of his tragic encounter with Michelangelo's towering statue, an encounter that personified his struggle with Jung, not yet at an end. Outwardly the same as ever, Jung would take up his pen on December 13, 1913, and turn to the journal he had abandoned when Emma had finally agreed to marry him. There he would document the struggle precipitated by his loss of Freud, a struggle years long, and one in which he would nearly lose his life.

CHAPTER SEVENTEEN

MINNA WAS glad Freud did not ask her to climb with him in the hot, dusty ruins of the Palatine Hill. She had joined her brother-in-law on the train from Bologna when the Munich Congress was over, and they had traveled on to Rome together. Always before, Freud had walked for days in the sun among ancient fallen temples, and the "incomparable beauty of Rome" had eased his spirit. But in the fall of 1913, Freud went less often to the Palatine. Instead, he walked up the steep steps from the Corso Cavour to "the lonely piazza where the deserted church stands," where he resumed a vigil begun on his last visit to Rome. Freud was drawn inside the church to the towering statue of *Moses* carved by Michelangelo four hundred years before.

Slight, nearly frail, the founder of psychoanalysis stood for hours every day before the seated giant of a man and sought himself. It had to do with Jung, this lonely sojourn by Moses' side. In Freud, as in

Moses, lay a singular passion. Freud's passion had shaped the concepts of psychoanalysis into a cause for which he would willingly give his life. His passion had transformed Carl Jung from a friend into his son and heir; his loss of Jung was the substance now of the long visits to the deserted church. Day after day as Freud witnessed the terrible anger of Moses, joined with it was his own. The story of Moses haunted Freud: according to the Old Testament, Moses would soon rise up in fury at the Israelites and cast down the tablets on which were carved the Ten Commandments. In a moment of uncontrollable rage Moses would risk the work of a lifetime. It was Freud's great fear. He was a man in whom self-control had long been achieved; yet in his bitterness over Jung, he did not trust himself. Freud stood in the shadow of the great statue fearing that he would do as the biblical Moses and risk the future of psychoanalysis in a single outburst of fury.

It is said that Michelangelo lived alone in a quarry for seven months while he searched for the perfect piece of marble for his *Moses*. When he finished the statue, Michelangelo gazed up into the face of Moses. "Speak!" he shouted. "Why don't you speak?" And he brought down his hammer hard on Moses' knee. Four hundred years later, Freud could see the scar on Moses' knee and he would know Michelangelo's despair. Freud pursued the mystery of the statue's meaning until his own struggle seemed to be resolved. He had begun to see a contradiction in Michelangelo's *Moses*: the motion of the upper body—the brow knitted in fury, the tangled beard, muscled arms and flowing robe—grew unaccountably still at the prophet's massive knee, rooted like a tree and immobile. Why, Freud wondered, if Moses were about to rise up in a terrible rage, was there no movement in his lower body? "I used to sit down in front of the statue in the expectation that I should now see how it would start up on its raised foot, dash the Tables of the Law to the ground and let fly its wrath," Freud wrote. "Nothing of the kind happened. Instead, the stone image became more and more transfixed, an almost oppressively solemn calm emanated from it."

Standing before the statue in September 1913, Freud confirmed his suspicion that Moses was holding the sacred tablets upside down, an improbable act in a respectful man. The haphazard positioning of the religious tablets convinced Freud that although Moses had wished to cast them away, self-restraint had supervened. The tables were askew because, in Moses' agitation, they had slipped. But Moses' lower body was at rest because he had succeeded at last in controlling his fury.

Freud was sure that Michelangelo's Moses was an altogether different man from the biblical Moses: he was the embodiment of self-control. "In his first transport of fury," Freud conceded, "Moses desired to act, to spring up and take vengeance and forget the Tables; but he has overcome the temptation, and he will now remain seated and still, in his frozen wrath and in his pain mingled with contempt. Nor will he throw away the Tables so that they will break on the stones, for it is on their especial account that he has controlled his anger; it was to preserve them that he kept his passion in check."

Like Moses, Freud would withstand his inner passion. "The giant frame with its tremendous physical power becomes only a concrete expression of the highest mental achievement that is possible in a man," Freud concluded, "that of struggling successfully against an inward passion for the sake of a cause to which he has devoted himself." Freud's inward passion was his anger over Jung's defection, and the cause was psychoanalysis. In Moses he had found expression for the unnameable agony of sacrifice and for passions that could not be.

The comparison did not end there. Freud knew that Michelangelo and Pope Julius II, in whose honor Michelangelo had carved the *Moses*, had once been close. The friendship had contained undercurrents of tension and they did not escape Freud's mention. "Julius II," Freud noted, "was akin to Michelangelo in this, that he attempted to realize great and mighty ends." But the relationship between Julius and Michelangelo was flawed. Julius "often made [Michelangelo] smart under his sudden anger and his utter lack of consideration for others." Michelangelo, Freud felt, "as the more introspective thinker, may have had a premonition of the failure to which they were both doomed."

Freud wrote down his observations in a little essay called "The Moses of Michelangelo." He completed the paper during the last days of December 1913 and decided to publish it anonymously, despite Abraham's vivid query: "Don't you think that one will recognize the lion's claw?" Freud wrote twenty years later, "My feeling for this piece of work is rather like that towards a love-child. For three lonely September weeks in 1913 I stood every day in the church in front of the statue, studied it, measured it, sketched it, until I captured the understanding for it which I ventured to express in the essay only anonymously. Only much later did I legitimatize this non-analytical child." Freud's essay was somber testimony to his despair. He thought Michelangelo had attempted the impossible: to portray Moses' private passion and, at the same time, to portray the calm Moses felt when he had sacrificed that passion. Perhaps, Freud concluded, it was too difficult, even for Michelangelo, to leave a wake of violent emotion clearly visible "in the ensuing calm." Perhaps not even Michelangelo could carve such torment into stone, but Freud could feel it.

DURING THE weeks in December 1913 that Freud was writing his essay on Moses, Jung felt his life slip from his grasp. "I was living in a constant state of tension," Jung remembered. "Often I felt as if gigantic blocks of stone were tumbling down upon me." He did yoga exercises to try to regain control of his emotions. Years later a friend described Jung's recommended procedure in such times: it was useful to lie down and breathe quietly for a while. To breathe with the sense that "the wind blew over one—the wind of disturbance blew over one."

Strange beings appeared to Jung in dreams and gave him no rest. "It was during Advent of the year 1913," Jung would remember, "12th December, to be exact—that I resolved upon the decisive step. I was sitting at my desk . . . thinking over my fears. Then I let myself drop." Carl Jung's son, Franz, said carefully years later, "My father writes that he *chose*. I do not believe that he chose. I believe he had no choice. Can you imagine what it must be to think that you might be going mad? That you might fall forever into the void?" Save for his analysis with patients, Jung could not work. He was unable to read a scientific book. He resigned his position at the University of Zürich, where he had lectured for eight years.

Diabolical images continually appeared, sometimes in hour-long visits and other times in dreams. In the name of unknown spirits Jung committed murder, and rivers of blood flowed interminably. A young blond boy drowned, a black snake pressed near and a leathery-skinned dwarf haunted Jung. There were caves and mud, dead bodies and through it all, unendurable guilt. The images terrified Jung. He could only abandon himself to them and describe their strange behavior in his journal, or take out his watercolor case and paint pictures of his dreams. Alphons Maeder once told Jung of a strange and frightening occurrence, a hallucination he had had. Jung was impressed by Maeder's experience. "What, you too?" Jung asked him.

"For years after he and Freud parted," Franz Jung said, "my father could do no work. He placed a gun in his nightstand and said that when he could bear it no longer he would shoot himself. Other people fell away, and he was alone. For seven years he did nothing really except his painting." Jung's children knew little of his turmoil. Only the eldest daughter, Agathli, nine years old in 1913 when Freud and her father parted, would one day say, "very vaguely I have the feeling that something happened." Franz as a child did not perceive his father's distress; but he has spent all of his life in the same part of Switzerland, and his memories of Jung are constant and close. Just as Franz, unknowing, helped his father build the small stone villages down by the lake, the little boy sat at the old table in the library where Jung painted his pictures. "I painted there, too," Franz said. "We were allowed sometimes, if we promised not to speak a word, to draw and paint. But I was not good at it, and it was hard to sit there in the chair opposite because my father was quite skilled at the painting he did."

Jung spent much time alone during these years. His children missed him, sometimes in a grave way. "My sister Marianne was born two years after I was," Franz said. "Since I was a boy, my father spent more of his time with me. One day—I think I was about ten and Marianne was eight—we were all of us out sailing. We stopped to get something in a village, and Father bought us all little cakes. When we got home, Marianne ran across the lawn to Mother and cried, 'Just look! Franz's father bought me a little cake.' Of course Mother immediately said, 'Now look, Marianne, you must understand that Franz's father is *your* father, too!' "

In summer the family went to Schaffhausen to stay with Emma's mother, and there the children spent time with their father as they did not during the rest of the year. "My grandmother had several carriages and two horses, a very fine house and many acres of land," Franz Jung said. "All summer long we played Indians against the English with my cousins. Father was the leader. He wore a Canadian Mountie's hat and a pair of cowboy boots from his visit to America with Freud. He looked like a sheriff. We built teepees and huts big enough to sleep in, and each side had a horse. We would light fires and burn down each other's teepees and steal the horses. This was Father's idea. He played with us all the time, although his brother-in-law did not approve." Nor did Franz's grandmother approve when Jung and the children dug tunnels in the soft, yellow earth. The tunnels were large enough to crawl into, and Frau Rauschenbach was afraid they would cave in on the children.

As a boy, Franz hiked a good deal with his father, sometimes in the hills around Schaffhausen, and sometimes near their house in Küsnacht. Later with his four sons, Franz walked the trails he had known since childhood and now he hiked a few of them with me. He would choose the route with care, for its element of surprise or beauty. Franz likes to climb mountains, but more than that he likes to go back down them at great speed. We have worked our way for hours up through dark wooded paths and then burst down a stony creek bed that opened, suddenly, onto a soft, spring valley as wide as one could see. Switzerland was always empty where we went, and always beautiful. One day Franz walked with me in the snowy forests high above the Zürichsee. A stand of huge beech trees, limbless for a hundred feet, arched up to the winter sky. Sunlight refracted through the snow crystals, stained glass in the ancient, vaulted space. "Think of my mother," Franz said into the silence. "Think of her. Can *you* imagine living with a man who slept with a gun by his bed and painted pictures of circles all day?"

FREUD DID not know that the man he had once loved like a son was struggling for his life. He did not know that the man he now feared as a dangerous rival was unable to work and spending hours by himself building little villages out of stones and drawing pictures of his dreams. Freud's anger against Jung lay like cold metal. "I was struck," he wrote Karl Abraham, "by the complete analogy that can be drawn between the first running away from the discovery of sexuality behind the neuroses by Breuer and the latest one by Jung. That makes it the more certain that this is the core of psycho-analysis." Ernest Jones was as uncompromising. "One is infuriated with Jung," he told Abraham, "until one discovers that he is simply crassly stupid, 'emotional stupidity,' as the psychiatrists term it." In Bergson, Freud felt, Jung had found another Jew for a father figure. "I am no more jealous," he told Jones acidly in June 1914. The anger lasted. A year later Freud would write James Putnam, "I found [Jung] sympathetic so long as he lived blindly, as I did. Then came his religious-ethical crisis with higher morality, 'rebirth,' Bergson, and at the very same time, lies, brutality and anti-semitic condescension towards me."

Freud and Jones had worried for some time that the psychoanalytic movement might turn to Jung. "It seems quite impossible for Vienna and Zurich to come to any kind of terms," Jones had written a colleague in November 1913 just after the Munich Congress. "So it will be better if they separate altogether, when each can develop without personal emotions on the lines that suit him best—and the best man win!" Freud had mixed feelings about the strength of Jung's position. "It may be that we overrate Jung and his doings. . . . He is not in a favourable position before the public when he turns against me, i.e., his past," he wrote Jones. But his confidence waned in the same letter and he finished it on a different note: "I expect no immediate success but incessant struggling. Anyone who promises to mankind liberation from the bondship of sex will be hailed as a hero, let him talk whatever nonsense he chooses."

Freud continued at moments to be unconvinced of the loyalty of even his closest friends. "I am very glad you show yourself inaccessible to Jung when he comes to London," Freud confessed to Ernest Jones. "He might try to flatter and compromise." Freud had long been concerned about his American colleagues: "There is no doubt all these men incline strongly to Jung or to put it correctly they tend away from [psychoanalysis]." In another letter to Jones, he wrote: "We know [Jung's] position is a very strong one, our only hope is still he will ruin it himself. You will have to fight him for the influence in England and America and it may be a long hard struggle." By the spring of 1914, though Freud was sure of the loyalty of only a few, Ernest Jones was one. "Otherwise," Freud reported to Ferenczi, telegraph-style, "only losses: Stanley Hall, of course, the complete Adlerian, Spielrein crazy, writes that I have something against her." Ferenczi told him that, after several "honeymoon years" in Budapest, resistance to psychoanalysis seemed to be on the rise.

In Switzerland, Bleuler fell away. An American studying in Germany had witnessed his defection without realizing it. W. J. Sweasey Powers attended a congress of German psychiatrists in Breslau and came away little impressed by the worn-out arguments raised against psychoanalysis. Later he understood why the meeting had been so dry. "The purpose," Powers was told, "was to give Bleuler the opportunity to publicly back-slide from the Freud-school as his name was considered to have had a great influence in keeping the Freud theories alive. The purpose was also to place the German psychiatricians [*sic*] on record as being against the Freud theories." Freud had not been surprised to see Bleuler go.

Ferenczi struggled to find a bright spot in the dark summer of 1914, with only moderate success. "Getting rid of Jung," he told Freud, "meant for you a return to your original way of working: taking everything into your own hand and not relying on 'co-workers.' The motto 'Après-moi le déluge' seems to be the only appropriate one in science."

For a moment that summer, it seemed to Freud that he might lose his youngest daughter as well. "I know from the best sources," he wrote Anna, who was vacationing in England, "that Dr. Jones has serious intentions to woo you." The thought of his young and fragile daughter living in England far from home with a sexually driven and complex man tormented Freud. "Jones is much less self-reliant and much more dependent than one's impression would lead one to believe," he told Anna gently. "He needs an experienced, perhaps even older woman. Left to himself—and this is the worst I can say about him—he shows a tendency to move into dangerous situations and then risk everything, which would not guarantee any security for you." He asked Anna not to see Jones alone. "He is not the right man for a delicate female being. He had to work his way out of a very small family and difficult situation . . . and failed to acquire the tact and fine discretions that a pampered and, what is more, very young and somewhat straight-laced girl would expect from her husband. You would have to be at least five years older to be able to appreciate him and to forgive him all kinds of things, and then he would be too old for you."

Freud turned for comfort that summer to Shakespeare. "Strange," he told Ferenczi, "I relinquished Macbeth to Jones years ago and now I take him back, so to speak. Dark powers are at play here." He ascribed his "Lear-like moods" to fatigue, but Freud was standing in Lear's shadow when he told Ferenczi that he did not want to lose Anna, his "Cordelia," "to an obvious act of revenge." Freud discouraged Ernest Jones. He told him that Anna, though the most gifted of his children, "does not claim to be treated as a woman, being still far away from sexual longings and rather refusing man. There is an outspoken understanding between me and her that she should not consider marriage or the preliminaries before she gets two or three years older. I don't think she will break the treaty." Freud wondered to Anna whether Jones's interest might be diverted to another woman, "to Mabel's sister, whom you like so much?" Freud cherished Anna, whom he needed and who would never marry.

In these days of shifting loyalties, Lou Andreas-Salomé remained loyal to Freud. She was practicing psychoanalysis just outside Göttingen, Germany. "Very nice," Anna Freud would write her father on a visit there. "Quite Mama's ideal of a small university town with little front gardens and green trees." Salomé lived in a house high on a hill, raising flowers and vegetables in her walled-in courtyard. But in 1914 the bucolic life of Germany changed, as it changed all over Europe. An Englishman staying in the German countryside that year saw structures difficult to describe. Standing on the roof of a house, he studied them through a pair of field glasses. The buildings were flat and yet they looked like warships or rooftops. Their use became ominously clear when German Zeppelins began flying overhead "dropping upon the targets . . . immense weighted objects which . . . appear to be some form of aerial torpedo." World War I had begun in the summer of 1914, and the Zeppelins were at target practice in the open fields, dropping dummy bombs.

Abroad, the frightening scope of the war was clear in a single New York headline on August 3, 1914: RUSSIA INVADES GERMANY; GERMANY INVADES FRANCE, BUT DOES NOT DECLARE WAR; ENGLAND'S DECISION TODAY; BELGIUM MENACED, LUXEMBURG AND SWITZERLAND INVADED; GERMAN MARKSMEN SHOOT DOWN A FRENCH AEROPLANE. Millions of lives were lost over the next four years, and the Europe that survived experienced terrible privations. Freud sent Lou Salomé money after the war because she could not afford fuel for a fire to write in the cold winter evenings. "And the voice of psychoanalysis is not heard in the world for the thunder of cannons," Freud wrote in November 1914.

CHAPTER EIGHTEEN

SOMEONE ONCE described Toni Wolff as a black pearl, and Jung had instantly agreed. Born in 1888, Antonia Wolff grew up in a wealthy family in Zürich. She suffered emotional difficulties when she was a girl and underwent treatment with Jung. Toni emerged from her analysis stronger and steadier, and Jung turned to her in his despair. As the horrors of World War I swirled around Switzerland's frontiers, Jung was engaged in a private battle.

Few people described Toni Wolff without first mentioning her eyes. "They were dark, with great depth," Carl Jung's son, Franz, remembered. "Toni was all spirit. It was almost as if she *had* no body." Toni was different from the Zürich housewives. "Seductive, not sexy," a woman analyst said without rancor. "She had a wonderful smile." Toni Wolff, twenty-six years old in 1914, would become a gifted analyst, although the portrait of her that emerged from her patients' descriptions rendered a solitariness in her nature. One patient never forgot the way Toni lighted a cigarette, always placing the match carefully in the ashtray to let its flame burn to the end like a little offering to a god known only to herself. Another recalled the refreshment served during the analytic hour: "The maid would bring a cup of tea—just one, for Miss Wolff—but never two."

Jung's colleague C. A. Meier had been told that Jung referred to Toni as the one case of schizophrenia he had been able to cure, but despite her great improvement, friends noticed that she was sometimes in mental distress. But Toni could help Jung. She knew the strange terrain that frightened him because she had seen its terrors herself. When Jung struggled to understand the psychotic images that rose unbidden from the depths of his unconscious, Toni was his guide. She was uncanny, direct and singular, and Jung would love her always. One day Jung would say to a patient, recommending an analyst: "You need someone who is clever like a serpent," and by this he meant Toni. "Not someone who is without fault, like a pigeon," Jung finished, and he meant his wife, an analyst then herself.

After the break with Freud, Jung told a friend, there was nothing to believe in. The onslaught of hallucinations was horrifying. "Fear crept over me," Jung wrote, "that the succession of such figures might be endless, that I might lose myself in bottomless abysses of ignorance." As madness threatened, Jung had to remind himself that his name was Carl Gustav Jung, that he was a respected physician with a wife and family and that he lived at 228 Seestrasse in Küsnacht. Looking back on those years, Jung wrote, "It is, of course, ironical that I, a psychiatrist, should at almost every step of my experiment have run into the same psychic material which is the stuff of psychosis and is found in the insane." Colleagues years later did not minimize the gravity of Jung's condition. "He was very near psychosis," said the analyst Liliane Frey-Rohn. "He didn't know how it would turn out." C. A. Meier said that "phenomenologically" Jung's breakdown could easily be classified "as a schizophrenic episode."

Jung emerged slowly from his years of emotional turmoil. He had been a professor of medicine, president of an international association, a prolific writer and a proper bourgeois. Several years later, as he sailed the waters of the Zürichsee, he was no longer a professor, no longer a president, no longer a model of Swiss propriety, which had, oddly, always mattered much. But he had recovered a lost part of himself and gained in the process an abiding respect for the power of the unconscious.

What Jung brought back from the terror and beauty of the unconscious was work for a lifetime. It would be twenty years before he understood a measure of what he had experienced. It was not what he had set out to do. "As a young man," he wrote, "my goal had been to accomplish something in my science. But then, I hit upon this stream of lava, and the heat of its fires reshaped my life." Within the rich imagery of hallucination and dream—scenes of horror and indescribable beauty—and in the waking nights of terror and remorse, Jung reached a fullness of understanding that would serve him in the years to come. When he was an old man, Jung was asked which of his concepts had given the most meaning to his life, and his reply was instantaneous. "Oh, that is the collective unconscious." Jung had become convinced that the lower depths of the psyche were comprised of universal and inherited patterns of behavior. "The deeper 'Layers' of the psyche," he felt, "lose their individual uniqueness as they retreat farther and farther into darkness. 'Lower down' . . . they become increasingly collective until they are universalised."

As Jung set about organizing his ideas, he was not always alone. Emma and Toni were privy to Jung's inner life. In order to work out his new concepts and their complicated relationship as well, Jung, Emma and Toni attempted a delicate experiment. "They studied their dreams on the problem," Frau C. A. Meier said. "It wasn't just a triangle situation as it is for ordinary people." Frau Meier and her husband knew both Emma Jung and Toni Wolff. Of Emma, C. A. Meier said, "I think she underwent the most spectacular transformation during their married life. More so than any of the women I saw. She was quite an exceptional person." Years later Toni Wolff, Emma Jung and Meier discussed their griefs and conflicts: "It was a mutual sort of thing. . . . We did group analysis for about a year," he said.

Emma Jung and Toni Wolff could not have been more different. Emma lived with wisdom and grace among the concerns of everyday life, and her warmth was tangible. "My mother was sure of herself," Franz Jung remembered, "and she was sure of her femininity, so she could deal with Toni." Physical reality confused Toni at times. She could not hammer a nail and she did not know how to plant a seed. The separate plights of these two women—and Carl Jung—were inextricably bound for over thirty years. "There isn't the slightest doubt in my mind," a family friend, Fowler McCormick, said, "that this relationship was a torture and a painful thing for Mrs. Jung to bear." A scene in the Jung household shocked him. "Mrs. Jung was helping to prepare the dinner, Miss Wolff was helping to prepare the dinner, Dr. Jung was there and there was no disturbance. . . . There were two people preparing the dinner as if both lived in the house." McCormick knew this was not so, but Franz and his sisters called Toni "Tante" because she was so often at their home.

"When I was a ripe man," Franz Jung said, "I felt sorry for Toni. She never knew what it was to be a wife and mother." But complex as the relationships were, Franz remembered only one disturbing scene. In 1925 his father was to return from months in Africa, and Emma and Toni disagreed over which of them would surprise Jung when his ship docked in Genoa. Emma settled the argument with the decision that Franz, then eighteen, should travel to Italy to meet his father. In later years, Emma and Toni were active members of the Psychology Club in Zürich. The writer and African expert Sir Laurens van der Post was present on an occasion when both women addressed the Club. "There was a bowl of beautiful, deep red roses placed on the table in front of Mrs. Jung to honor her," van der Post remembered. "After she had finished, Toni Wolff came up for her turn to speak, and do you know, the flowers were gone. It must have been very hard for Toni, if it were always like that."

Only after many years did the tight bonds of pain and love among the three finally loosen, although Jung's love for both women endured. A young friend sat one day over coffee in the garden in Küsnacht with Emma and Jung when they were old. "She was so nice," Sabi Tauber recalled of Frau Jung, "and let him do the things he felt he had to do as a man. . . . Sometimes she smiled quite slowly, he didn't look at this slow smile, but it was so nice. I felt that they both were in love with each other, even with all the difficulties." After Toni Wolff died in 1953, Jung carved Chinese characters into a little stone monument for her that stands among the shadows of old trees near the house in Küsnacht: "Toni Wolff. Lotus. Nun. Mysterious."

A friend who knew Toni well said of Jung, "One can say that he was a big spoon—he drank her soul." Fowler McCormick was asked what it was that had made Jung act so openly and cause such anguish. "He was so powerful. For creative people, you know there are, in many ways no laws. The law Jung was faithful to beyond anything else was the creative instinct in him. He would abandon everything for that."

THE PLATES that shift beneath the ocean floor are internally rigid and undergo changes only at their boundaries. Mountains and volcanoes are formed where plates collide; where they spread apart, ocean basins are opened and a new sea floor is made. For a brief moment in a long history, Freud and Jung had drawn together in a friendship of surpassing power. Their withdrawal from each other left new ground.

In 1915, two years after his break with Jung, Freud began six months of feverish work on twelve essays that he called "Introduction to Metapsychology." It was in large part an effort to chart the sea of the unconscious in all its transformations; it was intended as a summary of his thought, his legacy. But in its particulars and in its genesis, one paper resonated with the ideas of Carl Jung. In Freud's essay "A Phylogenetic Fantasy," he offered the view that certain states of mind, such as anxiety and paranoia, were remnants of responses once adaptive before and during the Ice Age. This was a view Jung held, roughly drawn, in which such emotions rose, not solely from early family conflicts, but out of the wellspring of inherited experience. It was a concept Freud had questioned in Jung's thought, only to see it now reflected, fleetingly, in his own. Jung was also present, behind the scenes, as Freud moved in his essay through the evolutionary stages of man. Turning the myth of Oedipus upside down in his essay, Freud, however momentarily "playful," stated that the primal father had castrated his rebellious sons.

Freud did not choose to publish this paper, nor did he publish six others of the twelve essays. At moments he denied that he ever wrote them. Perhaps he realized that he had been dictated too much by his emotions over the loss of men like Jung and not enough by his natural, creative instinct. Freud would move on, up to the last, to original and important work; but in at least one of the essays he wrote in 1915, the boundaries of new ground were sharply defined by memories of Carl Jung.

Jung was deeply troubled by the failure of his friendship with Freud. In 1921, after eight years of self-doubt and times of near psychosis, he published a work—*Psychological Types*—that was intimately connected with his break with Freud. How, Jung asked himself, could two intelligent and responsible men address themselves to the same scientific questions and come away with contradictory answers? There were, Jung finally concluded, two types of people. Both kinds were capable of living with equal security in the reality of their worlds. They were dissimilar only in the nature of their realities. For the introvert such as himself, the things that determined the progress of his life were subjective: the life and texture of his own thoughts. For the extrovert, and at the time Jung believed Freud one of these, reality lay outside the psyche. It was not Freud's thoughts that defined his science, but what he saw and heard in the world beyond his mind.

Jung's effort to understand what had come between himself and Freud had revealed to him worlds of difference. Jung would later seem to change his mind about Freud's orientation, finding him an "originally introverted feeling type"; but by then his theory had long been cast and was unaffected by this revision of Freud's type.

Jung's new work, wrung from years of anguish, invited some derision, not least from Freud. "A new production by Jung of enormous size 400 pages thick, inscribed 'Psychologische Typen,' " Freud announced to Ernest Jones in 1921, "the work of a snob and a mystic, no new idea in it. He clings to that escape he has effected or detected in 1913, denying objective truth in psychology on account of the personal differences in the observer's constitution." Years later, Freud told the French writer Romain Rolland, who had published a book on Hindu mysticism: "The distinction between 'extrovert' and 'introvert' derives from C. G. Jung, who is a bit of a mystic himself and hasn't belonged to us for years. We don't attach any great importance to the distinction and are well aware that people can [be] both at the same time, and usually are."

Smith Ely Jelliffe, in Europe in 1921, told his friend William Alanson White that Freud had referred to Jung's latest work as trash. "I am especially interested in what you say about Jung," White replied. "I am anxious to get a clear idea of what he is doing but many of the indications point to something woozy." Oskar Pfister wrote after several years of indecision, "I have completely finished with the Jungian manner. Those high-falutin interpretations which proclaim every kind of muck to be spiritual jam of the highest order and try to smuggle a minor Apollo or Christ into every corked-up little mind simply will not do." Jung had long felt beleaguered and misunderstood. "My view seems to be too indigestible to a scientific stomac [*sic*]," he had written Jelliffe darkly in 1913. Several years later he wrote him, "There is a large groupe [*sic*] of Freudians fighting against myself as if I were the devil."

But Freud heard that "yonder the pond," as he located the America he disliked, people seemed sympathetic to Jung's new views. "If America is really embracing Jungism . . ." he told Ernest Jones, "she will get what she deserves." Beneath the bitter humor, Freud worried. Jones had suggested that Freud publish his collected works in English, and at first Freud had rejected the idea. "Then on a sudden," Freud announced, "I grasped that you were right that psychoanalysis was better known in England by Jung's work than by my own and that [it] would mean much to the psychoanalytic movement if my collections were accessible to the English public." When he heard that Jones was planning to reprint a "blasphemous paper on the Holy Virgin" in English, Freud was all caution. "I think it would be foolish to provoke God and the pious stupidity of old England as long as our situation is not better insured in that remarkable island. It has its personal foes and so have you."

The differences between Freud and Jung seemed to increase with every theoretical step they took. Yet some people saw deep similarities. "I was very sorry when Freud and Jung parted company," Abraham Brill told the New York Academy of Medicine many years later in 1947. "Jung's analytic psychology though it differs theoretically in many respects from Freud's structure, is nonetheless psychoanalytic." Brill remained a loyal Freudian all his life, but he admitted that night, "Freud in the beginning said 'there are many ways and means of psychotherapy. All methods are good which produce the aim of the therapy.' " Nor did Sabina Spielrein ever abandon her belief that the similarities between Freud and Jung were of great significance. "You can understand Freud perfectly well if you wish to," she wrote Jung, "i.e., if your personal affect does not get in the way." To Freud she had stated with conviction: "You, Professor Freud, and he have not the faintest idea that you belong together far more than anyone might suspect."

"IT OFTEN happens," Freud wrote Oskar Pfister in 1922 on the subject of another man, "that excellent and serious men cannot help hurting each other, because otherwise they cannot give full expression to their love. It is not to be taken too seriously." Freud and Jung were serious men and each had hurt the other in a grave and lasting way. Their friendship had once been landfall. Over time the haven each man had been to the other was lost to view, but it existed in memory still.

Nearly a dozen years after the rupture between Freud and Jung, Karl Abraham warned Freud of the defection of Otto Rank, a member of his secret committee. Freud did not want to hear of Rank's derelictions, and he told Abraham so with some severity. Ernest Jones consoled Abraham. "The real tragedy," Jones said, "is this. I fear that Prof, with his clear mind, cannot be altogether blind to the unconscious tendency in Otto." It was only, Jones felt, that "he can hardly face the possibility of having once more to go through the Jung situation."

The theme of the lost comrade persisted. "Certainly I have had much that was good in life, but all in all it was hard," Freud told Ludwig Binswanger, who had come to Berggasse 19 with Jung on his first visit to Freud, and who had later agonized with Freud over the Kreuzlingen gesture when the friendship between Freud and Jung was in disarray. "I was very ready to be fond of others, like you, for example," Freud told Binswanger in 1923, "but many made it impossible for me."

One evening several years later, C. A. Meier was in Vienna and spent an hour alone with Freud among the hundreds of little artifacts gleaming in the study at Berggasse 19. "There was one topic of conversation," Meier remembered. "Jung. Freud was full of questions about Jung, about his family, his life and what he was doing. Every conceivable question," Meier said. "Because he still cared." Meier would find the same anguish in Jung. "He didn't like to talk about Freud because it was so painful." Another Swiss analyst agreed: "The wound was always there, it never healed. It was a tragedy." The hours that Freud and Jung had spent in the dim and quiet study lay in the past. The little statues had been present at scientific collaboration and theoretical schism, friendship and betrayal. In less than a decade, H.D. would come to Vienna and see the chalked swastikas leading to Freud's door and beyond. "Aye I am wistful for my kin of spirit," H.D.'s friend Ezra Pound wrote,"And have none about me save in the shadows."

The long ordeal of Freud and Jung was reminder and more that some piece of the human psyche was beyond comprehension. The moment when the world's first analysts, unable to alleviate their pain, played with stones at the edge of a dry lakeshore or stood for hours before the statue of an angry prophet, bore witness to the intransigent mystery of the human spirit. That mystery was the terrible beauty of the psyche, and they lived it, Freud and Jung, alone.

WORKS CITED

PUBLISHED SOURCES

Abraham, Karl, and Freud, Sigmund. *A Psycho-Analytic Dialogue: The Letters of Sigmund Freud and Karl Abraham 1907–1926*. Edited by Hilda C. Abraham and Ernst L. Freud. Translated by Bernard Marsh and Hilda C. Abraham. New York: Basic Books, 1965.

Alexander, Franz G., and Selesnick, Sheldon T. *The History of Psychiatry: An Evaluation of Psychiatric Thought and Practice from Prehistoric Times to the Present*. New York: Harper & Row, 1966.

Andreas-Salomé, Lou. *The Freud Journal of Lou Andreas-Salomé*. Translated by Stanley A. Leavy. New York: Basic Books, 1964.

Baedeker, Karl. *Switzerland and the Adjacent Portions of Italy, Savoy and Tyrol*. Leipsic: Karl Baedeker Publisher, 1895.

Bennet, E. A. *C. G. Jung*. London: Barrie and Rockliff, 1961.

———. *Meetings with Jung: Conversations Recorded During the Years 1946–1961*. Zürich: Daimon Verlag, 1985.

Works Cited

Bettelheim, Bruno. "Scandal in the Family." *New York Review of Books*, June 30, 1983, 39–44.

Billinsky, John. "Jung and Freud (The End of a Romance)." *Andover-Newton Quarterly* 1969, 10(2):39–43.

Binswanger, Ludwig. *Sigmund Freud: Reminiscences of a Friendship*. Translated by Norbert Guterman. New York: Grune & Stratton, 1957.

Breuer, Josef, and Freud, Sigmund. *Studies on Hysteria*. Edited and translated by James and Alix Strachey. Middlesex, England: Penguin Books, 1980.

Brill, A. A. *Freud's Contribution to Psychiatry*. New York: W. W. Norton, 1944.

———. *Lectures on Psychoanalytic Psychiatry*. New York: Alfred A. Knopf, 1946.

———. "Psychopathology and Psychotherapy on the Neuroses and Psychoses." *New York State Journal of Medicine* November 15, 1931, 31:1392–1397.

———. "Psychotherapies I Encountered." *Psychiatric Quarterly* 1947, 21:579–591.

Brome, Vincent. *Ernest Jones: Freud's Alter Ego*. New York: W. W. Norton, 1983.

———. *Freud and His Early Circle*. New York: William Morrow, 1968.

———. *Jung: Man and Myth*. New York: Atheneum, 1981.

Burnham, John C. *Jelliffe: American Psychoanalyst and Physician & His Correspondence with Sigmund Freud and C. G. Jung*. Chicago: University of Chicago Press, 1983.

Carotenuto, Aldo. *A Secret Symmetry: Sabina Spielrein Between Jung and Freud*. Translated by Arno Pomerans, John Shepley and Krishna Winston. New York: Pantheon, 1982.

Champernowne, Irene. *A Memoir of Toni Wolff*. San Francisco: C. G. Jung Institute of San Francisco, 1980.

Chekhov, Anton. *The Selected Letters of Anton Chekhov*. Edited by Lillian Hellman. New York: Farrar, Straus & Giroux, 1955.

Clark, Ronald W. *Freud: The Man and the Cause*. New York: Random House, 1980.

———. "Sigmund Freud's Sortie to America." *American Heritage* April 1980, 31:34–37.

Cocks, Geoffrey. *Psychotherapy in the Third Reich: The Göring Institute*. New York: Oxford University Press, 1985.

Eastman, Max. "A Significant Memory of Freud." *The New Republic*, May 19, 1941, 693–695.

Ellenberger, Henri F. *The Discovery of the Unconscious: The History and Evolution of Dynamic Psychiatry*. New York: Basic Books, 1970.

Engelman, Edmund. *Berggasse 19: Sigmund Freud's Home and Offices, Vienna 1938*. New York: Basic Books, 1976.

Federn, Ernst. "Letters to the Editor." *Journal of the Behavioral Sciences* January 1966, 2(1):76–77.

Fisher, David James. "Sigmund Freud and Romain Rolland: The Terrestrial

Animal and His Great Oceanic Friend." *American Imago* Spring 1976, 33(1):1–59.

Freud, Martin. *Sigmund Freud: Man and Father*. New York: Vanguard Press, 1958.

Freud, Sigmund. *An Autobiographical Study*. Translated by James Strachey. New York: W. W. Norton, 1952.

———. *The Complete Letters of Sigmund Freud to Wilhelm Fliess 1887–1904*. Edited and translated by Jeffrey Moussaieff Masson. Cambridge: Belknap Press of Harvard University Press, 1985.

———. *Five Lectures on Psycho-Analysis*. Edited and translated by James Strachey. New York: W. W. Norton, n.d.

———. *Group Psychology and the Analysis of the Ego*. Edited and translated by James Strachey. New York: W. W. Norton, 1959.

———. *The Interpretation of Dreams*. Edited and translated by James Strachey. New York: Avon Books, 1965.

———. *Letters of Sigmund Freud*. Edited by Ernst L. Freud. Translated by Tania and James Stern. New York: Basic Books, 1960.

———. "A Long-lost and Recently Recovered Letter of Freud." *The Israel Annals of Psychiatry and Related Disciplines* 13:2.

———. "The Moses of Michelangelo." *The Standard Edition of the Complete Psychological Works of Sigmund Freud*, vol. 13. Edited and translated by James Strachey. London: Hogarth Press, 1955. 211–238.

———. *On the History of the Psycho-Analytic Movement*. Edited by James Strachey. Translated by Joan Riviere. New York: W. W. Norton, 1966.

———. *A Phylogenetic Fantasy: Overview of the Transference Neuroses*. Edited by Ilse Grubrich-Simitis. Translated by Axel and Peter T. Hoffer. Cambridge: Belknap Press of Harvard University Press, 1987.

———. "Postscript." *The Standard Edition of the Complete Psychological Works of Sigmund Freud,* vol. 12. Edited and translated by James Strachey. London: Hogarth Press, 1973. 80–82.

Freud, Sigmund, and Abraham, Karl. *A Psycho-Analytic Dialogue: The Letters of Sigmund Freud and Karl Abraham 1907–1926*. Edited by Hilda C. Abraham and Ernst L. Freud. Translated by Bernard Marsh and Hilda C. Abraham. New York: Basic Books, 1965.

Freud, Sigmund, and Jung, C. G. *The Freud/Jung Letters: The Correspondence Between Sigmund Freud and C. G. Jung*. Edited by William McGuire. Translated by Ralph Manheim and R. F. C. Hull. Princeton: Princeton University Press, 1974.

Freud, Sigmund, and Pfister, Oskar. *Psychoanalysis and Faith: The Letters of Sigmund Freud and Oskar Pfister*. Edited by Heinrich Meng and Ernst L. Freud. Translated by Eric Mosbacher. New York: Basic Books, 1963.

Gay, Peter. *Freud: A Life for Our Time*. New York: W. W. Norton, 1988.

Gifford, George E., Jr. "Freud and the Porcupine." *Harvard Medical Alumni Bulletin* 1972, 4:28–32.

Groesbeck, C. Jess. "The Analyst's Myth: Freud and Jung as Each Other's Analyst." *Quadrant* Spring 1980, 13(1):28–55.

Guest, Barbara. *Herself Defined: The Poet H.D. and Her World.* New York: Quill, 1984.

H.D. *Tribute to Freud.* New York: New Directions, 1974.

Hale, Nathan G., Jr. *Freud and the Americans: The Beginnings of Psychoanalysis in the United States, 1876–1917.* New York: Oxford University Press, 1971.

Hannah, Barbara. *Jung: His Life and Work.* New York: Capricorn Books, 1976.

Herzstein, Robert Edwin. *Waldheim: The Missing Years.* New York: Arbor House/William Morrow, 1988.

Jaffé, Aniela. *Jung's Last Years and Other Essays.* Translated by R. F. C. Hull and Murray Stein. Dallas: Spring Publications, 1984.

Jensen, Ferne, ed. *C. G. Jung, Emma Jung and Toni Wolff: A Collection of Remembrances.* San Francisco: Analytical Psychology Club of San Francisco, 1982.

Jones, Ernest. *Free Associations: Memories of a Psycho-Analyst.* New York: Basic Books, 1959.

———. *The Life and Work of Sigmund Freud.* 3 vols. New York: Basic Books, 1953–1957.

Jones, J. Sydney. *Viennawalks.* New York: Holt, Rinehart and Winston, 1985.

Jung, C. G. *Letters*, vol. 1: *1906–1950.* Edited by Gerhard Adler and Aniela Jaffé. Translated by R. F. C. Hull. Princeton: Princeton University Press, 1973.

———. *Collected Papers on Analytical Psychology.* Translated by Constance E. Long. London: Ballière, Tindall & Cox, 1916.

———. *The Collected Works of C. G. Jung*, vols. 2, 6, 10, 17. Edited by William McGuire et al. Princeton: Princeton University Press, 1973–1979.

———. *Memories, Dreams, Reflections.* Recorded and edited by Aniela Jaffé. Translated by Richard and Clara Winston. London: Collins and Routledge & Kegan Paul, 1963.

———. "Psychic Conflicts in a Child." *The Collected Works of C. G. Jung*, vol. 17. *The Development of Personality.* 8–35.

———. "The Reaction-time Ratio in the Association Experiment." *The Collected Works of C. G. Jung*, vol. 2. *Experimental Researches.* 221–271.

———. "A Rejoinder to Dr. Bally." *The Collected Works of C. G. Jung*, vol. 10. *Civilization in Transition.* 535–544.

———. "General Description of the Types." *The Collected Works of C. G. Jung*, vol. 6. *Psychological Types.* 330–404.

———. "The State of Psychotherapy Today." *The Collected Works of C. G. Jung*, vol. 10. *Civilization in Transition.* 157–173.

———. *Word and Image.* Edited by Aniela Jaffé. Princeton: Princeton University Press, 1979.

Jung, C. G., and Freud, Sigmund. *The Freud/Jung Letters.* Edited by William McGuire. Translated by Ralph Manheim and R. F. C. Hull. Princeton: Princeton University Press, 1974.

Kenny, Anthony. *Wittgenstein.* Cambridge: Harvard University Press, 1973.
Koelsch, William A. *'Incredible Day-Dream': Freud and Jung at Clark, 1909.* Worcester, Mass.: The Friends of the Goddard Library, 1984.
Koonz, Claudia. *Mothers in the Fatherland: Women, Family Life and Nazi Ideology 1919–1945.* New York: St. Martin's Press, 1987.
Lief, Alfred. *The Commonsense Psychiatry of Dr. Adolf Meyer.* New York: McGraw-Hill, 1948.
McCully, Robert S. "Remarks on the Last Contact Between Freud and Jung." *Quadrant* 1987, 20(2):73–74.
McGuire, William. "Jung's Complex Reactions (1907)." *Spring* 1987, 3–17.
McGuire, William, and Hull, R. F. C. *C. G. Jung Speaking.* Princeton: Princeton University Press, 1977.
McIver, Elizabeth Putnam. "Early Days at Putnam Camp." Read at the Annual Meeting of the Keene Valley Historical Society, September 1941. 3–27. Privately printed.
Nunberg, Herman, and Federn, Ernst, eds. *Minutes of the Vienna Psychoanalytic Society,* vol. 1: 1906–1908. Translated by Margarete Nunberg. New York: International Universities Press, 1962.
Oeri, Albert. "Some Youthful Memories of C. G. Jung." Translated by Lisa Ress Kaufman. Spring 1970, 182–189.
Peterson, Frederick. "Credulity and Cures." *Journal of the American Medical Association* 73:1737–1740.
———. "A Talk on Morbid Psychology." *Journal of the Medical Society of New Jersey* 1908, 4(10):407–415.
Pfister, Oskar, and Freud, Sigmund. *Psychoanalysis and Faith: The Letters of Sigmund Freud and Oskar Pfister.* Edited by Heinrich Meng and Ernst L. Freud. Translated by Eric Mosbacher. New York: Basic Books, 1963.
Pound, Ezra. "In Durance." In *Collected Early Poems of Ezra Pound.* Edited by Michael John King. New York: New Directions, 1976. 86–87.
Putnam, James J. "Personal Impressions of Sigmund Freud and His Work with Special Reference to His Recent Lectures at Clark University." *The Journal of Abnormal Psychology* December 1909–January 1910, 4:293–310; March–April 1910, 5:372–379.
Riese, Hertha, ed. *Historical Explorations in Medicine and Psychiatry.* New York: Springer, 1978.
Robinson, Janice S. *H.D.: The Life and Work of an American Poet.* Boston: Houghton Mifflin, 1982.
Ruitenbeek, Hendrik M., ed. *Freud as We Knew Him.* Detroit: Wayne State University Press, 1973.
Russell, John. "The Brilliant Sunset of Vienna in Its Final Glory." *The New York Times,* June 29, 1986.
Sachs, Hanns. *Freud: Master and Friend.* Cambridge: Harvard University Press, 1944.
Schur, Max. *Freud: Living and Dying.* New York: International Universities Press, 1972.
Silverstein, Barry. " 'Now comes a Sad Story': Freud's Lost Metapsychological

Papers." In Paul E. Stepansky, ed. *Freud: Appraisals and Reappraisals.* Hillsdale, N.J.: Analytic Press, 1986. 143–195.

Sloane, Eugene H. "A Parapraxis of Freud's in Relation to Karl Abraham." *American Imago* Summer 1972, 29(2):123–159.

Steele, Robert S. *Freud and Jung: Conflicts of Interpretation.* Boston: Routledge & Kegan Paul, 1982.

Storr, Anthony. *C. G. Jung.* New York: Viking, 1973.

Sulloway, Frank J. "Freud as Conquistador." *The New Republic,* August 25, 1979. 25–31.

Taylor, Eugene. "C. G. Jung and the Boston Psychopathologists 1902–1912." *Voices: The Art and Science of Psychotherapy* 1985, 21(2):132–145.

Troyat, Henri. *Chekhov.* Translated by Michael Henry Hein. New York: E. P. Dutton, 1986.

van der Post, Laurens. *Jung and the Story of Our Time.* New York: Vintage Books, 1977.

von Franz, Marie-Louise. *C. G. Jung: His Myth in Our Time.* Translated by William H. Kennedy. New York: G. P. Putnam's Sons, 1975.

Winnik, H. Z. "A Long-lost and Recently Recovered Letter of Freud." *Israel Annals of Psychiatry and Related Disciplines* March 1975, 13(1):1–5.

Wittels, Fritz. *Sigmund Freud: His Personality, His Teaching, & His School.* Translated by Eden and Cedar Paul. London: George Allen and Unwin, 1924.

UNPUBLISHED MATERIALS

A. A. Brill Collection, Library of Congress, Washington, D.C.

C. G. Jung Biographical Archive, Francis A. Countway Library of Medicine, Boston, Massachusetts.

Jung Archive, Zürich, Switzerland.

Karl Abraham Papers, Library of Congress, Washington, D.C.

Los Angeles Psychoanalytic Society and Institute, Los Angeles, California.

Sigmund Freud Collection, Library of Congress, Washington, D.C.

AUTHOR'S INTERVIEWS

Brunner, Blanche. May 1985. Küsnacht, Switzerland.

Fichtl, Paula. July 1984 and February 1985. Salzburg, Austria.

Frey-Rohn, Liliane. February 1985. Zürich, Switzerland.

Jung, Franz. April and July 1984; February 1985; November 1987. Küsnacht, Switzerland.

Meier, C. A. April and July 1984. Zürich, Switzerland.

van der Post, Laurens. July 1984. Aldeburgh, England.

NOTES

CHAPTER ONE

page

3 Hilda Doolittle often . . . : Guest, *Herself Defined,* 40–43, 76, 177, 209–210.

3 in October 1934 . . . : H.D., *Tribute to Freud*, 4.

4 "They were the chalk ones . . .": Ibid., 59.

4 One of her . . . : Robinson, *H.D.,* 169.

4 "She is like . . .": Guest, *Herself Defined*, 73.

4 "Paula has opened . . .": H.D., *Tribute to Freud*, 96.

5 "But why did . . .": Ibid., 61.

5 "I paid a . . .": Freud and Pfister, *Psychoanalysis and Faith,* 139.

5 Freud knew that . . . : Hugo Knoepfmacher, "Sigmund Freud at Secondary School." Freud Collection. Box B27.

page

5 "The only thing . . .": Clark, *Freud,* 488.

5 Some seventy thousand . . . : Burnham, *Jelliffe,* 254–255.

5 "Well we had . . .": Guest, *Herself Defined,* 212.

6 Freud, too, had . . . : Jones, *Life of Freud,* vol. 3: 392–393.

6 "go backward or . . .": H.D., *Tribute to Freud,* 145.

6 "little statues and . . .": Ibid., 175.

6 "*This* is my . . .": Ibid., 68.

6 "to be venerated . . .": Ibid., 70.

6 "Mine," he said . . . : Sachs, *Freud,* 170.

7 The men had . . . : Jung, *Memories, Dreams, Reflections,* 146.

7 smoking cigars, picking . . . : Binswanger, *Sigmund Freud,* 3.

7 "I am by . . .": Freud, *Letters to Fliess,* 398.

7 "Jung was a . . .": Bennet, *C. G. Jung,* 56.

7 In 1933 there . . . : Jaffé, *Jung's Last Years,* 78–98; Alexander and Selesnick, *History of Psychiatry,* 407–409; Cocks, *Psychotherapy in the Third Reich,* 6, 43–49, 117, 127–134.

8 "I have fallen . . .": Jung, *Letters,* vol. 1: 157.

8 "The factual and . . .": Alexander and Selesnick, *History of Psychiatry,* 407.

8 "The Jew, who . . .": Jung, *Collected Works,* vol. 10: 165.

8 "That [Freud] hadn't . . .": "Frontier of Psychiatry." n.d., 3. *Roche Medical Image,* Freud Collection. Box B62.

9 "It is not . . .": H.D., *Tribute to Freud,* 59.

9 The year before . . . : Herzstein, *Waldheim,* 39–43.

9 "Life at my . . .": H.D., *Tribute to Freud,* 194.

CHAPTER TWO

10 "I slept very . . .": Interviews with Paula Fichtl. This quote and those to follow, as well as descriptions of household scenes in which Paula figures, unless otherwise noted, were given during these interviews.

11 "Quick, Paula—get . . .": Freud, M., *Sigmund Freud,* 205–206.

11 storm troopers in . . . : Schur, *Freud,* 495.

11 "God save Austria," . . . : Herzstein, *Waldheim,* 53.

11 Martin quickly saw . . . : Freud, M., *Sigmund Freud,* 206.

11 "Hitler in Vienna," . . . : Gay, *Freud,* 618.

12 room behind that . . . : Engelman, *Berggasse 19,* unpaged.

12 Martha took pleasure . . . : Freud, M., *Sigmund Freud,* 210–212.

12 Frau Freud invited . . . : Ibid., 210–211.

page
12 "That is more . . .": Sachs, *Freud*, 179–180.
13 John Cooper Wiley . . . : Clark, *Freud*, 502.
13 Bullitt was called . . . : *The New York Times*, February 16, 1967.
13 His thorough reports . . . : Ibid.
13 On the afternoon . . . : Freud, M., *Sigmund Freud*, 211–212.
13 Freud paced for . . . : Schur, *Freud*, 498.
14 At Jung's direction . . . : McCully, "Remarks on the Last Contact Between Freud and Jung," 73.
14 "I refuse to . . .": Hannah, *Jung*, 254–255.
14 A devoted friend . . . : Freud, M., *Sigmund Freud*, 214.
14 The princess, Anna . . . : Freud and Jung, *Letters*, xx.
15 Music drifts across . . . : Interview with Franz Jung.
15 his own design . . . : Interview with Adrian Baumann, May 1970. Jung Biographical Archive.
15 But an illness . . . : Jung, *Letters*, vol. 1: 244.
15 persisted, and this . . . : Hannah, *Jung*, 256.
15 The Nazis had . . . : Alexander and Selesnick, *History of Psychiatry*, 407; Koonz, *Mothers in the Fatherland*, 136; Clark, *Freud*, 489.
15 Hans Kuhn, would . . . : Jensen, *C. G. Jung, Emma Jung and Toni Wolff*, 16.
16 He had bought . . . : Jung, *Memories, Dreams, Reflections*, 223.
16 "Old Jung, down . . .": von Franz, *C. G. Jung*, 234.
16 Dressed as he . . . : Bennet, *Meetings with Jung*, 31, 85, 99–100.
16 "But this one . . .": Interview with Herr and Frau Franz Kuster and Rosa Wenk, January 1970. Jung Biographical Archive.
16 If friends were . . . : Interview with E. A. Bennet, February 1969. Jung Biographical Archive.
16 No one escaped . . . : Interview with Franz Jung.
16 Once at a . . . : Jensen, *C. G. Jung, Emma Jung and Toni Wolff*, 117.
17 "to make these . . .": Jung, *Word and Image*, 205.
17 "I call it . . .": Jung, *Memories, Dreams, Reflections*, 357.
17 "Where was that . . .": Jung, *Collected Works*, vol. 10: 166.
18 Jung did not . . . : van der Post, *Jung*, 148.
18 "The written word," . . . : Burnham, *Jelliffe*, 264.

CHAPTER THREE

19 "Wouldn't it be . . .": Clark, *Freud*, 510.
19 DR. JONES IS . . . : Ibid., 504–505.

page

19 Freud's son Martin . . . : Freud, M., *Sigmund Freud*, 214–215.

20 "You, Anna, have . . .": Ibid., 217.

20 "I can recommend . . .": Ibid.

20 "When I saw . . .": Clark, *Freud*, 513.

21 Wearing a green . . . : H. F. Pottecher, n.d. French news clipping, Freud Collection. Box B20.

21 dapper and smiling . . . : *The New York Times*, February 16, 1967.

21 "proud and rich . . .": Schur, *Freud*, 504.

21 "It's good to . . .": *New York Evening Sun*, June 6, 1938.

21 "If you want . . .": *London Daily Express*, clipping, n.d. Freud Collection. Box B20.

21 "The pain in . . .": Schur, *Freud*, 505.

21 "We are buried . . .": Jones, *Life of Freud*, vol. 3: 229.

21 "The Professor was . . .": Guest, *Herself Defined*, 246.

21 "I did not . . .": H.D., *Tribute to Freud*, 10.

21 "a deep shadow . . .": Freud to Simmel, June 26, 1938. Los Angeles Psychoanalytic Society and Institute.

22 "Register what?" he . . . : Freud to Anna Freud, August 1, 1938. Freud Collection.

22 "dinner jacket and . . .": "Aktuelles," *Zentralblatt für Psychotherapie* 1939, 11:1.

22 Jung maintained that . . . : Jaffé, *Jung's Last Years*, 79–82.

22 Jung's colleague C. A. Meier . . . : Interview with C. A. Meier, September 1970. Jung Biographical Archive; a related story is contained in Jung, *Letters*, vol. 1: 405 n.5.

22 "Hitler made upon . . .": McGuire and Hull, eds., *C. G. Jung Speaking*, 127–128.

22 Meier was never . . . : Interview with C. A. Meier, September 1970. Jung Biographical Archive; interview with Prof. C. A. Meier.

22 "It is extremely . . .": McGuire and Hull, eds., *C. G. Jung Speaking*, 131–132.

23 "I say let . . .": Ibid., 132–133.

23 "Today," he said . . . : Jung, *Collected Works*, vol. 10: 565.

24 THE TENTH INTERNATIONAL . . . : Interview with E. A. Bennet, February 1969. Jung Biographical Archive.

24 "The Oxford P.therapeutic . . .": Freud to Anna Freud, August 1, 1938. Freud Collection.

24 "It is really . . .": Anna Freud to Brill, December 27, 1939. Brill Collection.

24 "piled nearly a . . .": *PM*, December 1, 1940. Freud Collection. Box 58.

page

24 As the months . . . : Guest, *Herself Defined*, 260–262, 278–279.
25 The houses were . . . : Interview with Blanche Brunner.
25 Sometimes among the . . . : Interview with Franz Jung.
25 Brunner consulted with . . . : Interview with C. A. Meier.
25 "Yes," Jung's colleague . . . : Ibid.
25 "even for the . . .": Interview with Karl Schmid, May 1970. Jung Biographical Archive.
26 "Here is the . . .": Guest, *Herself Defined*, 270.
26 "the most delightful . . .": H. D., *Tribute to Freud*, vi.
26 Jung's letters to . . . : Freud and Jung, *Letters*, xx–xxxiv.
26 "He was an . . .": Interview with Franz Jung.
27 "My father would . . .": Ibid.

CHAPTER FOUR

31 In 1899, Sigmund . . . : Freud, *Letters to Fliess*, 366–367.
31 "there is some . . .": Freud, *Interpretation of Dreams*, 137.
31 The extent of . . . : Ellenberger, *Discovery of the Unconscious*, 451.
32 "I have great . . .": Freud, *Letters to Fliess*, 359.
32 but before Martha . . . : Ibid., 355–358.
32 "My old and . . .": Ibid., 363.
32 ("The rascals are . . .)": Ibid., 367.
32 "The deepest and . . .": Freud, *Interpretation of Dreams*, 280.
32 "And now," he . . . : Ibid., 138.
32 "a man who . . .": Jones, *Life of Freud*, vol. 1: 5.
33 "Why," his father . . . : Freud, *Interpretation of Dreams*, 460.
33 "My emotional life . . .": Ibid., 521.
33 "The boy will . . .": Ibid., 250.
33 his mother's choice . . . : Jones, *Life of Freud*, vol. 1: 3.
34 "Jew! get off . . .": Freud, *Interpretation of Dreams*, 230.
34 "Where was an . . .": Ibid., 459.
34 Freud drank black . . . : Knoepfmacher, "Freud at Secondary School." Freud Collection. Box B27.
34 "did not fail . . .": Freud, *Interpretation of Dreams*, 309.
35 "When the Professor . . .": Interview with Anna Freud Bernays, *Standard Star* (New Rochelle, N.Y.), September 1934. Freud Collection. Box B65.
35 Although he tunelessly . . . : Ruitenbeek, ed., *Freud as We Knew Him*, 144.
35 the sound of . . . : Jones, *Life of Freud*, vol. 1: 17.

page

35 Ludwig Wittgenstein, a . . . : Kenny, *Wittgenstein*, 8.
36 "on the crowded . . .": *Opera News*, February 5, 1972.
36 "I see the sun . . .": Jung, *Memories, Dreams, Reflections*, 21.
36 "I have guarded . . .": Ibid., 15.
36 Jung was often . . . : Interview with Mary Elliott, December 1969. Jung Biographical Archive.
37 "The muted roar . . .": Jung, *Memories, Dreams, Reflections*, 24.
37 "an unconscious suicidal . . .": Ibid., 23.
37 "dim intimations of . . .": Ibid., 22–23.
37 "*Alles Schweige, jeder* . . .": Ibid., 22.
37 "On the very . . .": Ibid., 26.
38 "All sorts of . . .": Ibid., 31.
38 "I see in . . .": Ibid., 32.
38 "I am sitting . . .": Ibid., 33.
38 "The tormenting sense . . .": Ibid., 34.
39 "A robust woman . . .": Jones, *Life of Freud*, vol. 1: 165.
39 "I really get . . .": Ibid., 132.
40 "I am like . . .": Freud, *Letters*, 53.
40 "the most unassuming . . .": Ellenberger, *Discovery of the Unconscious*, 432.
40 Bertha Pappenheim was . . . : Ibid., 480–482.
40 At times a . . . : Breuer and Freud, *Studies on Hysteria*, 74–89.
41 "grumbled about her . . .": Ibid., 88.
41 "Today I put . . .": Freud, *Letters*, 84.
41 Charcot had begun . . . : Ellenberger, *Discovery of the Unconscious*, 93.
41 "He used to . . .": Clark, *Freud*, 72.
42 "It seemed weird . . .": Freud, *Letters*, 217.
42 "I don't want . . .": Ibid., 216.

CHAPTER FIVE

43 the young doctor . . . : Troyat, *Chekhov*, 9–11.
43 "all six or . . .": Chekhov, *Selected Letters*, 140–142.
44 He contended that . . . : Freud, *Letters to Fliess*, 448.
44 Freud tried to . . . : Schur, *Freud*, 95, 143.
44 For a time . . . : Ibid., 25–26.
44 "I regard it . . .": Jones, *Life of Freud*, vol. 1: 162–163.
45 "I have often . . .": Jones, Ibid., vol. 1: 197.
45 "My 'unusualness,' Jung . . .": Jung, *Memories, Dreams, Reflections*, 72.

page
45 "More than ever . . .": Ibid., 71.
45 At the age . . . : Baedeker, *Switzerland*, 4–5.
45 The city had . . . : Riese, ed., *Historical Explorations*, 143.
46 At her home . . . : Interview with Franz Jung.
46 "The world is . . .": Jung, *Memories, Dreams, Reflections*, 47.
46 "How was that . . .": Ibid., 49.
46 "Yes, yes, that . . .": Ibid., 52.
46 "long since superseded . . .": Ibid., 57.
47 "Now you won't . . .": Ibid., 42.
47 "And how is . . .": Ibid., 43.
47 Moreover, in a . . . : Freud, *History of the Psycho-Analytic Movement*, 13–14.
47 "But in this . . .": Ibid.
48 "Be calm," Charcot . . . : Charcot to Freud, January 23, 1888. Freud Collection. Box B3.
48 Encouraged by his . . . : Jones, *Life of Freud*, vol. 1: 250.
48 "hysterical patients suffer . . .": Jones, Ibid., 273.
48 Two years later, . . . : Breuer and Freud, *Studies on Hysteria*, 26.
48 "Much will be . . .": Ibid., 393.
48 "Now listen to . . .": Freud, *Letters to Fliess*, 146.
49 "Freud's intellect is . . .": Steele, *Freud and Jung*, 75.
49 "You must read . . .": Jung, *Memories, Dreams, Reflections*, 68.
49 "The boy is . . .": Ibid., 90.
49 There was little . . . : Interviews with Jolande Jacobi, December 1969 and January 1970. Jung Biographical Archive.
49 "There was a . . .": Jung, *Memories, Dreams, Reflections*, 100.
50 His first talk . . . : Steele, *Freud and Jung*, 42–43.
50 "the handle lay . . .": Jung, *Memories, Dreams, Reflections*, 108.
50 "This possibility," Jung . . . : Ibid., 106.
51 He wanted, at . . . : Ibid., 104, 107.
51 "I denied myself . . .": Winnik, "A Long-lost and Recently Recovered Letter of Freud." 2.
51 Freud's hesitations about . . . : Federn, "Letters to the Editor." 76–77. Freud Collection. Box B60.
51 He would sit . . .: Oeri, "Some Youthful Memories." 188.
52 "My heart," Jung . . . : Jung, *Memories, Dreams, Reflections*, 111.
52 "I confess that . . .": Sulloway, "Freud as Conquistador." 26.
53 "Curious states incomprehensible . . .": Freud, *Letters to Fliess*, 254.
53 "I still do . . .": Ibid., 255.

page

53 "Many a sad . . .": Ibid., 274.

54 "I cannot convey . . .": Ibid., 269.

54 "It revolutioned my . . .": Freud to Jones, February 12, 1920. Freud Collection. Box D2.

54 "As Caesar loved . . .": Freud, *Interpretation of Dreams*, 459.

CHAPTER SIX

55 The Burghölzli Mental . . . : Hannah, *Jung*, 77.

55 The hospital was . . . : Interview with Manfred Bleuler, December 1969. Jung Biographical Archive.

55 The lives of . . . : Interviews with Jolande Jacobi, December 1969 and January 1970. Jung Biographical Archive.

56 A doctor paid . . . : Interviews with Manfred Bleuler, December 1969 and January 1970. Jung Biographical Archive.

56 A rare fusion . . . : Ellenberger, *Discovery of the Unconscious*, 667.

56 Before coming to . . . : Ibid., 287.

56 "The fact that . . .": Freud, *Letters to Fliess*, 461 n. 3.

56 Bleuler often told . . . : Brill, *Lectures*, 24.

57 "Understanding for it . . .": Freud, *Letters to Fliess*, 405.

57 "In those days . . .": Clark, *Freud*, 191.

57 "The attitude of . . .": Sachs, *Freud*, 73.

57 "I know that . . .": Freud, *Letters to Fliess*, 408.

57 "If you don't . . .": *Time* magazine, September 5, 1969.

58 The Vienna State . . . : Russell, "The Brilliant Sunset of Vienna in Its Final Glory."

58 "*I' bestimm' wer* . . .": Jones, *Viennawalks*, 108.

58 Freud saw that . . . : Freud, *Interpretation of Dreams*, 246.

58 "occurring to me . . .": Freud, Ibid., 523.

58 "There has never . . .": Freud, *Letters to Fliess*, 405–406.

58 "Explain to me, . . .": Ibid., 407.

59 "The sudden death . . .": Jones, *Life of Freud*, vol. 2: 447.

59 "In my life . . .": Freud, *Letters to Fliess*, 447.

60 "Because they know . . .": Brome, *Jung*, 73.

60 During his first . . . : Interview with Franz Jung.

60 "Ah, I was . . .": Storr, *C. G. Jung*, 24.

60 "to know how . . .": Jung, *Memories, Dreams, Reflections*, 114.

60 "would be better . . .": Jung, *Collected Papers*, 353.

61 Jung knew few . . . : Interview with Franz Jung.

page

62 "You see, Father . . .": Ibid.

62 "The Burghölzli is . . .": Brome, *Jung*, 84.

62 Late one evening . . . : Hannah, *Jung*, 80.

63 Sometimes, Jung noticed, . . . : Jung, *Memories, Dreams, Reflections*, 144.

63 "An overwhelming number . . .": Steele, *Freud and Jung*, 176.

63 "with every sign . . .": Carotenuto, *Secret Symmetry*, 158.

63 "Minds such as . . .": Ibid., 175.

64 "Freud, in his . . .": Freud, *Letters to Fliess*, 461 n. 3.

64 "I recently found . . .": Ibid., 461.

64 The little crosses . . . : Ibid., 382 n. 1.

64 Several months later . . . : Freud, M., *Sigmund Freud*, 76–90.

65 "Dear Sigmund," Fliess . . .: Freud, *Letters to Fliess*, 463–464.

65 Freud gradually revealed . . . : Ibid., 464–468.

65 "Won't you come . . .": Sachs, *Freud*, 43.

65 "it was C. G. Jung," . . . : Binswanger, *Sigmund Freud*, 1.

66 "Freud was definitely . . .": Jung, *Memories, Dreams, Reflections*, 145.

66 "This one," Bleuler . . . : Bleuler to Freud, June 9, 1905. Freud Collection. Box D1.

66 "It seems idiotic . . .": Bleuler to Freud, November 5, 1905. Freud Collection. Box D1.

66 "of the striking . . .": Jung, *Collected Papers*, 373.

66 "It appears, from . . .": Jung, *Collected Works*, vol. 2: 317.

66 Dear colleague, Many . . . : Freud and Jung, *Letters*, 3.

67 "it seems to . . .": Ibid., 4–5.

67 "Your writings have . . .": Ibid., 5.

67 "I beg of . . .": Ibid., 18.

67 "the lack of . . .": Ibid., 14.

67 "I know of . . .": Ibid., 17.

67 "Perhaps you will . . .": Ibid., 19.

67 One day that . . . : McGuire, "Jung's Complex Reactions." 3–17.

68 "We are here . . .": Ibid., 17.

68 Sigmund Freud left . . . : Bennet, *C. G. Jung*, 33.

CHAPTER SEVEN

71 The entrance to . . . : Binswanger, *Sigmund Freud*, 2.

71 Carl Jung was . . . : Freud and Jung, *Letters*, 95.

71 "Thick rich rugs," . . . : Eastman, "A Significant Memory." 693.

page

71 Freud sat quietly . . . : Binswanger, *Sigmund Freud*, 3.

72 The young Swiss . . . : Jones, *Life of Freud*, vol. 2: 31–33.

72 "Nevertheless," Jung remembered . . . : Jung, *Memories, Dreams, Reflections*, 146–147.

72 "For thirteen uninterrupted . . .": Bennet, *C. G. Jung*, 148.

72 "Freud was the . . .": Jung, *Memories, Dreams, Reflections*, 146.

72 "way of speaking . . .": Comments by Anne Federn. Freud Collection. Box B28.

72 Later Jung would . . . : Carotenuto, *Secret Symmetry*, 100.

72 "They were kindred . . .": Interview with C. A. Meier.

72 "Jung on these . . .": Freud, M., *Sigmund Freud*, 109.

72 but they liked . . . : Freud and Pfister, *Psychoanalysis and Faith*, 27.

72 "his liveliness, his . . .": Freud, M., *Sigmund Freud*, 109.

73 "Excuse me, please," . . . : Ibid.

73 "I, who grew . . .": Freud and Pfister, *Psychoanalysis and Faith*, 145–146.

73 "On Saturdays we . . .": Freud, M., *Sigmund Freud*, 14.

73 "They came out . . .": Interview with Leopold Stein, February 1969. Jung Biographical Archive.

74 As a child, . . . : Freud, M., *Sigmund Freud*, 70–71.

74 The little society . . . : Brome, *Freud and His Early Circle*, 18.

74 Jung did not . . . : Nunberg and Federn, eds., *Minutes of Vienna Psychoanalytic Society*, vol. 1: 138–145.

74 "perhaps we may . . .": Ibid., 132.

75 Another young man . . . : Jones, *Viennawalks*, 108, 235–236, 257–258; Herzstein, *Waldheim*, 29.

75 "I am no . . .": Freud and Jung, *Letters*, 26.

75 "Is it not . . .": Ibid., 25.

75 "I appreciate your . . .": Ibid., 28.

76 "Often I have . . .": Ibid., 49.

76 "Since I am . . .": Ibid., 36.

76 "There I found . . .": Brill, "Psychopathology and Psychotherapy," 1394.

76 "The object was . . .": Brill, *Lectures*, 11.

76 "There is more . . .": Ibid.

76 "was the first . . .": Ibid., 10–11.

76 "The way they . . .": Ibid., 10.

76 "degenerate stocks" and . . . : Peterson, "Talk on Morbid Psychology." 413.

77 "The trouble with . . .": Brill, *Freud's Contribution*, 29.

page

77 "It was inspiring," . . . : Ibid., 30.

77 "I feared lest . . .": Ibid., 33.

77 "I have unpleasant . . .": Freud and Jung, *Letters*, 78.

77 "all hearts open . . .": Ibid., 82.

77 "unconditional devotion to . . .": Ibid., 78.

78 "this child of . . .": Ibid., 76.

78 "Your lecture in . . .": Ibid., 77.

78 "hiking in the . . .": Ibid.

78 "Whether you have . . .": Ibid., 82.

78 Aschaffenburg had attacked . . . : Burnham, *Jelliffe*, 187.

78 "I remember," said . . . : Jones, *Life of Freud*, vol. 2: 113.

79 "a gang of . . .": Freud and Jung, *Letters*, 83.

79 "reign of terror," . . . : Ibid., 84–86.

79 "nothing for it, . . ." : Ibid., 87.

79 "great discussions" in . . . : Burnham, *Jelliffe*, 188.

79 "Actually—and I . . .": Freud and Jung, *Letters*, 95.

80 "What you say . . .": Ibid., 98.

80 "Let me enjoy . . .": Ibid., 122.

80 "We didn't invite . . .": Brome, *Jung*, 99.

80 While he was . . . : Jones, *Life of Freud*, vol. 2: 251.

80 On that particular . . . : Brome, *Jung*, 99–100.

80 *A town once* . . . : Poem read before Freud Society. Brill Collection. Box 2.

80 The "priceless doggerel," . . . : Freud and Jung, *Letters*, 101.

81 *Hence, Dr. Freud* . . . : Poem read before Freud Society. Brill Collection. Box 2.

81 "he could change . . .": Brome, *Jung*, 100.

81 "The meetings were, . . .": Brill, *Freud's Contribution*, 45.

81 Jones suspected Jung . . . : Brome, *Jung*, 100.

81 "He had an . . .": Interview with Manfred Bleuler, December 1969. Jung Biographical Archive.

81 "breezy personality," his . . . : Brome, *Ernest Jones*, 48–49.

81 "his unrestrained imagination. . . .": Jones, *Life of Freud*, vol. 2: 33.

CHAPTER EIGHT

82 "The Congress in . . .": Freud and Jung, *Letters*, 102.

82 "You deceive yourself . . .": Ibid., 103.

82 Freud had no . . . : Ibid., 104.

page

83 "felt distinctly nervous . . .": Brome, *Ernest Jones*, 52.
83 When Freud greeted . . . : Clark, *Freud*, 248.
83 "I came away . . .": Jones, *Free Associations*, 159–160.
83 "I don't expect . . .": Ibid., 123.
83 Early in 1906 . . . : Ibid., 145.
83 Jones had become . . . : Ibid., 150–151.
84 because he loved . . . : Ibid., 38–39.
84 "faster, more vivid . . .": *New York Post*, May 6, 1956.
84 "be careful with . . .": Freud to Jones, February 10, 1913. Freud Collection. Box D2.
84 "I admit at . . .": Freud and Jung, *Letters*, 78.
84 "I was predisposed . . .": Ibid., 79.
84 "I believe he . . .": Ibid., 109.
84 "Freud was naturally . . .": Jung, *Letters*, vol. 1: 7.
85 "Why not do . . .": Laforgue, "A Propos Des Règles Du Traitement Psychoanalytique." Freud Collection. Box B27.
85 "Apparently I was . . .": Ferenczi to Freud, January 2, 1909. Freud Collection. Accession number 19042.
85 "The colleagues behave . . .": Ferenczi to Freud, August 14, 1909. Freud Collection. Accession number 19042.
85 "I feel like . . .": Ferenczi to Freud, May 6, 1910. Freud Collection. Accession number 19042.
86 "forms the cornerstone . . .": Alexander and Selesnick, *History of Psychiatry*, 236.
86 "I had never . . .": Jones, *Free Associations*, 166.
86 "were the alternation . . .": Jones, *Life of Freud*, vol. 2: 42.
87 "a 'degenerate and . . .' ": Clark, *Freud*, 249–250.
87 "My eastern contingent . . .": Freud and Jung, *Letters*, 116.
87 "Here I must . . .": Ibid., 119.
87 "They were all . . .": Jones, *Free Associations*, 167.
87 "that Jung would . . .": Jones, *Life of Freud*, vol. 2: 44.
87 "how far he . . .": Brome, *Ernest Jones*, 55.
88 "a great success." . . . : Freud, *Letters*, 273.
88 "appropriation of it . . .": Freud and Jung, *Letters*, 150.
88 "My Salzburg manuscript . . .": Jones, *Life of Freud*, vol. 2: 49.
88 "be tolerant and . . .": Ibid., vol. 2: 48.
88 "I will do . . .": Ibid., 49–50.
89 "I have the . . .": Freud and Jung, *Letters*, 30.
89 "I am quite . . .": Ibid., 145.

page

89 "just seeing you . . .": Ibid., 158.

89 "I have a . . .": Ibid., 167.

89 "inaccessible solitude of . . .": Ibid., 170.

89 "I shall banish . . .": Ibid., 169.

89 "My selfish purpose," . . . : Ibid., 168.

89 How, Freud asked . . . : Jung, *Memories, Dreams, Reflections*, 128.

90 could "laugh down . . .": Interview with Franz Jung.

90 They talked all . . . : Jones, *Life of Freud*, vol. 2: 50.

90 "Now that we . . .": Freud and Jung, *Letters*, 178.

90 "You have . . . built . . .": Ibid., 206.

90 Yet not everything . . . : Jones, *Life of Freud*, vol. 2: 51–53.

90 "could still command . . .": Freud, M., *Sigmund Freud*, 15.

91 Freud was interested . . . : Freud and Jung, *Letters*, 226.

91 "The note of . . .": Ibid., 186.

91 "Until now I . . .": Ibid., 207.

91 "To be slandered . . .": Ibid., 210–211.

91 "You mustn't take . . .": Ibid., 212.

92 "I had a . . .": Jung, *Memories, Dreams, Reflections*, 152.

92 "When I left . . .": Freud and Jung, *Letters*, 216.

92 "my credulity, or . . .": Ibid., 218.

92 "I had the . . .": Ibid., 216.

92 "That last evening . . .": Ibid., 217.

92 "It is strange . . .": Ibid., 218.

93 "My last hope . . .": Carotenuto, *Secret Symmetry*, 93.

93 "I moved from . . .": Ibid., 94.

93 "too stupid that . . .": Freud and Jung, *Letters*, 232.

93 "I . . . deplore the . . .": Ibid., 236.

93 "has freed herself . . .": Ibid.

94 "Isn't it splendid . . .": Ibid., 233.

94 "Your being invited . . .": Ibid., 234.

94 "You, too, must . . .": Freud and Pfister, *Psychoanalysis and Faith*, 25.

95 "I hope you . . .": Hale, *Freud and the Americans*, 208.

CHAPTER NINE

96 After a heated . . . : Jones, *Life of Freud*, vol. 2: 55.

97 "Why are you . . .": Jung, *Memories, Dreams, Reflections*, 153.

97 The episode was . . . : Brome, *Freud and His Early Circle*, 98.

page

97 During the years . . . : Freud and Jung, *Letters*, 208.

97 "convinced," Jung thought . . . : Jung, *Memories, Dreams, Reflections*, 153.

97 Freud had told . . . : Jones, *Life of Freud*, vol. 2: 59.

97 "I had learned . . .": Ferenczi to Freud, October 5, 1909. Freud Collection. Accession number 19042.

97 "dissatisfaction with the . . .": Ibid.

98 "When I analyzed . . .": Groesbeck, "The Analyst's Myth." 38.

98 Jung was convinced . . . : Billinsky, "Jung and Freud." 39–43.

98 "I interpreted it . . .": Jung, *Memories, Dreams, Reflections*, 154.

98 The topic, Jung . . . : Interview with Karl Schmid, May 1970. Jung Biographical Archive.

98 "I cannot risk . . .": Jung, *Memories, Dreams, Reflections*, 154.

98 "Father was very . . .": Interview with Franz Jung.

98 "I never thought," . . . : Interview with E. A. Bennet, February 1969. Jung Biographical Archive.

98 "In the cave, . . .": Jung, *Memories, Dreams, Reflections*, 156.

99 "my first inkling . . .": Ibid., 157.

99 "I would not . . .": Ibid., 156.

99 Freud was pleased . . . : Jones, *Life of Freud*, vol. 2: 55.

99 "the mating cry . . .": Brome, *Freud and His Early Circle*, 100.

99 the news back . . . : *The New York Times*, August 29, 1909.

100 The *Mauretania* and . . . : *The New York Times*, September 10, 1909.

100 It took the . . . : Freud and Jung, *Letters*, 245.

100 Abraham Brill was . . . : Jones, *Life of Freud*, vol. 2: 55.

100 "The theories of . . .": Peterson, "Credulity and Cures." 1737.

100 "On this side . . .": Meyer to Jung, February 5, 1908. Jung Archive, Zürich.

100 "And thus I . . .": Burnham, *Jelliffe*, 70.

100 "This whole Freud . . .": Ibid.

100 camping on Staten Island . . . : *The New York Times*, August 1, 1909.

101 There were pictures . . . : *The New York Times*, August 22, 1909.

101 "an incredible dish . . .": Jung, *Word and Image*, 48.

101 The men found . . . : Jones, *Life of Freud*, vol. 2: 56.

101 "where all the . . .": Jung, *Memories, Dreams, Reflections*, 336.

101 "He is as . . .": Jung, *Word and Image*, 47.

101 a trained monkey . . . : *The New York Times*, August 1, 1909.

101 In fact, from . . . : Brome, *Ernest Jones*, 74.

page

101 The psychotherapeutic movement . . . : Hale, *Freud and the Americans*, 121.

102 New England was . . . : Ibid.

102 Sexual taboos were . . . : Freud and Jung, *Letters*, 316.

102 Putnam's mild manner . . . : Hale, *Freud and the Americans*, 206.

102 A speech Jones . . . : Brome, *Ernest Jones*, 66.

102 "A man who . . .": Ibid.

102 Freud wondered if . . . : Ibid., 74–75.

102 "I find the . . .": Freud and Jung, *Letters*, 165.

102 "One of the . . .": Freud and Pfister, *Psychoanalysis and Faith*, 29–30.

103 G. Stanley Hall was . . . : Hale, *Freud and the Americans*, 107.

103 "It was all . . .": Hannah, *Jung*, 92.

CHAPTER TEN

104 Worcester on the . . . : Freud, *Five Lectures on Psycho-Analysis*, 3.

104 He did not . . . : Hale, *Freud and the Americans*, 5–6.

104 "enthusiastic over the . . .": Clark, "Freud's Sortie to America." 41.

104 An hour or . . . : Jones, *Life of Freud*, vol. 2: 56.

104 At a suggestion . . . : Clark, *Freud*, 267.

105 They covered Freud's . . . : Hale, *Freud and the Americans*, 5.

105 Freud spoke on . . . : Freud, *Five Lectures on Psycho-Analysis*, 4.

105 "If it is . . .": Ibid., 9.

105 "the fingers turned . . .": Ibid., 15.

105 "in her terror . . .": Ibid.

105 "When she was . . .": Ibid., 19.

105 "We are the . . .": Jung, *Memories, Dreams, Reflections*, 337.

105 "front-page glamour." . . . : Lief, *Commonsense Psychiatry*, 230.

105 After Freud's third . . . : Jones, *Free Associations*, 192.

106 "First and foremost," . . . : Freud, *Five Lectures on Psycho-Analysis*, 40.

106 "People are in . . .": Ibid., 41.

106 At night he . . . : Jung, *Memories, Dreams, Reflections*, 337.

106 "Again and again," . . . : Ruitenbeek, ed., *Freud as We Knew Him*, 22–23.

106 One evening that . . . : *The New York Times*, September 7, 1909.

107 "We are rivals . . .": Ibid.

107 TOP OF THE . . . : Ibid.

107 HE PLANTED AMERICAN . . . : *The New York Times*, September 11, 1909.

page

107 "You don't know," . . . : *The New York Times*, September 7, 1909.

107 "I couldn't make . . .": Interview with Dora Kalff, January 1970. Jung Biographical Archive.

107 Like Freud, Jung . . . : Koelsch, '*Incredible Day-Dream*,' unpaged.

107 Only toward the . . . : Jung, *Collected Works*, vol. 2: 479.

108 "How did the . . .": Ibid., vol. 17: 27–29.

109 "regretted that the . . .": Freud and Jung, *Letters*, 348.

109 "In [Jung's] personal . . .": Freud to Ferenczi, August 17, 1910. Freud Collection. Accession number 19042.

109 "full of personality . . .": Putnam, "Personal Impressions of Sigmund Freud." 294.

109 "the grand old . . .": Hale, *Freud and the Americans*, 210.

109 "This outcry against . . .": Putnam, "Personal Impressions of Freud." 307.

109 "reacted with tragic . . .": Clark, "Freud's Sortie to America." 35.

109 "This is the . . .": Clark, *Freud*, 270.

109 "We are gaining . . .": Jung, *Memories, Dreams, Reflections*, 337.

109 "Freud is in . . .": Brome, *Freud and His Early Circle*, 106.

109 "He feared," Jones . . . : Brome, *Ernest Jones*, 74.

110 "You will find . . .": Ibid.

110 "I remember," said . . . : McIver, "Early Days at Putnam Camp." 9.

110 "a lamp to . . .": Ibid., 22–23.

111 "Everything is left . . .": Gifford, "Freud and the Porcupine." 29.

111 Freud, more formal, . . . : Ibid., 30.

111 "We took trails . . .": Ibid., 29.

111 "Freud assumes a . . .": Clark, "Freud's Sortie to America." 39.

111 "be described as . . .": Freud to Mathilde Freud, September 23, 1909. Freud Collection. Box B1.

111 "In America the . . .": Freud and Jung, *Letters*, 258.

111 "Low thinks," Jung . . . : Ibid., 305.

111 "The Americans are . . .": Freud to Jones, April 12, 1921. Freud Collection. Box D2.

112 Years later Freud . . . : Gifford, "Freud and the Porcupine." 31; Freud, *Group Psychology*, 33 n. 1.

CHAPTER ELEVEN

113 "The day after . . .": Freud and Jung, *Letters*, 248.

113 "Occasionally a spasm . . .": Ibid., 250.

page

113 In the fall . . . : Jung, *Memories, Dreams, Reflections*, 154.
114 On Freud's return . . . : Freud and Jung, *Letters*, 249.
114 He was pleased . . . : Ibid., 272.
114 "Your (that is, . . ."): Ibid., 268.
114 "In the end," . . . : Ibid., 249.
114 "I would invent . . .": Ibid., 256.
114 "A damned sight . . .": Ibid., 251.
114 "Today I resumed . . .": Ibid., 359.
114 "In my practice . . .": Ibid., 266.
114 Jung would one . . . : Ibid., 499.
114 Eugen Bleuler, an . . . : Jones, *Life of Freud*, vol. 2: 72.
115 "There will be . . .": Freud and Jung, *Letters*, 320.
115 "like embracing a . . .": Ibid., 417.
115 "a prickly eel, . . .": Ibid., 448.
115 Adler was paranoid . . . : Ibid., 376.
115 that Stekel, though . . . : Ibid., 259.
115 But, Freud conceded, . . . : Ibid., 404.
115 "I am bound . . .": Ibid., 418.
115 "Of course the . . .": Ibid., 325.
115 had mentioned to . . . : Ibid., 419.
115 "Sexual excitement," he . . . : Freud, *Letters to Fliess*, 276.
115 "My Indian summer . . .": Freud and Jung, *Letters*, 292.
115 His analysis with . . . : Ibid., 250.
115 In a burst . . . : Ibid., 247.
115 "really is enormous . . .": Ibid., 294.
116 "The prerequisite for . . .": Ibid., 289.
116 "Your Rat Man . . .": Ibid., 251.
116 "I am overjoyed . . .": Ibid., 254.
116 "Your remarks . . . are . . .": Ibid., 348.
116 "Archaeology or rather . . .": Ibid., 251–252.
117 "I was delighted . . .": Ibid., 260.
117 Four days later . . . : Ibid., 263.
117 "I have the . . .": Ibid., 279.
117 Freud was surprised . . . : Ibid., 282.
117 "I should like . . .": Ibid., 288.
117 "I imagine a . . .": Ibid., 294.
117 "Yes, in you . . .": Ibid., 295.

page

118 "I often wish . . .": Ibid., 270.

118 "The question of . . .": Ibid., 276.

118 "likely to play . . .": Ibid., 277.

119 "My attempt at . . .": Ibid., 279–280.

119 "It probably isn't . . .": Ibid., 259.

119 "Pater, Peccavi," Jung . . . : Ibid., 262.

119 "[I] still have . . .": Ibid., 297.

119 "I am merely . . .": Ibid., 300.

120 "like Herakles of . . .": Ibid., 275.

120 "It is a . . .": Ibid., 279.

120 "Whether I am . . .": Jung, *Letters*, vol. 1: 12.

120 "Won't mythology . . . be . . .": Freud and Jung, *Letters*, 292.

120 "I still have . . .": Ibid., 304.

120 At one point . . . : Brome, *Ernest Jones*, 76.

121 "I am not . . .": Ferenczi to Freud, January 3, 1910. Freud Collection. Accession number 19042.

121 "coffeehouse for very . . .": Ferenczi to Freud, October 24, 1909. Freud Collection. Accession number 19042.

121 "Obviously," Ferenczi told . . . : Ferenczi to Freud, January 3, 1910. Freud Collection. Accession number 19042.

122 "wise counselor" at . . . : Ibid.

122 "*You should stay* . . .": Ferenczi to Freud, October 24, 1909. Freud Collection. Accession number 19042.

122 Ferenczi's proposal at . . . : Jones, *Life of Freud*, vol. 2: 69.

122 "I was not, . . .": Ferenczi to Freud, April 5, 1910. Freud Collection. Accession number 19042.

122 "Most of you . . .": Wittels, *Sigmund Freud*, 140.

123 "fruition its hymn . . . ": Freud and Jung, *Letters*, 294.

CHAPTER TWELVE

124 On Christmas day . . . : Freud to Jones, January 22, 1911. Freud Collection. Box D2.

124 "the American fleet . . .": *The New York Times*, December 25, 1910.

124 "When Count Zeppelin . . .": Ibid.

125 "There is hardly . . .": Ibid.

125 "double-edged weapon." . . . : Freud to Ferenczi, April 24, 1910. Freud Collection. Accession number 19042.

page

125 "to keep two . . .": Ferenczi to Freud, June 12, 1910. Freud Collection. Accession number 19042.

125 "I hope you . . .": Freud and Pfister, *Psychoanalysis and Faith*, 37.

126 "blockheads," Freud had . . . : Freud and Jung, *Letters*, 331.

126 "The break with . . .": Ibid., 328.

126 "He dreamt he . . .": Ibid., 371.

126 "Jung was very . . .": Interview with C. A. Meier.

126 "coy new love, . . .": Freud and Jung, *Letters*, 285.

126 "Seclusion is like . . .": Ibid., 345–346.

126 "This is not . . .": Jones, *Life of Freud*, vol. 2: 109.

126 "that we Viennese . . .": Freud to Ferenczi, April 24, 1910. Freud Collection. Accession number 19042.

126 "Freud's work was . . .": Jones, *Life of Freud*, vol. 2: 109.

127 "You are right," . . . : Brome, *Ernest Jones*, 74.

127 But Jones would . . . : Ibid., 67–69.

127 "I wish," Freud . . . : Freud to Binswanger, November 6, 1910. Freud Collection. Box D1.

127 "As it is, . . .": Freud and Jung, *Letters*, 343.

127 "I realize now . . .": Ibid., 344–345.

127 "This would be . . .": Ibid., 375.

127 The "little intrigue" . . . : Freud to Binswanger, December 5, 1910, Freud Collection. Box D1.

127 "Please leave me . . .": Freud and Jung, *Letters*, 383.

128 "with breaks, however, . . .": Freud to Ferenczi, December 29, 1910. Freud Collection. Accession number 19042.

128 "he is just . . .": Ibid.

128 "So it looks" . . . : Freud to Binswanger, n.d. Freud Collection. Box D1.

128 He had spent . . . : Interview with Herr and Frau Lutz Niehus. April 1970. Jung Biographical Archive; interview with Franz Jung.

128 "I poured out . . .": Freud to Ferenczi, December 29, 1910. Freud Collection. Accession number 19042.

128 "The same paranoia, . . .": Freud and Jung, *Letters*, 376.

128 "Adler is a . . .": Freud to Ferenczi, December 16, 1910. Freud Collection. Accession number 19042.

128 "I have had . . .": Freud and Jung, *Letters*, 380.

128 "since Fliess's case . . . ,": Jones, *Life of Freud*, vol. 2: 83.

128 "I have now . . .": Freud to Ferenczi, December 16, 1910. Freud Collection. Accession number 19042.

129 "significant researches." . . . : Freud to Binswanger, n.d. Freud Collection. Box D1.

page

129 "I don't know . . .": Freud and Jung, *Letters*, 388.

129 "I am glad," . . . : Freud to Ferenczi, December 29, 1910. Freud Collection. Accession number 19042.

129 "was entirely splendid . . .": Ibid.

129 "I am more . . .": Freud and Jung, *Letters*, 384.

129 "Bleuler has now . . .": Ibid.

129 "He has created . . .": Freud and Pfister, *Psychoanalysis and Faith*, 48.

129 "If the kingdom . . .": Freud to Binswanger, March 14, 1911. Freud Collection. Box D1.

130 "The difficulties in . . .": Freud to Binswanger, April 20, 1911. Freud Collection. Box D1.

130 "palace revolution in . . .": Freud and Jung, *Letters*, 403.

130 "a time full . . .": Ibid., 439.

130 "I have been . . .": Ibid., 438.

130 "So you too . . .": Ibid., 441.

130 "the outlook for . . .": Ibid., 460.

131 "Invoked or not . . .": Bennet, *C. G. Jung*, 146.

131 "We Swiss live . . .": Bennet, *Meetings with Jung*, 63.

131 Possibly Jung's two . . . : Carotenuto, *Secret Symmetry*, 15–16.

131 Freud had been . . . : Freud and Jung, *Letters*, 372.

131 It seemed to . . . : Hannah, *Jung*, 90.

131 Besides, she knew . . . : Freud and Jung, *Letters*, 456.

131 "This, I think, . . .": Interview with Franz Jung.

132 "Even if it . . .": Ibid.

132 "my father always . . .": Ibid.

132 "The women are . . .": Freud and Jung, *Letters*, 465.

132 When the weather . . . : Interview with Adrian Baumann, May 1970. Jung Biographical Archive.

132 Jung was fascinated . . . : Freud and Jung, *Letters*, 450.

132 "had long been . . .": Ibid., 456.

133 Jung "was a . . .": Interview with Alphons Maeder, January 1970. Jung Biographical Archive.

133 Freud's paper, his . . . : Clark, *Freud*, 303.

133 The audience was . . . : Brome, *Ernest Jones*, 80.

133 "unconscious contains not . . .": Jones, *Life of Freud*, vol. 2: 86.

133 "[These remarks] may . . .": Freud, *Complete Psychological Works*, vol. 12: 82.

134 "On page 7 . . .": Freud to Jones, March 21, 1926. Freud Collection. Box D2.

page

134 "At the end . . .": Jones to Freud, March 25, 1926. Freud Collection. Box D2.

134 "The days in . . .": Freud and Jung, *Letters*, 448.

CHAPTER THIRTEEN

137 "fully as a . . .": Ferenczi to Freud, October 19, 1911. Freud Collection. Accession number 19042.

137 "the profound after-effects . . .": Ibid.

138 "occultism or libido." . . . : Ferenczi to Freud, October 23, 1911. Freud Collection. Accession number 19042.

138 "Dear Professor Freud, . . .": Freud and Jung, *Letters*, 452.

138 "as if I . . .": Freud to Ferenczi, October 30, 1911. Freud Collection. Accession number 19042.

138 "Why in God's . . .": Freud and Jung, *Letters*, 459.

138 "I knew how . . .": Ibid., 456.

139 "The couple," Freud . . . : Freud to Ferenczi, November 5, 1911. Freud Collection. Accession number 19042.

139 "Comprehension is dawning . . .": Freud to Ferenczi, November 13, 1911. Freud Collection. Accession number 19042.

139 Possibly Freud's silence . . . : Freud to Jones, November 5, 1911. Freud Collection. Box D2.

139 "One of the . . .": Freud and Jung, *Letters*, 459.

139 "Do not think . . .": Ibid., 457.

139 "The President of . . .": Ibid., 365–366.

140 "The essential point . . .": Ibid., 471.

140 "I am all . . .": Ibid., 472.

141 "Your demonstration of . . .": Ibid., 480.

141 "Man should not . . .": Freud to Ferenczi, November 17, 1911. Freud Collection. Accession number 19042.

141 "You can see . . .": Freud to Ferenczi, January 23, 1912. Freud Collection. Accession number 19042.

141 "I certainly knew . . .": Ibid.

142 "I suspect in . . .": Ferenczi to Freud, January 20, 1912. Freud Collection. Accession number 19042.

142 "Of course I . . .": Freud and Jung, *Letters*, 491.

142 "The indestructible foundation . . .": Ibid., 492.

142 Jung, however, had . . . : Ibid., 502.

143 His friend Ludwig . . . : Binswanger, *Sigmund Freud*, 39.

143 "On the evening . . .": Freud and Jung, *Letters*, 508.

page

143 There was every . . . : Binswanger, *Sigmund Freud*, 42.

143 "The fact that . . .": Freud and Jung, *Letters*, 509.

143 "It is a . . .": Freud and Pfister, *Psychoanalysis and Faith*, 56–57.

143 "Even if we . . .": Freud and Jung, *Letters*, 510.

143 "I had a . . .": Ibid.

143 a now familiar . . . : Interview with Frau C. A. Meier, March 1970. Jung Biographical Archive.

144 "Now I can . . .": Freud and Jung, *Letters*, 511.

144 "For all its . . .": Freud to Binswanger, July 22, 1912. Freud Collection. Box D1.

144 "The most interesting . . .": Freud to Jones, July 22, 1912. Freud Collection. Box D2.

144 "After everything that . . .": Ferenczi to Freud, August 6, 1912. Freud Collection. Accession number 19042.

CHAPTER FOURTEEN

145 Jung offered to . . . : Freud and Jung, *Letters*, 512.

145 "There is no . . .": Carotenuto, *Secret Symmetry*, 116.

146 "What took hold . . .": Freud to Jones, August 1, 1912. Freud Collection. Box D2.

146 Ludwig Binswanger's response . . . : Freud to Binswanger, September 2, 1912. Freud Collection. Box D1.

146 "Fortunately you are . . .": Freud to Binswanger, July 29, 1912. Freud Collection. Box D1.

146 "Nothing," Freud told . . . : Freud to Ferenczi, August 8, 1912. Freud Collection. Accession number 19042.

146 "I felt increasing . . .": Freud to Jones, September 7, 1912. Freud Collection. Box D2.

146 Ernest Jones had . . . : Jones, *Life of Freud*, vol. 2: 94, 143.

146 Now, sitting alone . . . : Freud to Jones, September 7, 1912. Freud Collection. Box D2.

147 Jung had interpreted . . . : Alexander and Selesnick, *History of Psychiatry*, 241.

147 Freud arrived in . . . : Freud to Jones, September 22, 1912. Freud Collection. Box D2.

147 "All I ask, . . .": Freud to Binswanger, September 22, 1912. Freud Collection. Box D1.

147 Freud craved solitude . . . : Freud, *Letters*, 293.

147 "Bring my deepest . . .": Freud to Jones, November 15, 1912. Freud Collection. Box D2.

page

147 "To be sure . . .": Freud to Jones, September 22, 1912. Freud Collection. Box D2.

147 "I have finally . . .": Freud to Binswanger, September 22, 1912. Freud Collection. Box D1.

147 Freud hoped Jung . . . : Freud to Jones, September 22, 1912. Freud Collection. Box D2.

147 "really too bad" . . . : Ibid.

148 Freud's walks among . . . : Freud, *Letters*, 293.

148 There would be . . . : Freud and Jung, *Letters*, 497.

148 "such a suggestion . . .": Freud to Ferenczi, June 23, 1912. Freud Collection. Accession number 19042.

148 "A small, unknown . . .": Ibid.

148 Jung would end . . . : Freud and Jung, *Letters*, 515.

148 In May 1912, . . . : Minutes of the New York Psychoanalytic Society, Tuesday, May 28, 1912. Brill Collection. Box 3.

148 "I do not . . .": Jung, *Collected Works*, vol. 4: 119, 125; Freud and Jung, *Letters*, 515.

148 "So we're opening . . .": Freud to Ferenczi, October 17, 1912. Freud Collection. Accession number 19042.

148 "three regrettable misunderstandings . . .": Freud to Ferenczi, October 2, 1912. Freud Collection. Accession number 19042.

148 "Jung's rebellion"; . . . : Freud to Ferenczi, July 4, 1912. Freud Collection. Accession number 19042.

148 "If he were . . .": Freud to Jones, November 17, 1913. Freud Collection. Box D2.

149 "creating new and . . .": Freud to Ferenczi, October 20, 1912. Freud Collection. Accession number 19042.

149 "Your Kreuzlingen gesture . . .": Freud and Jung, *Letters*, 515.

149 "Dear Dr. Jung, . . .": Ibid., 517.

149 Dear Sir: It . . . : Ibid., 521.

149 Freud was one . . . : Ibid.

149 "We left each . . .": Freud to Jones, October 28, 1912. Freud Collection. Box D2.

150 Why, Freud asked, . . . : Freud to Ferenczi, November 26, 1912. Freud Collection. Accession number 19042.

150 Jung said he . . . : Freud to Binswanger, January 1, 1913. Freud Collection. Box D1.

150 "He brought out . . .": Freud to Ferenczi, November 26, 1912. Freud Collection. Accession number 19042.

150 "I had a . . .": Freud and Jung, *Letters*, 510.

page

150 "What would you . . .": Freud to Ferenczi, November 26, 1912. Freud Collection. Accession number 19042.

150 "absolutely beaten" and . . . : Ibid.

151 "No," Jung replied . . . : Interview with Jolande Jacobi, December 1969. Jung Biographical Archive.

151 "had conjured up . . .": Freud to Ferenczi, November 26, 1912. Freud Collection. Accession number 19042.

151 "Jung was very . . .": Freud to Binswanger, November 28, 1912. Freud Collection. Box D1.

151 "Everybody was charming . . .": Freud and Jung, *Letters*, 522.

151 When Freud and . . . : Jones, *Life of Freud*, vol. 2: 146–152.

152 The discussion then . . . : Sloane, "A Parapraxis of Freud's." 126–140.

152 "I have misgivings . . .": Jones, *Life of Freud*, vol. 2: 454.

152 Ernest Jones noticed . . . : Jones, Ibid. vol. 1: 317.

152 "Yes, he did," . . . : Clark, *Freud*, 327–328.

152 "Take care that . . .": Freud and Jung, *Letters*, 491.

152 Perhaps only Ferenczi, . . . : Jones, *Life of Freud*, vol. 2: 146; Ferenczi to Freud, November 28, 1912. Freud Collection. Accession number 19042.

CHAPTER FIFTEEN

153 Ernest Jones, sitting . . . : Jones, *Free Associations*, 222; Jones, *Life of Freud*, vol. 1: 317.

153 He had the . . . : Freud and Jung, *Letters*, 522.

153 Carrying him from . . . : Jung, *Memories, Dreams, Reflections*, 153.

153 "How sweet it . . .": Jones, *Life of Freud*, vol. 1: 317.

154 "You will find . . .": Freud to Ferenczi, November 26, 1912. Freud Collection. Accession number 19042.

154 Freud slept well . . . : Ibid.

154 "Writing table and . . .": Freud, *Letters*, 294.

154 "Reports of my . . .": Binswanger, *Sigmund Freud*, 49.

154 "repressed feelings, this . . .": Ibid.

154 "I saw Munich . . .": Freud to Jones, December 8, 1912. Freud Collection. Box D2.

154 Moreover, while sometimes . . . : Schur, *Freud*, 269.

154 Ernest Jones thought . . . : Jones, *Life of Freud*, vol. 1: 317.

154 Another attack, Jones . . . : Jones, *Free Associations*, 222.

154 "unruly homosexual feeling." . . . : Freud to Jones, December 8, 1912. Freud Collection. Box D2.

page

154 "in supposing that . . .": Freud to Jones, December 26, 1912. Freud Collection. Box D2.

154 Freud confessed to . . . : Groesbeck, "The Analyst's Myth." 37.

155 "who are wrecked . . .": Jones, *Life of Freud*, vol. 2: 146.

155 "In spite of . . .": Ferenczi to Freud, December 26, 1912. Freud Collection. Accession number 19042.

155 Lou Andreas-Salomé . . . : Andreas-Salomé, *Freud Journal*, 58.

155 "a will to . . .": Ibid., 46.

155 "Freud has returned . . .": Ibid., 58.

156 "I have been . . .": Freud and Jung, *Letters*, 522.

156 "According to my . . .": Ibid., 524.

156 Jung told Freud . . . : Ibid., 525.

156 "I am writing . . .": Ibid., 526.

156 "Let each of . . .": Ibid., 529.

156 "He behaves like . . .": Freud to Jones, December 8, 1912. Freud Collection. Box D2.

157 "Even Adler's cronies," . . . : Freud and Jung, *Letters*, 533.

157 "But are you . . .": Ibid., 534.

157 "Your technique of . . .": Ibid., 534–535.

157 "As regards Jung . . .": Freud to Jones, December 26, 1912. Freud Collection. Box D2.

157 "florid fool and . . .": Freud to Ferenczi, December 23, 1912. Freud Collection. Accession number 19042.

157 "could take so . . .": Freud to Jones, December 26, 1912. Freud Collection. Box D2.

157 "The reaction to . . .": Freud to Ferenczi, December 23, 1912. Freud Collection. Accession number 19042.

158 "I cannot suffer . . .": Freud to Jones, December 26, 1912. Freud Collection. Box D2.

158 "The letter to . . .": Freud to Ferenczi, December 30, 1912. Freud Collection. Accession number 19042.

158 "I'm in the . . .": Freud to Ferenczi, December 25, 1912. Freud Collection. Accession number 19042.

158 "The harmony established . . .": Freud to Binswanger, January 1, 1913. Freud Collection. Box D1.

158 He liked the . . . : Comments by Theodor Reik. Freud Collection. Box B28.

158 "Your letter," he . . . : Freud and Jung, *Letters*, 539.

158 "I'm letting you . . .": Freud to Ferenczi, January 7, 1913. Freud Collection. Accession number 19042.

page

158 "I accede to . . .": Freud and Jung, *Letters*, 540.

158 "It is quite . . .": James Putnam to Fanny Bowditch, December 9, 1912[?]. Jung Biographical Archive.

159 Fanny was a . . . : Crossman, "Preliminary Inventory: Fanny Bowditch Katz (1874–1967) Letters and Papers." Jung Biographical Archive.

159 "This is a . . .": James Putnam to Fanny Bowditch, February 11, 1912. Jung Biographical Archive.

159 " 'Manic-depressive insanity' . . .": James Putnam to Fanny Bowditch, June 2, 1912[?]. Jung Biographical Archive.

159 Increasingly, Putnam worried . . . : Taylor, "C. G. Jung." 136–140.

159 "It is a . . .": James Putnam to Fanny Bowditch, December 1, 1912. Jung Biographical Archive.

159 "After the parting . . .": Jung, *Memories, Dreams, Reflections*, 165.

160 "Since I know . . .": Ibid., 168–169.

160 "Father would be . . .": Interview with Franz Jung.

160 "It was a . . .": Jung, *Memories, Dreams, Reflections*, 168.

CHAPTER SIXTEEN

161 Freud found the . . . : Freud to Ferenczi, January 7, 1913. Freud Collection. Accession number 19042.

161 "Jung attempted to . . .": Freud, *Autobiographical Study*, 100–101.

161 "to behave 'diplomatically' . . .": Andreas-Salomé, *Freud Journal*, 58.

161 "It is beginning . . .": Ibid., 78.

161 "I recollect vividly, . . .": Jones, *Free Associations*, 223.

162 "Theory is by . . .": Andreas-Salomé, *Freud Journal*, 37.

162 "Jung is right . . .": Ibid., 150–151.

162 "One is sometimes . . .": Ibid., 43.

162 "As long as . . .": Ibid, 130.

163 The poet Rainer . . . : Ibid., 9.

163 "Her interests are . . ." : Freud to Ferenczi, March 20, 1913. Freud Collection. Accession number 19042.

163 " 'My new friend' . . .": Anna Freud to Freud, April 30, 1922. Freud Collection.

163 "a female of . . .": Freud to Ferenczi, October 31, 1912. Freud Collection. Accession number 19042.

163 "stared as if . . .": Andreas-Salomé, *Freud Journal*, 44.

163 had spoken "falteringly." . . . : Ibid., 106.

163 Salomé and Freud . . . : Ibid., 114.

163 On Lou's last . . . : Ibid., 131.

page

163 "I am deeply . . .": Brome, *Ernest Jones*, 97.

163 "I would rather . . .": Ferenczi to Freud, March 9, 1913. Freud Collection. Accession number 19042.

163 "Naturally everything that . . .": Freud to Ferenczi, May 8, 1913. Freud Collection. Accession number 19042.

164 "Certainly," Ferenczi replied . . . : Jones, *Life of Freud*, vol. 2: 149.

164 "It is very . . .": Freud to Ferenczi, May 4, 1913. Freud Collection. Accession number 19042.

164 "These fights . . . are . . .": Jones, *Life of Freud*, vol. 2: 455.

164 "Putnam . . . may easily . . .": Ferenczi to Freud, August 6, 1912. Freud Collection. Accession number 19042.

164 "We are and . . .": Bettelheim, "Scandal in the Family." 44.

164 "I am not . . .": Freud to Jones, April 9, 1913. Freud Collection. Box D2.

164 "Abraham has been . . .": Jones, *Life of Freud*, vol. 2: 153.

165 "I think it . . .": Freud to Ferenczi, May 13, 1913. Freud Collection. Accession number 19042.

165 "I shall not . . .": Carotenuto, *Secret Symmetry*, 120.

165 "I was completely . . .": Ibid., 184.

165 "I am sorry . . .": Ibid., 119.

165 "His recent conduct . . .": Brome, *Ernest Jones*, 97.

165 "Jung is crazy," . . . : Freud and Abraham, *Psycho-Analytic Dialogue*, 141.

165 "As regards . . . the . . .": Freud to Jones, August 29, 1913. Freud Collection. Box D2.

166 "It is like . . .": Freud to Jones, October 30, 1913. Freud Collection. Box D2.

166 "Don't forget," Freud . . . : Freud to Jones, August 29, 1913. Freud Collection. Box D2.

166 Lou Salomé arrived . . . : Andreas-Salomé, *Freud Journal*, 168.

166 There were many . . . : Brome, *Jung*, 151.

166 "Good morning, Herr . . .": Interview with Alphons Maeder, January 1970. Jung Biographical Archive.

166 "Two years ago," . . . : Andreas-Salomé, *Freud Journal*, 168–169.

166 "a blond fellow . . .": Ibid., 37.

166 "Clever and dangerous," . . . : Ibid., 169.

166 "I have never . . .": Ibid., 168–169.

167 "Then I saw . . .": Interview with Alphons Maeder, January 1970. Jung Biographical Archive.

167 Salomé thought Jung . . . : Andreas-Salomé, *Freud Journal*, 169.

page

167 "All sorts of . . .": Jones, *Life of Freud*, vol. 2: 102.

167 The Congress pleased . . . : Jones, *Free Associations*, 224.

167 "The best thing . . .": Andreas-Salomé, *Freud Journal*, 189–190.

167 "which," Salomé noticed . . . : Ibid., 169.

167 "looked back to . . .": Ibid., 108.

168 "We dispersed," Freud . . . : Freud, *On the History of the Psycho-Analytic Movement*, 45.

168 "If the real . . .": Freud to Hall, *Time* magazine, September 5, 1969.

168 Freud could not . . . : Freud to Jones, March 25, 1914. Freud Collection. Box D2.

168 "I have visited . . .": Freud to Jones, September 21, 1913. Freud Collection. Box D2.

CHAPTER SEVENTEEN

169 Minna was glad . . . : Freud to Jones, September 21, 1913. Freud Collection. Box D2.

169 She had joined . . . : Jones, *Life of Freud*, vol. 2: 103.

169 "incomparable beauty of . . .": Freud and Abraham, *Psycho-Analytic Dialogue*, 147.

169 But in the . . . : Freud to Jones, September 21, 1913. Freud Collection. Box D2.

169 "the lonely piazza . . .": Freud, *Complete Works*, vol. 13: 213.

170 The story of . . . : Ibid., 233.

170 Freud stood in . . . : Jones, *Life of Freud*, vol. 2: 367.

170 He had begun . . . : Freud, *Complete Works*, vol. 13: 220.

170 "I used to . . .": Ibid., 220–221.

170 Standing before the . . . : Ibid., 227–230.

170 But Moses' lower . . . : Ibid., 221.

171 "In his first . . .": Ibid., 229.

171 "The giant frame . . .": Ibid., 233.

171 For Freud, his . . . : Jones, *Life of Freud*, vol. 2: 366–367.

171 "Julius II," Freud . . . : Freud, *Complete Works*, vol. 13: 233–234.

171 "Don't you think . . .": Gay, *Freud*, 314.

171 "My feeling for . . .": Jones, *Life of Freud*, vol. 2: 367.

172 "in the ensuing . . .": Freud, *Complete Works*, vol. 13: 236.

172 "I was living . . .": Jung, *Memories, Dreams, Reflections*, 170–171.

172 Years later a . . . : Interview with Fowler McCormick, April 1969. Jung Biographical Archive.

page

172 "It was during . . .": Jung, *Memories, Dreams, Reflections*, 172.

172 "My father writes . . .": Interview with Franz Jung.

172 Save for his . . . : Jung, *Memories, Dreams, Reflections*, 185.

172 Diabolical images continually . . . : Ibid., 169–177.

172 He could only . . . : Ibid., 171, 180.

172 "What, you too?" . . . : Interview with Alphons Maeder, January 1970. Jung Biographical Archive.

172 "For years after . . .": Interview with Franz Jung.

173 "very vaguely I . . .": Interview with Agathe Niehus-Jung, April 1970. Jung Biographical Archive.

173 "I painted there . . .": Interview with Franz Jung.

173 "My sister Marianne . . .": Ibid.

173 "My grandmother had . . .": Ibid.

174 "Think of my . . .": Ibid.

174 "I was struck," . . . : Freud and Abraham, *Psycho-Analytic Dialogue*, 151.

174 "One is infuriated . . .": Jones to Abraham, December 29, 1913. Abraham Papers. Box 2.

174 "I am no . . .": Freud to Jones, June 2, 1914. Freud Collection. Box D2.

174 "I found [Jung] . . .": Clark, *Freud*, 333.

174 "It seems quite . . .": Burnham, *Jelliffe*, 193.

174 "It may be . . .": Freud to Jones, May 17, 1914. Freud Collection. Box D2.

175 "I am very . . .": Freud to Jones, July 7, 1914. Freud Collection. Box D2.

175 "There is no . . .": Freud to Jones, November 17, 1913. Freud Collection. Box D2.

175 "We know [Jung's] . . .": Freud to Jones, November 22, 1913. Freud Collection. Box D2.

175 "Otherwise," Freud reported . . . : Freud to Ferenczi, May 16, 1914. Freud Collection. Accession number 19042.

175 "honeymoon years" in . . . : Ferenczi to Freud, February 9, 1914. Freud Collection. Accession number 19042.

175 "The purpose," Powers . . . : Burnham, *Jelliffe*, 74.

175 "Getting rid of . . .": Ferenczi to Freud, July 20, 1914. Freud Collection. Accession number 19042.

175 "I know from . . .": Freud to Anna Freud, July 16, 1914. Freud Collection.

176 "Strange," he told . . . : Freud to Ferenczi, July 17, 1914. Freud Collection. Accession number 19042.

page

176 "Lear-like moods" . . . : Freud to Ferenczi, July 22, 1914. Freud Collection. Accession number 19042.

176 Anna, his "Cordelia," . . . : Gay, *Freud*, 433.

176 "to an obvious . . .": Freud to Ferenczi, July 17, 1914. Freud Collection. Accession number 19042.

176 "does not claim . . .": Freud to Jones, July 22, 1914. Freud Collection. Box D2.

176 "to Mabel's sister, . . .": Freud to Anna Freud, July 22, 1914. Freud Collection.

176 "Very nice," Anna . . . : Anna Freud to Freud, April 30, 1922. Freud Collection.

176 "dropping upon the . . .": *The New York Times*, December 2, 1914.

177 RUSSIA INVADES GERMANY . . . : *The New York Times*, August 3, 1914.

177 "And the voice . . .": Freud to Ferenczi, November 9, 1914. Freud Collection. Accession number 19042.

CHAPTER EIGHTEEN

178 Someone once described . . . : Interview with Aline Valangin, September 1970. Jung Biographical Archive.

178 "They were dark, . . .": Interview with Franz Jung.

178 "Seductive, not sexy," . . . : Interview with Liliane Frey-Rohn.

179 One patient never . . . : Interview with William Alex, May 1969. Jung Biographical Archive.

179 "The maid would . . .": Jensen, *C. G. Jung, Emma Jung and Toni Wolff*, 10.

179 Jung's colleague C. A. . . . : Interview with C. A. Meier, September 1970. Jung Biographical Archive.

179 "You need someone . . .": Interview with Regula Rohland-Oeri, May 1970. Jung Biographical Archive.

179 "Fear crept over . . .": Jung, *Memories, Dreams, Reflections*, 177.

179 "It is, of . . .": Ibid., 181.

179 "He was very . . .": Interview with Liliane Frey-Rohn.

179 "phenomenologically" Jung's breakdown . . . : Interview with C. A. Meier, September 1970. Jung Biographical Archive.

180 "As a young . . .": Jung, *Memories, Dreams, Reflections*, 190.

180 "Oh, that is . . .": Bennet, *Meetings with Jung*, 101.

180 "The deeper 'Layers' . . .": Jung, *Memories, Dreams, Reflections*, 357.

180 "They studied their . . .": Interview with Frau C. A. Meier, September 1970. Jung Biographical Archive.

page

180 "I think she . . .": Interview with C. A. Meier, September 1970. Jung Biographical Archive.

180 "It was a . . .": Ibid.

180 "My mother was . . .": Interview with Franz Jung.

180 "There isn't the . . .": Interview with Fowler McCormick, April 1969. Jung Biographical Archive.

181 "Tante" because she . . . : Interview with Franz Jung.

181 "When I was . . .": Ibid.

181 "There was a . . .": Interview with Sir Laurens van der Post.

181 "She was so . . .": Interview with Sabi Tauber, September 1970. Jung Biographical Archive.

181 "Toni Wolff. Lotus. . . .": Champernowne, *Memoir of Toni Wolff*, 4.

181 "One can say . . .": Interview with Jolande Jacobi, December 1969. Jung Biographical Archive.

181 "He was so . . .": Interview with Fowler McCormick, April 1969. Jung Biographical Archive.

182 In 1915, two . . . : Silverstein, " 'Now Comes a Sad Story.' " 143, 145, 147.

182 In Freud's essay . . . : Freud, *Phylogenetic Fantasy*, xii, 13–18.

182 "playful," stated that . . . : Ibid., 19.

182 Freud did not . . . : Silverstein, " 'Now Comes a Sad Story.' " 144.

182 At moments he . . . : Ibid., 149.

182 Perhaps he realized . . . : Ibid., 191.

183 "originally introverted feeling . . .": Jung to unnamed Swiss colleague, February 18, 1957.

183 "A new production . . .": Freud to Jones, May 19, 1921. Freud Collection. Box D2.

183 "The distinction between . . .": Fisher, "Sigmund Freud and Romain Rolland." 36.

183 "I am especially . . .": Burnham, *Jelliffe*, 205 n. 4.

183 "I have completely . . .": Freud and Pfister, *Psychoanalysis and Faith*, 86–87.

183 "My view seems . . .": Burnham, *Jelliffe*, 194.

183 "There is a . . .": Ibid., 200.

183 "yonder the pond," . . . : Freud to Jones, January 15, 1919. Freud Collection. Box D2.

183 "If America is . . .": Freud to Jones, May 24, 1920. Freud Collection. Box D2.

183 "Then on a . . .": Freud to Jones, June 4, 1922. Freud Collection. Box D2.

page

184 "I think it . . .": Freud to Jones, April 6, 1922. Freud Collection. Box D2.

184 "I was very . . .": Brill, "Psychotherapies I Encountered." 589–590.

184 "You can understand . . .": Carotenuto, *Secret Symmetry*, 85.

184 "You, Professor Freud, . . .": Ibid., 112.

184 "It often happens," . . . : Freud and Pfister, *Psychoanalysis and Faith*, 86.

184 "The real tragedy," . . . : Jones to Abraham, April 8, 1924. Abraham Papers. Box 2.

184 "Certainly I have . . .": Freud to Binswanger, May 12, 1929. Freud Collection. Box D1.

185 "There was one . . .": Interview with C. A. Meier.

185 "Aye. I am . . .": Pound, "In Durance." 86–87.

INDEX

Index

Index

Index

Index

Index

Index

Grateful acknowledgment is made to the following for permission to reprint previously published material:

Excerpt from Jung: Man and Myth by Vincent Brome. Copyright © 1960 by Sigmund Freud Copyrights, Ltd., London. Reprinted by permission of Atheneum Publishers, an imprint of Macmillan Publishing Company.

The Letters of Sigmund Freud and Karl Abraham, ed. by Hilda C. Abraham and Ernst L. Freud. Copyright © 1966 by Hilda C. Abraham and Ernst L. Freud.

The Life and Work of Sigmund Freud, vols. 1, 2, and 3 by Ernest Jones. Copyright © 1953, 1955, and 1957, respectively, by Ernest Jones.

The Freud Journal of Lou Andreas-Salomé, trans. with an Introduction by Stanley A. Leavy. Copyright © 1964 by Basic Books, Inc., Publishers.

The Interpretation of Dreams by Sigmund Freud. Trans. from the German and ed. by James Strachey. Published in the United States by Basic Books, Inc. by arrangement with George Allen & Unwin Ltd., and The Hogarth Press, Ltd.

Psychoanalysis and Faith: The Letters of Sigmund Freud & Oskar Pfister, ed. by Heinrich Meng and Ernst L. Freud. Copyright © 1963 by Sigmund Freud Copyrights, Ltd.

The Discovery of the Unconscious: The History and Evolution of Dynamic Psychiatry by Henri F. Ellenberger. Copyright © 1970 by Henri F. Ellenberger.

Free Associations: Memories of a Psychoanalyst by Ernest Jones. Copyright © 1955 by Katharine Jones. Reprinted by permission of Basic Books, Inc., Publishers.

Excerpt from *Sigmund Freud: Reminiscences of a Friendship* by Ludwig Binswanger. Copyright © 1957 by Grune & Stratton, Inc. Reprinted by permission of Grune & Stratton, Inc.

Excerpt from *The Complete Letters of Sigmund Freud to Wilhelm Fleiss,* ed. by Jeffrey Masson. Copyright © 1985 by Sigmund Freud Copyrights, Ltd., and J. M. Masson. Reprinted by permission of Harvard University Press.

Excerpt from *Viennawalks* by J. Sidney Jones. Copyright © 1985 by J. Sidney Jones. Reprinted by permission of Henry Holt and Company, Inc.

Excerpt from *A Memoir of Toni Wolff* by Irene Champernowne. Copyright © 1980 by C. G. Jung Institute of San Francisco. Reprinted by permission of the C. G. Jung Institute of San Francisco.

Excerpt from *Tribute to Freud* by H. D. Copyright © 1956, 1974 by Norman Holmes Pearson. Reprinted by permission of New Directions Publishing Corp.

Excerpts from *A Secret Symmetry: Sabina Spielrein Between Jung and Freud* by Aldo Carotenuto, trans. by Krishna Winston, Arno Pomerans, and John Shepley. Copyright © 1982 by Random House, Inc. and *Freud: The Man and the Cause* by Ronald Clark. Copyright © 1980 by E. M. Partners, A. G. Reprinted by permission of Random House, Inc.

Excerpt from *Memories, Dreams, Reflections* by C. G. Jung, recorded and ed. by Aniela Jaffe, trans. by Richard and Clara Winston. Copyright © 1961, 1962, and 1963 by Random House, Inc. Reprinted by permission of Pantheon Books, a Division of Random House, Inc.

Excerpts from *The Freud/Jung Letters: The Correspondence Between Sigmund Freud and C. G. Jung,* ed. by William McGuire, trans. by Ralph Manheim and R. F. C. Hull, Bollingen Series XCIV. Copyright © 1974 by Sigmund Freud Copyrights, Ltd. and Erbengemeinschaft Professor Dr. C. G. Jung and C. G. Jung, *Word and Image,* ed. by Aniela Jaffe, Bollingen Series XCII: vol. 2. Copyright © by Princeton University Press. Reprinted by permission of Princeton University Press.

And special thanks to:
Tom Roberts of Sigmund Freud Copyrights, Colchester, England, for use of material from the Sigmund Freud Collection in the Library of Congress.
Edmund Brill, for permission to quote from the correspondence of Abraham Brill.
Gerda Niedieck, of Niedieck Linder, A. G.
Richard Wolfe of the Countway Library in Boston.
Grant Allan, for use of material from the correspondence of Ernest Jones.